The Infants Lawyer:

OR, THE

LAW

(Ancient and Modern)

Relating to

INFANTS.

Setting forth

Their Priviledges; their ſeveral Ages for divers Purpoſes; Guardians and *Procheiu amy*, as to Suits and Defences by them; Actions brought by and againſt them, with the manner of Declarations and Pleadings; Fines and Recoveries, and other Matters of Record ſuffered or acknowledged by them, how reverſable; Conveyances and Specialties, how bound by them or not; Contracts, Promiſes, *&c.*

ALSO

Treating of Infant-Executors, Adminiſtrator *durante minori Ætate*; Actions and Suits brought by them and againſt them, with the manner of Declaring and Pleading.

LIKEWISE,

Of Deviſes by and to Infants, Apprentices, Cuſtom of *London*, and Pleadings, Orphans, Tryals of Infancy, Portions and Legacies, and Reſolutions and Decrees at Common Law and *Chancery* concerning the ſame.

With an APPENDIX, *of the Forms of Declarations and Pleadings concerning* INFANTS.

The Second Edition:

With many Additions of late adjudged Caſes in Common Law and *Chancery*; and the Explication of all the late Statutes relating to INFANTS.

NEW INTRODUCTION BY

MORRIS L. COHEN

Professor Emeritus of Law and Professional Lecturer in Law at Yale Law School

THE LAWBOOK EXCHANGE, LTD.

Clark, New Jersey

ISBN 978-1-58477-833-2

Lawbook Exchange edition 2008, 2017

The quality of this reprint is equivalent to the quality of the original work.

THE LAWBOOK EXCHANGE, LTD.
33 Terminal Avenue
Clark, New Jersey 07066-1321

Please see our website for a selection of our other publications and fine facsimile reprints of classic works of legal history:
www.lawbookexchange.com

Library of Congress Cataloging-in-Publication Data

The infants lawyer, or, The law (ancient and modern) relating to infants : setting forth their priviledges, their several ages for divers (sic) purposes, guardians and prochein amy, as to suits and defences by them, actions brought by and against them, with the manner of declarations and pleadings, fines and recoveries, and other matters of record suffered or acknowledged by them, how reversable, conveyances and specialties, how bound by them or not, contracts, promises, &c ... concerning the same ; with an appendix, of the forms of declarations and pleadings concerning infants / new introduction by Morris L. Cohen.
p. cm.
Originally published: 2nd ed., with many additions of late adjudged cases in common law and chancery, and the explication of all the late statutes relating to infants. [London] in the Savoy :
Printed by J. Nutt, assignee of E. Sayer, for St-John Baker, 1712.
ISBN-13: 978-1-58477-833-2 (cloth : alk. paper)
ISBN-10: 1-58477-833-4 (cloth : alk. paper)
1. Children--Legal status, laws, etc.--England. 2. Guardian and ward --England. 3. Actions and defenses--England. 4. Children--Legal status, laws, etc.--England--Forms. I. Title: Infants lawyer. II. Title: Law (ancient and modern) relating to infants.
KD735.I54 2007
346.4201'35--dc22 2007003326

Printed in the United States of America on acid-free paper

Introduction

The Infants Lawyer: or, the Law (Ancient and Modern) Relating to Infants was first published in London in 1697 by the Assigns of R. and E. Atkins, Esquires, for Robert Battersby. This second edition was printed in 1712 in London by the law printer, John Nutt, as Assignee of E. Sawyer for St. John Baker, and a third edition was issued in London, in 1726, with the imprint, "Printed by the Assigns of Edw. Sayer, Esq; for James Crokatt." In none of the editions is there any indication of the identity of the author, and neither Halkett and Laing[1], nor Holdsworth[2] suggest an attribution. The Stationers' Company Registers for the 1690s do not show an entry for the book.[3]

It seems clear from the quality of the writing and the research on which it is based that the author was a trained lawyer — and, from the breadth of the sources cited, a learned one. Those conclusions are reinforced by the fact that this is a pioneering work; it seems to be the first English treatise on this subject. It is clearly not a paste-pot job put together quickly by a venture some printer or bookseller. The issuance of two subsequent editions after the first in 1697 and the lack of significant competition in the form of other

---

[1] Halkett, Samuel & John Laing, *A Dictionary of Anonymous and Pseudonymous Publications in the English Language* (Edinburgh: Oliver and Boyd, 1926–1962; 3rd rev. & enl. Ed., Harlow : Longman, 1980–).

[2] Holdsworth, William, *A History of English Law* (London: Methuen; Sweet and Maxwell, 1972–1992.

[3] Stationers' Company. *A Transcript of the Registers of the Worshipful Company of Stationers, from 1640–1708 A.D.* (London, Privately printed, 1914) Vol. III, 1675–1708.

publications certainly suggests the acceptance of this work as an authoritative statement of the law.

Fortunately, a clue in the Harvard Law Library copy of the 1697 edition suggests that the author is most probably Samuel Carter (baptized 1641, died 1713),[4] a Cambridge graduate, and a barrister of the Inner Temple who was subsequently appointed "library keeper" of that Inn. Carter was also a law reporter and a prolific writer of law books. The clue to the authorship in the Harvard copy is a manuscript note opposite the title page which states in a late 17th or early 18th century hand: "Saml Carter Esq. Inner Temple the Author of this book." The anonymous publication of this volume is less surprising when one notes that most of Carter's books were published with just the simple designation on the title page: "S.C., barrister at law." At least two of his books had not even that clue and perhaps he wrote others which have not yet been attributed to him. I have been unable to find any edition of any of his books that carries his full name as author.

The work is a sophisticated treatise covering a wide range of both common law and statutory law topics on the English law relating to infants. The second edition, reprinted here, is described on its title page as having "many Additions of late adjudged Cases in Common Law and Chancery; and the Explication of all the late Statutes relating to Infants." The title page itself describes in detail the contents of the work which includes "An Appendix of the Forms of Declarations and Pleadings concerning Infants." The extensive jurisdiction of the Chancery Court in matters affecting children is reflected in the book's substantial coverage of equity and equitable remedies. Along with the expected treatment of relevant areas of the law of contracts, wills and estates, real property,

---

[4] For a biographical article, see *Oxford Dictionary of National Biography*, v. 10 (2004), p. 368.

custody, and variant ages for different legal purposes, it also includes coverage of guardians and wards, masters and apprentices, and litigation involving infants. In addition to discussing the leading cases and relevant statutes, the author cites many of the leading authorities of early English law.[5]

The author's sympathetic view toward children is suggested by the title, *The Infants Lawyer*. The book might have been called *Children Under the Law* or *The Law Governing Children*. The title chosen places the reader, at least initially, in the mindset of the infant's advocate or counselor, rather than in a more removed and uninvolved position. That attitude is spelled out even more clearly in the author's prefatory note, "To the Reader," as follows:

> It is a frequent Saying in our Law-Books, *De minimis non curat Lex*, which is true if it be understood of petty Things and minute Circumstances, but if we apply it to Persons, it is not so; for it is most certain, that our Law hath a very great and tender Consideration for Persons naturally disabled, and especially for Minors. The Law protects their Persons, preserves their Rights and Estates, excuseth their Laches, and assists them in their Pleadings . . . *The Judges are their Counsellors, the Jury are their Servants . . . and the Law is their Guardian*. And let me add, They are under the special Aid and Protection of his [i.e., the King's] Equity, who is no less than Keeper of the King's Conscience.

This tone and the anonymous publication of the treatise seem to be suggested by the last sentence of that prefatory note: ". . . it [this

---

[5] For example, *Doctor and Student*; Doderidge's *English Lawyer*; Fitzherbert's *Nova Brevium*; Coke's *Institutes*; Rolle's *Abridgment*; Hale's *Pleas of the Crown*; Dalton's *Country Justice*.

book] appears without either a *Parent or a Patron*; and therefore, as an *Orphan*, claims *Pity*, and hopes for a *favourable* Construction."

Considering the wide-ranging scope of the English law of infants, it is surprising that this is the first full-scale treatment of the subject. Although there are occasional references to infants in specialized treatises, there is no single-focused examination of the many legal problems facing children. Occasionally, when infants are the subject of a specific legal discussion, they are linked to other classes subject to legal disabilities, e.g., insane people, women, and Jews. Even so important a work as Edward Coke's *Institutes of the Laws of England*[6] gives only brief and scattered references to infants. The 1632 treatise, *The Lawes Resolutions of Women's Rights: or the Lawes Provision for Women*[7]. . . , where one might have expected to find some treatment of infants, there is almost nothing of note. Aside from the three editions of *The Infant's Lawyer*, it is not until William Blackstone's *Commentaries on the Laws of England*[8] do we get a substantial treatment of this subject. Blackstone devotes *Chapter the Sixteenth. Of Parent and Child* (pp. 434–445 of the first edition) and *Chapter the Seventeenth. Of Guardian and Ward* (pp. 448–454) to infants.

The following is one scholar's explanation for the timing of this book's publication:

> Towards the end of the seventeenth century, a particular need was perceived within the internal legal culture to collect and to explain civil law concerning a particular social group: children. This development reflects the growing professionalism of lawyers, but it also expresses

---

[6] London: Printed for the Societie of Stationers, 1628–1644.

[7] *London: Printed by the assignes of John More . . . 1632.*

[8] Oxford, Printed at the Clarendon Press, 1765–1769.

> changed societal attitudes towards children in the late seventeenth and early eighteenth centuries. Thus, the concept of the 'child' became important as a heuristic category . . . A legal treatise of 1697, the *Infants' Lawyer*, explained why it was necessary to publish a book on the legal status of children . . .[9]

Focusing on those "changed social attitudes" at the end of the seventeenth century, we can see the beginning of fundamental changes in the way people in England viewed children. Some scholars suggest that the development of a concept of childhood, as a distinct period of human life, arose at that time. Previously, children were viewed as small adults without any special consideration or provision being made for their needs and limitations. They were unfinished creatures who had to be whipped into shape to become fully developed adults. Toward the end of the seventeenth century and through the eighteenth century, people began to see children as constituting a unique stage in human development requiring different treatment and understanding appropriate to their level of intellectual, emotional and physical maturity. As a result, many aspects of their lives were changed—their clothes, their education and discipline, their responsibilities in the home and family, and even their books and games.

> Slowly, at a pace which varied from class to class and from individual family to individual family within each class, there took place in England between about 1660 and 1800 a

---

[9]Anna-Christina Giovanopoulos, "The Legal Status of Children in Eighteenth-Century England" in *Fashioning Childhood in the Eighteenth Century*, edited by Anja Muller (Burlington, Vt.: Ashgate Publishing, 2006) p. 45.

> remarkable change in accepted child-rearing theory, in standard child-rearing practices, and in affective relations between parents and children.[10]

It was inevitable that change occurred as well in the way the law dealt with children.

This transitional period was also undoubtedly a significant factor in stimulating the writing and publication of *The Infant's Lawyer*, a work which reflected that change. And, in return, perhaps we can assume that this relatively enlightened treatise contributed to the improved treatment of children under English law.

Morris L. Cohen
Yale Law School
November 30, 2007

---

[10] Stone, Lawrence, *The Family, Sex and Marriage in England 1500–1800* (New York, Harper & Row, 1977) p. 405.

The Infants Lawyer:

OR, THE

LAW

(Ancient and Modern)

Relating to

INFANTS.

Setting forth

Their Priviledges; their ſeveral Ages for divers Purpoſes; Guardians and *Procheiu amy*, as to Suits and Defences by them; Actions brought by and againſt them, with the manner of Declarations and Pleadings; Fines and Recoveries, and other Matters of Record ſuffered or acknowledged by them, how reverſable; Conveyances and Specialties, how bound by them or not; Contracts, Promiſes, *&c.*

ALSO

Treating of Infant-Executors, Adminiſtrator *durante minori Ætate*; Actions and Suits brought by them and againſt them, with the manner of Declaring and Pleading.

LIKEWISE,

Of Deviſes by and to Infants, Apprentices, Cuſtom of *London*, and Pleadings, Orphans, Tryals of Infancy, Portions and Legacies, and Reſolutions and Dec rees at Common Law and *Chancery* concerning the ſame.

With an APPENDIX, *of the Forms of Declarations and Pleadings concerning* INFANTS.

The Second Edition:

With many Additions of late adjudged Caſes in Common Law and *Chancery*; and the Explication of all the late Statutes relating to INFANTS.

In the *Savoy*: Printed by J. Nutt, Aſſignee of *Edw. Sayer* Eſq; for St-John Baker, at *Thavies-Inn-Gate* in *Holborn*, 1712.

TO THE
READER.

IT is a frequent Saying in our Law-Books, *De minimis non curat Lex*, which is true if it be underſtood of petty Things and minute Circumſtances, but if we apply it to Perſons, it is not ſo; for it is moſt certain, that our Law hath a very great and tender Conſideration for Perſons naturally diſabled, and eſpecially for *Minors*. The Law protects their Perſons, preſerves their Rights and Eſtates, excuſeth their Laches, and aſſiſts them in their Pleadings. And as it is ingenuouſly obſerved in *Holford* and *Platt*'s Caſe, 2 *Roll*. Rep. 18. *The Judges are their Counſellors, the Jury are their Servants*, (for they ought to find the Title at large in an Aſſize) *and the Law is their Guardian*. And let me add, They are under the ſpecial Aid and Protection of his Equity, who is no leſs than Keeper of the King's Conſcience.

To the Reader.

It hath been computed by ſome (whoſe Genius lies that Way), That Infants make up a Third Part of the Nation; which if ſo, (as the Gueſs ſeems not very improbable) then I ſuppoſe a Treatiſe of this Kind (and never before attempted) may be acceptable.

It is but Small, and therefore more analogous to the Subject of it; and yet the Matter is full of Weight and Variety.

The Method which I have uſed is, I conceive, as proper and apt as a Treatiſe of this Sort is capable of. And indeed it is the Nature of the Subject, which ought to direct the Method.

But be that as it will, it appears without either a *Parent* or a *Patron*; and therefore, as an *Orphan*, claims *Pity*, and hopes for a *favourable* Conſtruction.

THE CONTENTS.

CHAP. I.

Of Infants en Ventre sa Mere.

ing

CHAP. II.

Priviledges of Infants, or not.

The CONTENTS.

CHAP. IV.

Of Guardian *and* Prochein amy.

CHAP. V.

Of Actions by Infants.

to

CHAP. VI.

Actions brought against Infants.

CHAP.

The CONTENTS.

CHAP. VII.

Of Fines levied by Infants.

CHAP.

The CONTENTS.

CHAP. VIII.

Of Common Recovery, and other Matters of Record suffered by Infants.

Recovery against Infant by Vertue of a Privy Seal. Infants permitted to suffer Recoveries by the Court: And the Reasons thereof. The manner of passing such Recoveries. Recovery suffered by Infant of Four Years of Age. If Infant appear by his Guardian, and suffer a common Recovery, it cannot be reversed for Error: But if in such Case he appear by Attorney, it may be reversed after his full Age, and why. And if he appear in Person it may be reversed within Age, but not after full Age, and why. Difference where Infant comes in on single Voucher, and where on double Voucher. Recovery by Infant in Person, may be avoided in Error before full Age, but at full Age he cannot avoid it by Entry. Judgments in Courts not to be subverted by Matters in Pais. *If Infant suffered a Recovery by Attorney, he in Remainder may vouch it for Error, and why. The Appearance by a* Feme Covert *within Age in a Recovery by Attorney is Error.* Regula *as to* Baron *and* Feme, *as in respect of the Inheritance of the Wife, being impeached by the Husband. Difference between Matters of Record, and Matters of Fait as to their being void or voidable for Infancy, and how and when to be avoided. Infants shall avoid Matters in Fait within Age, or at full Age. Statutes and Recognizances are avoided by*

Audita

The CONTENTS.

CHAP. IX.

Of Conveyances and Specialties.

The CONTENTS.

CHAP.

The CONTENTS.

CHAP. XI.

Of Acts in Law.

CHAP. XII.

Of Declarations and Pleadings.

The CONTENTS.

CHAP. XIII.

Of Infant Executors and Administrators.

CHAP. XIV.

Of Devises.

CHAP.

The CONTENTS.

The CONTENTS.

CHAP.

The CONTENTS.

CHAP. XVII.

Orphans.

CHAP. XVIII.

Trial, Judgment, Execution.

THE

THE INFANTS LAWYER.

CHAP. I.

Of Infants en Ventre sa Mere.

What Consideration the Law hath of an Infant in Ventre sa Mere. *Killing an Infant in* Ventre sa Mere, *Murder. Of a Devise to an Infant in* Ventre sa Mere. *Of a Surrender to the Use of Infant in* Ventre sa Mere. *Issue born afterwards affirms a voidable Lease by Acceptance of Rent. Of an Usurpation of an Infant in* Ventre sa Mere. *By what Acts in Law Infants in* Ventre sa Mere *shall be bound, and by what not, as by Voucher, Descent, Forejudger and Acquittal,* Bastard eigne *and* Mulier puisne. *By* Stat. 10 & 11 W. 3. c. 16. *Son or Daughter, Posthumous Children, born after the Decease of the Father, may take such Estate as if born in his Life-time,* &c. *altho' there be no Limitation to Trustees to preserve contingent Remainders. When an Infant, as to the Computation of its Time in the Womb, shall be said to be Legitimate or not. The exact Time of a Man's being at full Age. A Case of a Bond to save harmless of a Bastard Child in the Womb,* 1 Lutt. 669.

INcipiendum est ab Ovo: And I shall in the first Place shew what Consideration is to be had of Infants before they are born, and how an Infant *en Ventre sa Mere (in Ventre Matris)* stands in the Eye of the Law; as also of a *Privement enseint*; and then treat of the Writ *De Ventre inspiciendo*, being a grave Provision in our Law for the preventing Bastards and Supposititious Births inheriting Estates.

Infant in *Ventre sa Mere*, how consider'd in Law, and why.

Altho' *Filius in Utero Matris, est Pars Viscerum Matris*, and has been look'd upon as not *in esse*; yet the Law in many Cases hath Consideration of him in respect of the apparent Expectation of his Birth. He seems to have a real Essence, and therefore is something more than a meer Fiction in Law; tho' to some Purposes the Law imputes Acts to and by him by way of Fiction, as an Infant in *Ventre sa Mere* may be vouched, 38 *Ed.* 3. 39.

Killing a Child in the Womb, Murder.

It hath been the Opinion, that the Killing of an Infant in *Ventre sa Mere* is not Felony, 3 *Ass. Pl.* 2. *Stamf. Pleas of the Crown.* But it was resolv'd in *Syms*'s Case, *Mich.* 39 & 40 *El.* A Man wounds such Infant, which after is born, and the Wounds appear, and that it died within the Year of these Wounds, that this is Murder. *Vid. infra* 7 *Rep.* Earl of *Bedford*'s Case.

Of a Devise to an Infant in *Ventre sa Mere*.

It hath been a great Question in our Books, Whether a Devise to an Infant in *Ventre sa Mere*

Mere be good or not? It hath been denied, but with this Difference, in *Simpson* and *Southern*'s Case, 2 *Bulstr.* 274. An immediate Devise to an Infant in *Ventre sa Mere* is void; but if it be in Remainder, it's good. The same Difference is taken by *Windham* in *Snow* and *Cutler*'s Case, 16 *Car.* 2. *B. R.* That a present Devise to an Infant *en Ventre sa Mere* is void; but if it be devised to him when he shall be born, it's good; as was *Farmer* and *Fosset*'s Case, in *Banc. Com.* 1655. A Devise, That if the Child with which the *Feme* was *enseint*, should be born, he shall have a Share with the rest, is good; for this is Executory. And the Case in *Dyer* 303. which is contrary, is held not to be Law, and the Roll doth not warrant that Case. But now it's held, That a present Devise to an *Infant en Ventre sa Mere* is good, tho' it hath been a wavering Point in all Ages; and the Words in the Statute of 34 *H.* 8. *c.* 5. *To devise to any one Person or Persons, do not hinder such a Devise*; these Words being put in to shew the Power and Largeness of the Statute, and therefore not restrained to Persons *in esse*: And it hath been clearly resolv'd, A Devise to an Infant when he shall be born, or to a Daughter when she shall be married, is good, and the Land shall descend to the Heir in the mean time. But it seems to be resolved in *Chudleigh*'s Case, such a Devise is not good by the Statute of 32 & 34 *H.* 8. *Of Wills*; for those Statutes do not provide for putting of Lands in Abeyance, and so a Conveyance to the Use of an Infant in *Ventre sa Mere* is void; but now it's held good in a Devise, as Executory Devise, 2 *Bulstr.* 247. *Simpson* and *Southern*, 16 *Car.* 2. B. R. *Snow* and *Cutler*, *Farmer* and *Fosset*'s Case, *Dyer* 303. *Siderf.* 153.

Devise to an Infant in *Ventre sa Mere.*

J. M. by his Will devised the Rents, Issues and Profits of all his Messuages, during his Interest therein, to his Wife for Life, and if she died before the Determination of his said Interest, the same to come amongst his Four Children equally; and the Testator conceiving his Wife with Child, devised to the Child in *Ventre sa Mere* a Lease of Two Houses, and order'd the Moiety of the Profits to be put out for a Stock, and the other Moiety for Maintenance; and by his Will further declared, That if all his Children should die before Marriage, or Twenty one Years of Age, then the Premisses devised to his Children should remain to his Brothers and Sisters Children. The Four Children died before Marriage or Twenty one, and the Child (*Alice*) who was not born at the Time of the Testator's Death, is only living. *Per Cur.* The Collateral Line hath nothing to do with the Estate of the Testator during the Life of *Alice*, 1 *Rep. in Chap.* 76. *Marsh* and *Kirby*. And yet I have read a Case to this Purpose: *A.* gives 700 *l.* to the Children of her Daughter, and wills it to be paid amongst them after the Decease of her Daughter, and that the Daughter shall have the Interest during her Life. The Daughter hath Three Children at the Decease of *A.* and hath one Child more after. One of the Three Daughters dies, and *J. S.* takes

takes Administration of his Estate, and then the Daughter dies. Lord Chancellor held, That the Child born after the Devisor's Death could have no Benefit of the Devise, because that this was a present Devise *sol-vend. in futur.* and the Words [amongst them] apportion the Thing, and the Administrator of the dying Child shall have a Share.

And now Estates are usually settled in such Manner, not only where there is an actual *Enseintment*, but long before, even upon a Marriage Settlement, and the Uses shall rise as they come *in esse*.

It's a Rule at Common Law, If the immediate Grantee be not *in Rerum Natura*, and able to take by Vertue of the Grant, it's void presently. But now, in case of Surrender of a Copyhold, tho' at the Time of the Surrender the Grantee is not *in esse*, or not capable of a Surrender, yet if he be *in esse*, and capable at the Time of the Admittance, it is sufficient. As a Surrender to him that shall be Heir to *J. S.* or to the Use of the next Child of *J. S.* tho' at the Time of Surrender *J. S.* had no Child, yet if afterwards he hath a Child, the Child may come into Court, and compel the Lord to admit him. The Reason given is, because the Surrender is a Thing Executory, and is executed by the subsequent Admittance; and therefore if at the Time of the Admittance he be capable to take, it is sufficient, *Co. Copyholder*. *Regula.*

Now whether the Surrender to the Use of an Infant in *Ventre sa Mere* be good, hath been much questioned, *Cro. Jac.* 376. 1 *Rol. Rep.* Of Surrender to the Use of an Infant in *Ventre sa Mere.*

Rep. 109, 131. 2 *Rol. Abr.* 415, 416. 2 *Bulstr.* 274, 275. *Simpson* and *Southern*, Some are for it, and some are against it. I conceive the better Opinion is, That it is good, as well as a Devise to an Infant *en Ventre sa Mere*; but it's agreed by all, That a Surrender to the Use of *J. S.* for Life, the Remainder to the Use of an Infant *en Ventre sa Mere*, is good.

A Father, at or under the Age of 21 Years, by his last Will, or by his Deed executed in his Life-time, may dispose of the Custody or Tuition of his Child or Children unmarried, or of Infants *en Ventre sa Mere*, to any Person or Persons whatsoever, other than to Papists, and this *per Stat.* 12 *Car.* 2. *cap.* *Vide infra.*

Privement enseint, and the Relation to it.

If Tenant in Tail makes a voidable Lease, *rendant* Rent, and after takes Wife and dies *sans Issue*, the Wife *privement enseint* with a Son, and the Wife recovers Dower; she, before the Birth of the Son, shall not avoid the Lease, for her Estate is *quodammodo* a Continuance of Part of the Estate Tail; for she shall be attendant for a Third Part of the Services, and is in the *Per* by her Husband, 31 *Ass.* 26. *Dyer* 51. 7 *Rep.* 9. *Earl of Bedford's* Case.

Issue born after affirms a voidable Lease by Acceptance of Rent.

If Tenant in Tail makes a Lease for 40 Years, rendring Rent, which is voidable by the Issue in Tail, and afterwards Tenant in Tail dieth without Issue, his Wife with Child of a Son, by which the Donor entereth, and as to him avoideth the Lease, and afterwards the Son is born, the Lessee reentreth, the Son at his full Age accepteth the

the Rent, the same doth affirm the Lease; for the Lease was never absolutely void, but voidable, and by Matter *ex post Facto* was defeated for a Time: And altho' *Filius in Utero Matris* is *Pars Viscerum Matris*, yet the Law in many Cases hath Consideration of him in respect of the apparent Expectation of his Birth, *Saunders* and *Brown*'s Case in *Stowell*'s Case, *Plo. Com.*

It was the Opinion of my Lord *Hobart*, That if an Usurpation be had upon one in *Ventre sa Mere*, that at the next Term after his Birth he shall be reliev'd by *Stat. W.* 2. *c.* 5. 'For (saith he) suppose the Heir then '*in esse*, being a Daughter, were relievable in 'respect of her Nonage; Were it reasonable 'that the Son after born (to whom the 'Wrong is now done) should lose that Re-'lief? And (saith he) for Prelates to be re-'liev'd against Usurpation in the Vacation 'of their Prelacies (as they are) is altogether 'of the like Nature and Reason.' And it is held by *Crooke*,' If Land in Fee be mortgaged on Condition, if Mortgagor or his Heirs pay, *&c.* Mortgagor dies, leaving a Daughter Heir, his Wife *privement enseint*, and she pays the Money, and after a Son is born, she shall retain the Estate; *Terra transit cum Onera.*

In respect of Usurpation on Infant in *Ventre sa Mere.*

In case of Acquittal of the Tenant by the *Mesne*, where the Tenant receiveth his Acquittal in a Writ of *Mesne*, if he be not acquitted afterwards, he shall have a *Distringas ad acquietandum* against the *Mesne*; and if he come not, he shall be fore-judged by his

In respect of Fore-judger to Acquittal.

his Default: But if the Daughter, the Son being in *Ventre sa Mere*, be fore-judged, it shall bind the Son born afterwards, because he had no Right at the Time of the Fore-judgment.

In respect of *Bastard eigne* and *Mulier puisne* Discent.

A Man seised of Lands in Fee, and hath Issue *Bastard eigne* and *Mulier puisne*, and dies; if the *Bastard* entreth, and the *Mulier* dies, his Wife *privement enseint* with a Son, and the Bastard hath Issue, and dies seised, the Son is born, his Right is bound for ever: But if the Bastard dies seised, his Wife *enseint* with a Son, the *Mulier* enters, the Son is born, the Issue of the Bastard is bar'd; for there must not be only a Dying seised, but a Discent to his Issue. *Note*, This Discent differeth from other Discents: Other Discents take away the Entry only of him that hath Right, and leaveth him to his Action; but this Discent bars the Right of the *Mulier*, 1 *Inst*. 224.

If the Wife be *privement enseint*, the Heir may not plead Detinue of Charters.

Where a Felonious Act done to the Child in the Womb shall be Murder.

If a Woman be quick with Child, and by a Potion (or otherwise) killeth it in her Womb; or if a Man beat her, whereof the Child dieth in her Body, and she is deliver'd of a dead Child, this is a great Misprision, but no Murder: But if the Child be born alive, and dieth of the Potion, Battery, *&c.* this is Murder; for in Law it is accounted a Reasonable Creature *in Rerum Natura*, when it is alive.

If a Man counsel a Woman to kill a Child in her Womb when it shall be born, and after

after she is deliver'd she kills it, the Counseller is an Accessary to the Murder; and yet at the Time of the Commandment or Counsel, no Murder could be committed of the Child in *Utero Matris*, 3 *Inst.* p. 50, 51. 7 *Rep. Earl of Bedford's* Case.

The Act 10 & 11 *W.* 3. *c.* 16. is to enable Posthumous Children to take Estates as if born in their Fathers Life-time. *Note.*

Before this Act, when by Marriage, or other Settlements, Estates were limited in Remainder to the Use of the Sons and Daughters, the Issue of such Marriage, with Remainder over, without limiting an Estate to Trustees to preserve the contingent Remainder, if they happen'd to be born after the Death of the Father, were in Danger to be defeated of their Remainder by the next in Remainder after them, and left unprovided for by such Settlements.

It is enacted, That where any Estate already is, or shall hereafter, by any Marriage, or other Settlement, be limited in Remainder to or to the Use of the first or other Son or Sons of the Body of any Person lawfully begotten, with any Remainder or Remainders over to or to the Use of any other Person or Persons, or in Remainder to or to the Use of a Daughter or Daughters lawfully begotten, with any Remainder or Remainders to any other Person or Persons, that any Son or Sons, or Daughter or Daughters, of such Person or Persons lawfully begotten or to be begotten, that shall be born after the Decease of his, her

Son or Daughter born after the Decease of the Father, may take such Estate as if born in his Life-time, &c. although there be no Limitation to Trustees, &c.

or

or their Father, shall and may, by Vertue of such Settlement, take such Estate so limited to the first and other Sons, or to the Daughter or Daughters, in the same Manner as if born in the Life-time of his, her or their Father, altho' there shall happen no Estate to be limited to Trustees after the Decease of the Father to preserve the contingent Remainder to such after-born Son or Sons, Daughter or Daughters, until he, she or they come *in esse*, or are born to take the same.

Writ De Ventre inspiciendo, *and the Proceed-*

This is a Writ for the searching of a Woman that saith she is with Child, and thereby withholds Land from him that is next Heir at Law, *Reg. of Writs, fol.* 227. 1 *Inst. fol.* 8. *b.*

De Ventre inspiciendo, and the Sheriff's Proceedings thereon, in the Case of a Widow.

Sir *Francis Willoughby* died seised of a great Estate of Inheritance, having five Daughters, leaving *Dorothy* his Wife, who at the Time of his Death pretended her self to be with Child by Sir *Francis*, which, if it were a Son, all the five Sisters should thereby lose the Inheritance descended to them. They prayed a Writ *De Ventre inspiciendo* out of *Chancery*, directed to the Sheriff of *London*, That he should cause the said *D.* to be view'd by 12 *Knights*, and to be searched by 12 Women in the Presence of the 12 Knights, and *ad tractand' per Ubera, & ad Ventrem inspiciend'*, whether she were with Child, and to certify the

the ſame into the *Common Bench*; and if ſhe were with Child, to certify for how long Time in their Judgments, *& quando ſit paritura*. Whereupon the Sheriff cauſed her accordingly to be ſearched, and returned, that ſhe was Twenty Weeks gone with Child, and that within Twenty Weeks *fuit paritura*. Whereupon another Writ iſſued out of the *Common-Bench*, commanding the Sheriff ſafely to keep her in ſuch an Houſe, and that every Day he ſhould cauſe her to be viewed by ſome of the Women named in the Writ, (Ten being named therein) and ſome to be preſent at her Delivery, and to view the Birth, whether it be Male or Female. And the Sheriff returned, that ſuch a Day ſhe was deliver'd of a Daughter, *Cro. El. p.* 566. *The Lady Willoughby*'s Caſe.

The like Circumſtances and Proceedings were in *Theaker*'s Caſe, *Paſch.* 22 *Jac.* 1. with this Difference: *Willoughby*'s Caſe was in the Caſe of a Widow; but this was in the Caſe of a *Feme Covert*, who was married within a Week after the Death of her firſt Husband, who is ſuppoſed to get the Child: For here ſhe was a *Feme Covert*, and ſhe ought to inhabit with her Husband. They did not take ſuch a Courſe as in the Lady *Willoughby*'s Caſe, of taking her into the Sheriff's Cuſtody, but left her with her Husband, he entring into a Recognizance that ſhe ſhould not remove from the Houſe wherein they inhabited, and that one or two of the Women might ſee her every Day, and two or three be preſent at her Travel: For it was ſaid, That

And in the Caſe of a *Feme Covert*.

That this Iſſue might be well ſaid to be the Child of the firſt Husband, and ſhould inherit the Land. And after this Courſe obſerved, ſhe was deliver'd of a Female Child, who was afterwards by Inquiſition found to be the Daughter and Heir of the firſt Husband, *Cro. Jac. p.* 685. *Theaker's* Caſe.

Computation of the Time in the Womb.

Infant was born 40 Weeks and 10 Days after the Death of the Husband, and was held Legitimate. So Adjudged in the Caſe of Dr. *Andrews*, who died of the Plague, upon Conference with Phyſicians: And the Doctors held, That 20 Days backward, *&c.* or 20 Days forward, doth not take away Legitimation, tho' 40 Weeks is the *Tempus conſtitutum*, *Palmer* 9.

And in *Alſop's* Caſe, the Wife after 40 Weeks and 8 Days, was deliver'd of a Daughter. By the Doctors, it may be Legitimate; for as an *Antenatus* might be Heir in a Child born at the End of 7 Months, ſo a *Poſtnatus* actually born after 40 Weeks: And they held, a Child may be Legitimate, though it be born the laſt Day of the 10th Month after the Conception, accounting the Months *per Menſes Solares*, not *Lunares*, *Godb.* 281. 1 *Roll.* 356. 2 *Cro.* 541. *Alſop* and *Stacy*.

The exact Time of a Man being at full Age.

H. born on the 16th Day of *February*, 1608, is on the 16th Day of *February*, 1629, One and twenty Years of Age; and in whatever Hour of the Day he was born, is not material, there being no Fraction of Days. But in *Siderfin*, in the ſame Caſe, the accounting of the Age, the Day of the Birth ſhall be reckon'd reckon'd exclusive: And if one is born the 15th of *February* (this Month 21 Years) he is of full Age the 14th of *February*.

As to a Supposititious Birth, I shall cite you at large *Buckworth*'s Case out of *Siderfin*'s Reports, because it's remarkable, and of late I have heard it often mentioned. The Case was this: Information was exhibited against *B.* and others for Perjury, and others for Subornation. Mr. *Dormer* being Tenant for Life of several Lands in *Lincolnshire*, with Remainder to his first Son in Tail, and so to his first Daughter, *&c.* took Wife, and they came to *London*, and were Lodgers in *Chancery-Lane*, where *Dormer* dies; but about the Time of his Death, his Wife said she was deliver'd of a Child, which was a Daughter. There was a Trial in *B. C.* between the Infant and he in Remainder. The Manner of the Delivery of the Infant was proved by Circumstances and by Marks, the Infant being strip'd in Court. But *B.* who was the Midwife, gave in Evidence, That this Infant was not the Child of the said Woman, but of a poor Woman in St. *Giles*'s, which was procured by *Dormer*'s Wife, and bought for 2 *s.* 6 *d.* by the Midwife, and by Appointment the Infant was to be privately brought to *Dormer*'s Wife, and then there was to be an Outcry, and the Infant was put into her Bosom, and drawn out by the Thighs when the Woman came to the supposed Labour, and that there was a Bladder of Blood and Lamb's Appurtenances provided, and shewed to those which came to the Labour. And for giving this Evidence,

B.

B. was indicted for Perjury; and the Circumstances to prove her guilty, was the cutting the Navel-strings, the Colour of the Skin of the Infant, *&c.* and that *B.* had several Sums of Fifty Pounds, *&c.* given to her by the Direction of *G.* who was next in Remainder. On the other Side, there was the poor Woman and others, that said, That the Midwife had her Child at this Time, and that no Account could be given of the Child, unless this were the Child: And there was great Proof, That the poor Woman, after her Child was Christen'd at St. *Giles*'s, gave it to the Midwife; and it appeared, that Money was given to the Witnesses on both Sides. And the Jury acquitted the Defendants of Perjury, and the Parties were left at Law to try their Right. And after, 21 *Car.* 2. there was a Trial at Bar for these Lands by a *Lincolnshire* Jury, and Verdict *pro Querente, (viz.)* That this was a Supposititious Child, *Siderfin, p.* 378. *The King* and *Buckworth, and others.*

Bond to save harmless of a Bastard Child in the Womb.

Debt on Obligee, with Condition, That the Defendant shall pay to the Plaintiff 10 *l.* 8 *Jan.* ensuing, Provided that the Plaintiff save harmless, *&c.* one *T. S.* of all Costs, Trouble, *&c.* which might accrue to him by reason that the Plaintiff was then *enseint. Bar,* That the Plaintiff had sworn before a Justice of the Peace that the said *T. S.* was Father of the said Child, whereby the said *T. S.* was taken and forced to find Bail. *Replic.* That the Plaintiff, 1 *Aug.* 8 *Will.* 3. was deliver'd of a Child, who was a Bastard begotten by the ſaid *T. S.* and that the ſaid *T. S.* was never damnified by reaſon of the Maintenance of the ſaid Infant. Demurrer, and Judgment for the Plaintiff; for that the Intent of the Condition was only to ſave *T. S.* harmleſs of the Maintenance of the Child, but not to ſave him harmleſs againſt legal Proſecution, to prevent which, it was not in the Power of the Plaintiff or Defendant; and if the Proviſo in the Condition of the Obligation had been to ſuch expreſs Purpoſe, it had been repugnant to the firſt Part of the Condition, becauſe againſt Law, 1 *Lutt.* 669. *Briggs* verſus *Maund.*

CHAP.

CHAP. II.

Privileges of Infants, or not.

Where the Nonage of an Infant shall not stay an Inquest. Infant may ward his Demurrer to a Declaration, and plead to Issue. Infants more favoured at Common Law than Feme Coverts, and why. The Law protects the Persons of Infants: They are not to be amerced except in Special Cases; nor imprisoned. The Reason of finding Pledges in Actions. Custom of a manner of Surrender be made to the Use of another, and he doth not come in to be admitted after Three Proclamations, to be forfeited. If this Custom shall bind an Infant, well argued. After Surrender of Copyhold, he may enter at full Age. If the Custom be, that the Lord may grant the Custody of an Infant Copyholder, the Father may not dispose it by the Stat. 12 Car. 2. *Infant outlaw'd. Failure* de *Record, in account against Infant, as Bayliff. Auditors not to commit him if he be found in Arrear. Statutes which give Corporal Punishment shall not extend to Infants generally. If a Lease of Infant Copyholder without Licence be a Forfeiture in Judgment against him by Default, how to be understood. Of Confession by Infant, all Judgments are in Four Manners. What Acts shall bind Infant or not. To bind himself Apprentice. Of a Lease made to him. To make Letter*

Letter of Attorney to take Livery for him. In what Cases Laches shall be prejudicial to an Infant, or not. Not priviledged in case of Criminal Actions or Torts; nor in Cases of Rents, Services, Tenures, Conditions or Charges on Lands. Interest lost, decreed in the Case of an Infant. What Act shall amount to a Forfeiture. What Offices or Functions an Infant is capable of. Office of Trust. Judicial Offices not grantable to Infant; nor Ministerial Offices which concern the Administration of Justice. Not be an Attorney. May be a Mayor. May be a Prebend. By what Acts of Parliament Infants are bound, or not. Infancy shall not excuse him against the Statute of Fraudulent Conveyances. He is bound in respect of the Publick Repose, concerning Men's Freeholds. He is bound to the Custom of a Manor or Place. He is bound by Prerogative. Infant Inn-keeper, no Action against him for Robbery of his Guests Goods.

Where the Nonage of the Infant shall not stay an Inquest.

BY *Stat. Glouc. 6 Ed. 1. c. 2.* If a Child within Age be holden from his Heritage after the Death of his Father, Grandfather or Great Grandfather, whereby he is driven to his Writ, and his Adversary comes into Court, and for his Answer alledgeth a Feoffment, or pleadeth some other

Parole shall not demur where the Justices award an Inquest.

other Thing whereby the Justices award an Inquest; there whereas the Inquest was deferred unto the full Age of the Infant, now the Inquest shall pass as well as if he were of full Age. This Act relieves Infants against Delay to their Prejudice. In a Writ of *Mort d'ancestor*, *Ayel les aile Cosinage*, such Pleading, Trial and Proceeding, shall be as if the Plaintiff were of full Age. *Vide*, for the Explication of the Statute, 2 *Inst*. 290. 6 *Rep*. 3. 1 *Bulst*. 137.

Our Common Law looks upon Infancy as an Age of Impotence, Weakness and Disability, not capable of managing their Concerns with Discretion, and for their better Profit and Advantage; and therefore is very favourable to them in preserving their Rights and Estates, inabling them in their Suits, assisting them in their Pleadings, excusing their Laches, and in protecting their Persons. In short, as it is expressed in *Holford* and *Platt*'s Case, 2 *Rolls Rep*. 18. The Judges are their Counsellors, the Jury are their Servants, for they ought to find the Title at large in an Assize, and the Law is their Guardian, 2 *Roll. Rep*. 18. 5 *Ed*. 3. *per Stat.*

May wave his Demurrer to the Declaration, and plead to Issue.

If Action be brought against Infant, and in Law he demurs to the Declaration, he may afterwards wave his Demurrer and plead to Issue, 31 *Ed*. 3. *Fitz*. Infants Case: And so was it adjudged in *Kirton* and *Elliot*'s Case.

Caſe. An Infant may wave his Demurrer at another Day after he hath demurred; but this ought to be in the ſame Term. 2 *Bulſt*. 69.

Now Infants and Feme Coverts, as to the Diſability of their Perſons, are generally ranked together. But my Lord *Hobart*, in *Môre* and *Huſſey*'s Caſe, *fol.* 95. ſaith, That Infants are more favoured at Common Law than Feme Coverts; and that Coverture was not at Common Law ſo far protected as was Infancy, and ſome other Diſabilities, as *non ſane Memorie, ouſter le mere, &c.* As for Inſtance, upon the *Stat.* 21 *Ed.* 1. which is; If in Aſſize the Tenant pleads Jointenancy with a Stranger, who being called in and maintains it, and it be found falſe, he ſhall be impriſoned a Year. In 21 *Aſſ. pl.* 28. Aſſize was brought againſt the Husband, who pleads Jointenancy with his Wife by Deed, and ſhe being called in, maintain'd it, and it being found falſe, it was adjudged, That ſhe ſhould be impriſoned according to that Statute; but upon *Stat. W.* 2. *c.* 21. If Infant fail in Aſſize of a Record by him pleaded, he ſhall not be thereupon adjudged a Diſſeiſor within that Law, *Hob.* 95. *More* and *Huſſey*'s Caſe.

Infants more favoured at Common Law than Feme Coverts.

Failure of Record.

In *Lechford*'s Caſe, 8 *Rep.* The Cuſtom of the Manor was, That if a Copyhold diſcend to the Heir, that Proclamation ſhall be made at Three ſeveral Courts; that he ſhall come in to be admitted, and if he come not in, it ſhall be forfeited to the Lord; yet

Proclamation.

yet an Infant ſhall not be comprehended within this Cuſtom, for he by Intendment of Law is not of Diſcretion to make his Claim, but in ſuch Caſe Feme Covert might be; becauſe her Husband might do it; and at the Common Law a Feme Covert was ouſted of her Non-claim on a Fine, which an Infant was not, but the Statute 4 *Hen.* 7. *c.* 24. excepts Feme Coverts, 8 *Rep.* 100. *Lechford*'s Caſe. This Caſe is more fully reported.

Cuſtom of a Manor is, That if a Surrender be made to the Uſe of another, and he doth not come in to be admitted after Three Proclamations at Three Courts, that the Bailiff of the Manor may, by Command of the Lord, ſeiſe ſuch Tenement as forfeited: Such Surrender was to the Uſe of *J. S.* and Three Proclamations, and none came in to be admitted; *J. S.* before the firſt Proclamation died, leaving *J. N.* his Son and Heir then and yet an Infant; it was adjudged in *B. C.* That the Cuſtom did not bind an Infant. Error was brought in *B. R.* and the Judgment was affirmed by Three Judges, *contra Ch. J. Holt.*

Where an Infant hath not Privilege.

It's true in ſome Caſes Infant hath no Priviledge, as in Caſes of Church, Life and Liberty, 1 *Inſt.* 233, 234. Where the Statute gives a Remedy by Action, he is bound; *aliter*, in caſe where an Entry is given: In Sir *R. Lechford*'s Caſe, the Cuſtom is to be intended ſo as the Heir be of full Age, and ſafe Memory. 1 *Leon.* 100. *Rumney* and *Eve*'s

Eve's Case. Infant is not bound to come to any Court for Admittance during his Nonage. If the Surrendree be before Admittance, the Heir shall have the Land, 2 *Sid.* 37. *Noy* 92. *Jones* 157. Infants Feoffment doth not make a Forfeiture, much less shall an Omission. Not bound to be admitted during Nonage.

Dolbin J. said in his Argument, That he was Steward of 26 Copyhold Manors, and in every one of them was this Custom; and the constant Entry was, *Nulla Proclamatio quia Enfans*, by most Copyhold Customs the Lord appoints a Guardian for an Infant, and he himself is bound to come in within Three Proclamations after he is of Age. *Holt Ch. J.* Opinion was, That till the Heir of the Surrendree be admitted, the Estate of the Copyhold remains in the Surrendree, and then the Infancy of the Heir of the Surrendree cannot affect this Case; and here is no Loss to the Infants Inheritance in this Case. *Shower* 83. *King* and *Dilliston*.

The Lord of a Manor may not grant the Custody of an Infant Copyhold without Custom, but such a Custom is not controlled by the Statute 12 *Car.* 2. and therefore in such Case the Father may not dispose the Custody of such Infant, *Latch* 1189, 1190.

Infant of 10 Years outlaw'd, he was not awarded to Prison for the Tenderness of his Age. 38 *Ed.* 3. 5. *b.* Outlaw'd.

Failure de Record. Infant named a Disseisor, voucheth a Record and fails, he shall not be imprison'd on the Statute *W.* 2. *cap.* 25. *Com.* 364. *a.*

So if Infant be Bail, *&c.* and on Account he is found in Arrear, the Auditors may not commit him to the next Gaol, upon the Statute of *W.* 2. *c.* 11.

The Law protects the Persons of Infants. As to the Favour the Law shews in protecting the Person of an Infant, it's generally owned, that an Infant shall not find Pledges, and consequently shall not be amerced. It's a Rule, That in all Actions Original, Real or Personal, Pledges are to be found except in Two Cases, 3 *Bulst.*

Pledges, where not to be found. 1. For the Dignity of the Person, as the King.

2. For the Imbecillity of the Person, as in case of an Infant; but if the Infant comes to his full Age hanging the Writ, he shall find Pledges, or be amerced. Now there are Two Reasons for the finding of Pledges: *1st.* For the Party; If Judgment be given against the Plaintiff, the Judgment ought not to be prolonged without Cause. *2dly.* For the King; For that the Plaintiff hath troubled the Court without Cause. Now the Defendant (Infant) shall not be amerced, but the Entry shall be *pardonatur quia Infans*, 8 *Rep.* 62. 2 *Leon.* 4. 185, 186.

Reasons for the finding of Pledges in all Actions.

Treason, Felony. He is not guilty of Felony till the Age of Discretion, 3 *Inst.* 4, 5.

He

He at 11 Years of Age may be Grantee of an Office, after an Estate for Life, *excercendum per se vel per sufficientem Deputatum suum* as *Register Office*; and a Deputy is allowed always in Ministerial Offices, to be approved of by the Judges of that Court: And as an Infant may have an Office by Discent, as to be Steward or Warden of the *Fleet*, *&c.* so he may by Grant, *vide plus Cr. Car.* 279. *Young* and *Steell* 55. *b.* Office.

Infant may be a Purchaser.

He shall be amerced in some Cases, *sed pardonatur quia Infans*, *vide infra.*

He cannot be an Approver, 3 *Inst.* 129.

Judgment *quod capiatur* against an Infant is reversed, for an Infant shall not be imprisoned in this Case. Infant is found a Disseisor, so that he ought to be imprisoned, *sed pardonatur quia Infans.* In case of Felony he shall be imprison'd, *Br. tit. Impris.* 75. 1 *Bulst.* 172. *Daby* and *Holb.* Not imprisoned.

It's said generally, Statutes which give Corporal Punishment shall not extend to Infants. But 30 *Ass.* 18. Infant brought an Attaint, and the first Verdict was affirmed, and the Infant was awarded to Prison.

He is disabled to take a Church, *Hob.* 325.

Infant shall not be of a Jury, 1 *Inst.* 157, 172.

Note, The King cannot be a *Minor*, and therefore shall not avoid his grant by Nonage, 5 *Rep.* 27. 7 *Rep.* 10, 12.

Estates and Rights of Infants protected.

As to the protecting of his Estate and Rights.

Infant should have been bound by the Statute of 4 *Hen.* 7. of Fines, if there had not been an express Saving for him in the *Stat.* 3 *Rep.* 87.

If Infant had not been excepted in the Statute of Fore-judgment, the Fore-Judgment had bound him. *Doct. & Stud.* 148. *b. Dyer.* 104. *b.*

It seems to be a Rule in Law, That an Infant cannot be protected by the Law in any Case, but where his Right which he had while an Infant, and discended to him, might have been barred and interrupted by Non-claim; and so it is in case of Forfeiture. The Reason of the Rule is, because the Law conceives he will have that Knowledge to preserve his Right when he is of full Age. *Vide plus ad hoc infra sub titulo Fines,* &c. *Carter*'s *Rep.* 86. in *Smith* and *Painton*'s Case.

Infant not bound to pay Admittance.

If a Copyholder dies, his Heir within Age, he is not bound to come into any Court during his Nonage to pay Admittance, or tender his Fine, 1 *Leon. p.* 100. *pl.* 128. *Rumus* and *Eaves.*

May enter at full Age into Copyhold Estate he surrendred.

So an Infant, who surrenders his Copyhold Land within Age, may enter at his full Age, without being put to any Suit for it. Nay, if he surrender to another when he is within Age, it's not good in *Chancery*, *M.* 9 *Jac.* *Hayles* and *Carpenter*, *Pop. Rep. p.* 39.

Infant,

Infant Copyholder in Fee makes a Leaſe for Years without Licence, rendering Rent, at full Age he accepts the Rent, and after *ouſts* the Leſſee, Leſſee brings Eject-ment; and Judgment for Leſſee: It was adjudged, *1ſt.* That this Leaſe by the Infant without Licence is no Forfeiture. *2dly.* Acceptance of Rent at full Age makes it good, 8 *Rep.* 44. *Noy* 92. Leaſe by him without Licence no Forfeiture.

This Caſe is in *Latch* 199. *Aſhfield*'s Caſe, *per Crawley* Serjeant. He may well ouſt his Leſſee, though it be true a Leaſe by Infant rendering Rent is but voidable, yet in the Caſe of a Copyholder it is otherwiſe, becauſe the Leaſe ſhall be a Diſſeiſin to the Lord, and a Forfeiture of his Eſtate; but *e contra* it was ſaid, That this is a Leaſe till it be avoided, and if a Copyholder makes a Leaſe it is a Forfeiture: *Eaſt* and *Harding*'s Caſe.

Copyholder makes a Leaſe for Years, to commence *in futuro*: This is a good Leaſe, but a Forfeiture in caſe of Infant; becauſe, if the Lord enter upon him, he may re-enter, as in 8 *Rep.* The Court agreed, That this was no Diſſeiſin to the Lord; but the Qu. was, If it was void in reſpect of Forfeiture? and adjudged, That the Leaſe is not void; but Judgment was given againſt the Infant for the Declaration, *Latch* 199. *Vide* 1 *Jones* 157. *Read* 188. *Godb.* 364. *Pop.* 188.

As

Judgment cannot be against him by Default.

As to the Priviledges of an Infant in respect of Feoffments, Leases, Contracts, Statutes, Bonds, *&c. Vide infra*, under the respective Titles.

How to be understood.

It is commonly said, an Infant cannot have Judgment against him by Default. But as to that, I shall examine it by that Case of *Holdford* and *Plott*, which was learnedly argued by the Judges, and is reported in 2 *Rolls Rep.* and in *Cro. Jac.* 464. 2 *Rolls Rep.* 17. *Holdford* and *Plott*.

Error was brought to reverse a Judgment in a Writ of Entry against the Earl of *Newport*, an Infant, where he appeared by his Guardians; wherein they vouched the common Vouchee upon his Default after Appearance: The Error assigned was, That the Judgment was given by Default, he being an Infant. *Per Cur.* This is not Error, for the Judgment is not given upon the Default of the Infant, but upon the Departure of the Vouchee in despight of the Court, and the Court is trusted that they will not admit a Guardian but such as shall answer to the Infant for his Loss, if he have any, *Crok.* 1. 224. Earl of *Newport* and Sir *H. Mildmay*.

If Judgment be given in *dum fuit infra ætatem*, or other Action against Infant by Default; after Default he shall have a Writ of Error, and reverse the Judgment for his Nonage. Yet if Infant after Appearance make Default, Judgment shall be given against him, and he shall not reverse it for Error. *Dyer* 104.

In

In Aſſize of *Novel Diſſeiſin*, the Tenant pleads a Recovery in a former Aſſize againſt him. The Demandant replies, That he was an Infant, and avers, That he was not Tertenant at the Time of the Recovery, but that *P.* was Tenant, and that it was a Recovery by Default. The Replication was held by the better Opinion to be good. In this Caſe the Infant cannot have Error or Attaint, and therefore he may falſify the Recovery. *Firſt*, Here is a Title and Judgment pleaded againſt an Infant, whereas his Title is not diſcovered, which ought to be done, and that might be Two Ways: 1. By Appearance; or, 2. By Default. Upon his Appearance in Two Manners, (*viz.*) upon *Confeſſion*, or *Nient dedire*. If the Infant in Aſſize will confeſs, the Court ſhall not receive his Confeſſion; and if he will not plead, the Jury ſhall not enquire upon the Point of Seiſin, but at large. If he make Default, and ſo will not diſcover his Title, his Default is *mera negligentia*, and that will not prejudice him, or it is *negligentia cum contemptu*, and is in the ſame Degree as a Departure in deſpight of the Court; as if he appear and after make Default, there Judgment ſhall be given againſt him. If an Infant be eſſoined in *ſervitio Regis*, and make Default in not bringing in his Warrant: So if he make Default in a *Petit Cape*, theſe are Defaults with Contempt, and Judgment ſhall be given againſt him. But Judgment by Default in Aſſize ſhall not bind an Infant,

Confeſſion by Infant.

Defaults with Contempt.

How Judgment by Verdict or Trial shall bind an Infant.

fant, but Judgment by Verdict or Trial shall bind him, but with this Difference, if the Judgment be upon Appearance; but if there be not Appearance, it shall never bind him.

What Acts shall bind an Infant, or not.

Acts made for his Advantage, *Perk.* 4. *a.* as to pay for his necessary Diet, *&c.*

So if he bind himself Apprentice.

Infant of 12 Years may be Appprentice by Covenant, 38 *H.* 8. 22. *a.*

If Infant hath a Lease made to him and Manures the Land, Debt lies against him for the Rent, because it is for his Avail, 21 *H.* 6. 31. *b.*

If Infant Feoffee make a Letter of Attorney to *A.* to take Livery for him, this is good, because for his Avail.

If Infant present to a Benefice, this binds him, otherwise Lapse would incur against him, 1 *Inst.* 172. *a.*

Trespass lies against Infant of the Age of Discretion, *Doct. & Stud.* 149. *a.* and by *Wangford* it lies against Infant of Four Years of Age, 35 *H.* 6. 11. *b.* But *Bro. Corone* 6. makes a Quære of this.

If his Goods are estray'd or wasted, and proclaimed and not claimed, he shall be barred of them, 5 *Rep.* 108. *Com.* 364. *b.*

So in case of Wreck.

So

So the taking of his Goods and Sale in open Market, *Com*. 160. *b*.

Every Thing that an Infant is bound to do by Law ſhall bind him. 1 *Inſt*. 172. *a*. as if Infant Executor, upon Payment of a Debt, makes Acquittance; but Acquittance without Payment is void.

Vide infra, Acts in Law as to Warranty.

If Infant be Receiver, and enter into Account before Auditors, he ſhall be charged in Debt on Account, 10 *H*. 6. 14. *b*. for *non patet de recordo*: Now if he were within Age, or not, and it ſeems he may not have for Plea in Debt *ſur* account, that he was within Age *tempore compoti*, for it is a Judgment paſs'd before againſt him. *Quære*, Account doth not lie againſt an Infant, 1 *Inſt*. 172. *a*.

Infant may not wage his Law, 1 *Inſt*. 295. *a*.

If Judgment be given againſt an Infant upon *Laches*, he may have a Writ of Error, and alledge, that he was an Infant, and it was given againſt him by Default, and the other ſhall not plead in *nullo eſt erratum*, but the Iſſue ſhall be upon the Nonage. So in *Crok*. *Jac*. 64. 651. If Judgment be given againſt an Infant by Default, after the Default he ſhall have a Writ of Error, and reverſe the Judgment for his Nonage; and yet if an Infant after Appearance make Default, Judgment ſhall be given againſt him, and he ſhall not reverſe it. But in the principal

Writ of Error.

cipal Case of *Holdford* and *Plott*, it was the Opinion of *Dodderidge*, That the Infant could not help himself by Writ of Error, because the Judgment was not given against him upon the Default, but the Assize was upon the Default, as in 6 *Rep*. *Ferrer*'s Case.

Regularly Bar in Assize is a Bar in Action of the same Nature, except in Three Cases.

By *Mountague* Chief Justice, regularly a Bar in Assize is a Bar in an Action of the same Nature. But this Rule hath Three Exceptions: 1. In case of a Parson Prebend, or Tenant in Tail. 2. If he can from any Title. 3. If he be an Infant.

All Judgments are in Four Manners.

A Judgment against an Infant shall not bind him, for all Judgments are either

By { Award, Confession, Default, Trial.

1. Judgment by Award shall not bind an Infant, 8 *Ass. pl.* 17. he may plead a Release in Bar after the Assize awarded; so 10 *H.* 6. 14. Judgment against an Infant on Account, that he shall account, binds him not, if he do not enter into the Account.

2. Upon Confession, 9 *Ed.* 3. 38. 28 *Ass. pl.* 52. the Court will not receive his Confession. Judgment shall never be given against an Infant upon his Confession, but the Jury shall enquire at large of all Circumstances.

cumstances. So upon *Nihil dicit*, 2 *Roll. Rep.* 17.

3. Upon Trial by Default, 3 *H.* 6. 10. *Vide supra.* And the Difference.

4. Judgment upon Trial shall not bind an Infant, the Book of 33 *H.* 6. 21. That if there be a Trial by Verdict it shall bind an Infant, is to be expounded by 7 *H.* 4. 25.

In all Real Actions, Infant shall have his Age, *Vide infra, sub titulo Pleadings*, several Exceptions. Infant to have his Age.

Infant cannot lose by Default in Dower, except by Guardian. *Per Cur.* If a Writ of Dower be brought against an Infant, who loseth by Default at the Grand Cape, yet he may reverse the same by Writ of Error. But where an Infant appeareth by Guardian, and afterwards loseth by Default, there he shall never avoid it; and if any Default be in the Guardian, the Infant shall recover against him in a Writ of Disceit. And if the Infant brings Assize by his Guardian, although the Infant disavow the Suit in proper Person, yet no Nonsuit shall be awarded, 2 *Leon. p.* 579. *Dyer* 104. 39 *Ass. pl.* 1. Nonsuit.

In what Cases Laches shall be prejudicial to an Infant, or not.

The Rule, That no Laches or Negligence shall be adjudged in an Infant is true, where he is thereby to be barred of his Entry in respect of a former Right, as by a Descent, or No Laches prejudicial to Infants, how to be understood.

or of his former Right, as by a Warranty where his Entry is congeable. But otherwise it is of Conditions, Charges, Penalties going out, or depending upon the Original Conveyance; for Laches ſhall be adjudged in thoſe Caſes as well in the Infant as any other, *Plow. Com. Stowell's* Caſe, *per tot.* 355. *Vide* 1 *Inſt.* 380. *b.*

But if the Infant be within Age at the Time of the Alienation with Warranty, and becomes of full Age before the Deſcent of the Warranty, the Warranty ſhall bar him for ever, *Vide infra tit. Acts in Law.*

But though an Infant is generally favoured in the Law, (as hath been repreſented to you) yet this Favour doth not extend to all Caſes; the Conſideration whereof ſhall be the Subject of the next Section.

In what Caſes an Infant is not favoured in the Law.

An Infant ſhall not have any Benefit of his Nonage where he claims as a Purchaſer, the Law protecting Infants only in Caſes of Diſcents. *Carter* 87, 88. *vide.*

Not favoured in Contempt. He is not priviledged in caſe of Contempt to the Court. And therefore Judgment by Default after Appearance ſhall bind him, for the Default amounts to a Departure in deſpight of the Court, *Vide ſupra.*

its

It's a General Rule, That an Infant ſhall not be amerced; and this is the Cauſe that he ſhall not find Pledges; yet we find in our Books many Caſes wherein he ſhall be amerced: As, In what Caſes he ſhall be amerced.

In a *Quare Impedit* againſt an Infant, if the Plaintiff had a Writ to the Biſhop, the Infant ſhall be amerced, 44 *Ed.* 3. *tit. Amerc.* 10.

If an Infant brings an Action, and this abates for his Infancy, he ſhall be amerced, 41 *Aſſ.* 14.

If Infant brings Action by *Prochein Amy*, and hanging the Action, comes of full Age and makes an Attorney, and after is Nonſuit, he ſhall be amerced, *Dyer* 338.

Infant brought Action of Treſpaſs by his Guardian againſt Two, and the Defendants plead Not guilty, and at *Niſi prius* the Plaintiff appears in Perſon, and a Verdict is found for the Plaintiff for Part, and Not guilty for the Reſidue, and one of the Defendants Not guilty. And Judgment is given for the Plaintiff for that for which the Verdict is given for him, and *quod nil capiat per billam* for the Reſidue, and him that is found Not guilty, *ſed nihil de miſericordia pro falſo clamore, &c. quia querens tempore tranſgreſſionis præd' factæ infra ætatem exiſtebat*; yet this is good, and no Error, and the Court took a Difference between this and a Nonſuit.

But when an Infant is amerced, he ſhall be pardoned of Courſe. But pardoned.

May be Out-law'd. Infants above the Age of Fourteen may be Outlaw'd, for this is a flying from the Law, and no Reason he should be favoured by it.

Shall pay Cost. Infant Lessor in Ejectment shall pay Costs, 3 *Keb.* 347.

Leygager. Infant may not wage his Law, because he cannot make Oath, 11 *H.* 6. 40 *b.*

Not favour'd in Criminal Acts. 2. In case of Criminal Actions, and Wrongs and Injuries done to the Person or Estate of another, an Infant shall not be priviledg'd, for in such Cases *Malitia supplet Ætatem*; but then he must be of the Age of Discretion.

If an Infant be Tenant by the Courtesy, or Lessee for Life or Years, he shall answer for Wast done by a Stranger, by *Stat. Glocest. c.* 5. If he doth Wast, and the Lessor recover in Wast, it shall bind him, 3 *Inst.* 301. 8 *Rep.* 44.

Infants, or Feme Coverts, Keepers of Gaols, shall be charged with Escapes, 2 *Jac.* 382.

3. Infant is not favoured in Cases of Rents, Tenures or Services, or other Charge upon the Land, for *transit Terra cum Onere*, 2 *Inst.* 11.

Gorge did, by Articles sealed, agree to pay *Hilliard*, the Plaintiff's Father, 2100 *l.* for his Interest in a Plantation in *Barbadoes*, with Covenants to enter into seven Bonds for the Money, 300 *l.* each Bond. *Gorge* enjoy'd the Plantation, but no Conveyance made to him. But *Hilliard* died, and made *Speak* and *Hely* Executors, *&c.* in Trust for the Plaintiff, an Infant. 600 *l.* was paid. *Hely* (five of the Bonds being due) deliver'd them

them up, and takes Bonds of the same Sums in the Name of himself and his Co-executor, pretending that *Gorge* had received a Commission from the King to go to *Suranam*, &c. and so to mend the Security, he took five new Bonds. But by this 500 *l.* Interest was lost to the Infant.

Interest lost, decreed in the Case of an Infant.

It was decreed, That Payment should be made according to the Times of Payment in the first Articles, and *Gorge* and *Hely* to be charged therewith, notwithstanding that *Hely* had on taking the new Bonds releas'd *Gorge* of the Articles, 2 Cases in *Chancery* 235. *Hilliard* versus *Gorge*.

Infancy shall not excuse the Breach of a Condition. And a Condition in a Deed obligeth Infants as much as others. *Vide* 8 *Rep.* 42. *Wittingham*'s Case. As to this between Conditions in Fact, and Condition in Law; Infant is bound by all Conditions in Deed, tho' not by all Conditions in Law. *Plow. Com.* 57. is against it; but *Br. Cond. Pl.* 114. that Case is said to be no Law, 1 *Vent.* 200. *Porter and Fry.*

What Act by Infant shall amount to a Forfeiture. *Vide infra Tit. Conveyance* and *Feoffment.* An Infant may do Homage, but not Fealty, because that is to be done upon Oath, 1 *Inst. lib.* 2. *cap.* Homage. In a *per quæ Servitia* against an Infant, he shall be compelled to Attorn; for he shall not be prejudiced by it, because at full Age he may disclaim to hold of him, or that he held by lesser Services; but there should be a greater Mischief to the Lord, if the Attornment of the Tenant should not be good, for he ſhould loſe his Services in the mean time. If an Infant be Leſſee, he ſhall be compelled to Attorn in a *Quid Juris clamat*, 9 *Rep*. 125. *b*. *Coney*'s Caſe.

If Land deſcend to an Infant, this being held in Socage, he ſhall pay a Relief; and after the Death of Tenant in Socage, Relief is due preſently, be the Heir of what Age he will, and though he be not paſt Fourteen, *Doct*. and *Stud*. 14. *b*. 2 *Rolls Abr*. 59. 1 *Inſt*. 127.

As to other Charge, *Vide infra Tit. Law Acts, Conditions*, &c.

What Offices or Functions an Infant is capable of.

Not to be employ'd in publick Offices.

4. In Caſes of Offices and publick Adminiſtration, an Infant ſhall not be employed therein, in reſpect of his Non-ability to undergo *Ardua Regni* or *Negotia Curiæ*. But this indeed is rather a Favour to him, the Law not permitting an Infant to attempt Things beyond his Strength and Capacity, leſt *Phaeton* like, he raſhly overturn the Frame of Adminiſtration.

Not to be Steward of a Manor.

He ſhall not be Steward of a Manor, or Bailiff or Attorney; but he may be an Attorney to give Livery and Seiſin.

Infant not to be elected Knight or Burgeſs for Parliament, tho' it is too often done to the contrary.

He is not capable to perform grand Serjeanty at the Coronation.

As

As to Offices, of what Offices, and the Execution thereof, an Infant is capable, or not.

Of his Forfeiture by Condition in Law. *Vide* 8 *Rep.* 44.

It's a good Distinction in the first Institutes as to Conditions in Law, which are annexed to Offices. One Condition in Law is Skill and Confidence. Another Condition in Law is, That if he alien a greater Estate than he hath, it's a Forfeiture. Now to apply it, If an Office of Partnership be granted or descend to an Infant, or Feme Covert, if the Condition in Law annexed to this Office, which requires Skill and Confidence, be not observed and fulfilled, the Office is lost for ever; for it is as strong as an express Condition. But if a Lease for Life be made to an Infant, and he by Charter of Feoffment aliens in Fee, the Breach of this Condition in Law is no absolute Forfeiture of his Estate. So of a Condition in Law given by the Statute, 1 *Inst.* 233. *b.* 8 *Rep.* *Whittingham*'s Case.

Grant of an Office of Trust to an Infant to execute by Deputy, is good; or a Grant to him in Reversion, is good; for it may be granted in Fee, and so descend to an Infant; or a Feme Covert may have such an Office, because by Possibility she may have an Husband who may execute it, *March* 38. *Young* and *Fowler*. Infant ought to execute by sufficient Deputy. He may be chargeable for Escape, and by Forfeiture of his Office.

M. 40, 41 *El. Scambler*'s Case, Infant not capable of Stewardship of a Manor.

Judicial Offices may not be granted to an Infant, 1 *Inst.* 3. *b.* But they may diſcend to an Infant, for it may be granted in Fee, *March Rep.* 42, 43. *per Inſt. Crook* and *Barkley.*

Miniſterial Offices, which concern the Adminiſtration of Juſtice, may not be granted immediately to an Infant, as Steward of a Manor, 1 *Inſt.* 3. *b.* But it may be granted to an Infant in Reverſion, and ſhall be good, if he be of full Age when it falls, and accordingly ſo was it adjudged in the Caſe of the Regiſterſhip of the Biſhop of *Rocheſter, March Rep.* 38, 39.

One may not be Attorney within Age, becauſe he cannot be ſworn, *March Rep.* 92. And becauſe an Attorney may not make a Deputy.

Infant may be Mayor, 21 *Ed.* 4. 13, 14. 13 *H.* 8. 12. *b.*

Infant may be a Prebend, *Bro. Age,* 80.

Grant of a Parkerſhip to an Infant is good, *March* 41.

Infant, before *Stat.* 10 *Eliz.* might have been preſented to Benefice, and he was Parſon *de Facto, March* 43. But this is intended to be of an Infant who was at the Age of Diſcretion.

Per Stat. 13 *Eliz. c.* 12. None ſhall be made Miniſter, or admitted to preach or adminiſter the Sacraments, being under the Age of 24.

Note, It was in a Manner agreed by all the Juſtices in *B. C.* in the Time of Queen *Mary,* That if a Parſon, Prebend, or the like,

like, within the Age of 21 Years makes a Lease of his Benefice, that this shall bind him; for where he is admitted by Law of Holy Church to take it within Age, so the Common Law will enable him to demise his Benefice within Age, 4 *Mary*, *Bro. Age*, 80.

It has been continually seen, that the Prebends are given to Infants, and yet they are not Priests, nor have they any Orders; but it is for that they have not Cure of Souls. *Per Conisby*, 21 *H.* 7. 2. *a*. *b*.

5. In Cases of publick Utility and Safety of the Common Weals, an Infant shall not be favoured no more than others; his House may be blown up in case of a general Fire, and to stop the spreading of the Conflagration. He is bound to contribute to repair Bridges, to pay publick Taxes, and the like, 2 *Inst*. 703. Publick Safety.

And here I shall briefly observe, in and by what Acts of Parliament an Infant is bound or not. By what Acts of Parliament Infant is bound or not.

It's a Rule in *Dyer* 104. an Infant is bound by every Statute Law, if he be not excepted, as the Statute of Fore-judger, *Cessavit*, Fines, with Proclamations, &c.

In the Argument of *Stowell* and *Zouch*, *Plow*. 394. it is well distinguish'd, that in some Cases where the Statutes are general, yet they shall not extend to the Infants, and in some Cases they shall, *Plow*. 364. *Zouch* and *Stowell*.

The Statute of Non-claim shall not bind Infant, 2 *Ass*. 6. But if Part of the Year be in the Time of his Ancestor; now if the Statute of Non-claims.

 Heir

Heir within Age doth not enter during that Year, he ſhall be barred, 370, 371. in *Stowell*'s Caſe. Q.

Corporal Puniſhment.

Statutes which give Corporal Puniſhment, ſhall not extend to Infants, contrary of other Statutes, 36 *Ed.* 3. If Infant be Keeper of a Priſon, and ſuffer an Eſcape, he ſhall be ſubject to the Eſcape.

If Infant be found a Diſſeiſor, yet it was held his Impriſonment ſhall be remitted; but *vid.* 30 *Aſſ.* 18. where an Infant brought Attaint, and the firſt Verdict was affirm'd, and the Infant was awarded to Priſon. *Ex quo Nota,* That an Infant was within a Statute that gave Corporal Puniſhment, 43 *Ed.* 3. *Fitzh. Tit. Impriſonment.*

The *Stat. W.* 2. *c.* 11. That if Bailiffs or Receivers be found in Arrearages upon their Account, that the Auditors may ſend them to Priſon to the next Gaol. It's the Opinion of *Sanders, Plo. Com.* 364. That an Infant is out of that Statute, becauſe the Statute gives Impriſonment.

Poulter and others againſt *Wiſeman* and others. Bill exhibited on 27 *El. c.* 4. of Fraudulent Conveyances. It was reſolved, that the Infancy of one of the Defendants ſhall not excuſe him of the Penalty, he being of 16 Years, and privy to the Conveyance, and having juſtified that he made *bona Fide,* and for that he ſhall be puniſh'd as if he were of full Age, *Noy Rep. p.* 105.

Statute of Fraudulent Conveyances.

An Infant is within the Statute of Waſt, for Waſt done by himſelf, but not for Waſt done by a Stranger, 8 *Rep.* 44.

It

It is said in some of the Books, That an Infant is bound by all Statute Laws, if they be not by Name excepted; *sed Q.* of the Generality of this Rule.

Where Infant comes in as a Purchaser, he is bound by Condition without Notice, 2 *Lev.* 21.

By *W.* 2. *c.* 25. If one named a Disseisor, vouch a Record, and fail at the Day, he shall be imprison'd for a Year; yet if an Infant named a Disseisor, vouch a Record, and fail, he shall not be imprisoned; for that he hath not Discretion, and though he be comprehended in the Letter, yet it is not intended in the Sense. So if an Infant is Bailiff or Receiver, and he accounts before Auditors assigned, and is found in Arrearages, the Auditors may not commit him to the next Gaol, and yet the Stat. *W.* 2. *c.* 11. is general in such Case, That they may commit all Bailiffs and Receivers; but an Infant which had not the Age of Discretion, was not intended to be bound by the Act. And yet an Infant shall be bound by the Statute 20 *Ed.* 3. of *Resceipts*, to put in Security according to the Statute for the Value, because the Security is *à Latere*, and the Words of the Statute are generally *(if any.)* 33 *H.* 6. *b.*

It is said in *Godb.* 80. That a General Act of Parliament shall bind an Infant if he be not excepted. But an Infant shall be bound by the Statute of *Cessavit* and *Wast*, and such like, tho' the Statutes are General, for the Ces-

Cesser is an Injury to the Lord, and Wast is injurious to the Lessor; *Plow.* 364. *b.*

Diversity as to Conditions in Law by Force of a Statute.

And there is a good Difference in 1 *Inst.* *p.* 233. *b.* of Conditions in Law by Force of a Statute. If an Infant (or Feme Covert) with her Husband, aliens by Charter of Feoffment in *Mortmain*, this is no Bar to the Infant, or Feme Covert. But if a Recovery be had against an Infant (or Feme Covert) in an Action of Wast, there they are bound and barred for ever.

Presentation to a Church.

Laches shall be adjudged in an Infant, if he present not to a Church within six Months; for the Law respects the Priviledge of the Church, that the Cure be served, more than the Priviledge of Infancy.

If an Infant be a Mayor, and he and the Commonalty make an Alienation after he comes of full Age, he shall not have a *Dum fuit infra Ætatem*, because it was not his Act, but the Act of the Body Politick, 13 *H.* 8. 12. *b.*

He is bound in respect of the publick Repose concerning Men's Freeholds.

The Law respects the publick Repose of the Realm concerning Men's Freeholds and Inheritances, before the Priviledge of Infancy, in the Case of a Fine, where the Time begins in the Time of his Ancestor, *Plow.* 372. The Non-claim of a Villain of an Infant by a Year and a Day, who had fled into ancient Demesne, shall take away the Seisure of the Infant. And if an Infant bring not an Appeal of the Death of his Ancestor within a Year and a Day, he is barred of his Appeal for ever; for the Law

Law reſpects more Life and Liberty, than the Priviledge of Infancy. And ſo the Law reſpects Prerogative more than Infancy, as if, the King die ſeiſed of Land, and the Lands deſcend to his Succeſſor, this ſhall bind an Infant, 1 *Inſt*. 246. *a*. He is bound by Prerogative.

6. By reaſon of the Cuſtom of the Place, Manor, Court, *&c.* an Infant ſhall not be priviledged more than others. Cuſtom, That the Lord may take the Profits during the Non-age of the Infant Tenant, good, 1 *Leon*. 266.

But this is not regularly true, as in the Caſe above cited: If Heir of Copyholder come not in and pray Admittance at the third Proclamation in Court, he ſhall loſe his Eſtate; this doth not extend to Infants. Neither muſt Cuſtom deprive the Law of Nature. By the Cuſtom of ſome Cities and Places, an Infant of 15 Years old, (for in pleading an Age certain muſt be ſet down, and is not to be left to the counting of twelve Pence, or meaſuring an Ell of Cloth, (as ſome Books are) that ſo the Court may judge it an Age of Diſcretion, for Cuſtom muſt not deprive the Law of Nature) may make a Feoffment of his Lands lying there. But if ſuch an Infant would make a Grant to the King by Deed enrolled, the Statute of 31 *H*. 8. of Monaſteries, would not make it good, *Hob*. 225. *Needler*'s Caſe.

If an Inn comes to an Infant, and he keeps it, and his Gueſts are robbed, yet no Action lies againſt the Infant, *M*. 40 *&* 41 *El. B. R. Croſſe* and *Andrews*. Infant Inn-keeper.

CHAP.

CHAP. III.

Of the several Ages of Infancy.

Of the several Ages of Infants in the Law, for several Purposes. What is accounted the Age of Discretion. Of the Age for Consent to Marry. Of full Age. When Marriage infra Annos nubiles *shall be ratified by Agreement, or defeated by Disagreement. Of* Baron *and* Feme de Facto. *Information for seducing a young Girl to Marry,* 1 Lev. *What amounts to an Agreement. The Age of an Heir in Socage, and what he may then do. At what Age a Woman is Dowable. When an Infant may make a Will of Goods, Chattels or Lands.*

MY Lord *Hobart* hath a fine Notion in his Argument of *Needler* and *the Bishop of Winchester*'s Case. The Age of One and twenty Years is set by our Law for the Time of full Age, and thereby Grants are perfected. ‘ Now (saith he) tho' it be true ‘ that the Age of Twenty one is not set for ‘ Granting by the Law of Nature, yet be- ‘ cause it is by the Law of the Land set as ‘ the Term and Period that the Law of Na- ‘ ture judgeth of the Disability of Minors to ‘ give or grant, all Statutes of this Land shall ‘ equally be judged in Favour of Minors, ‘ even to that Age, in Imitation of the

‘ Com-

'Common Law, except in ſpecial Caſes, 'ſecundum quid: As an Infant to contract 'for meer Neceſſities; and the Age of Four- 'teen for the Heir in Socage; and the 'Age of Twelve and Fourteen for the 'Marriage of the Male and Female, &c. 'Hob. 224.

As to the Ages of Infants, in reſpect of Wardſhips, there are very many Reſolutions in our Books, both as to their Times of Marriage, and of taking their Eſtates into their own Hands, and ſuing out Liveries, and the like: But the Statute having taken away the Court of *Wards*, all theſe great Titles in our Books are vaniſhed and render'd uſeleſs, and as ſuch I ſhall not ſtand to treat of them.

One and twenty is accounted the full Age in our Law, and Twenty five by the Civil Law, for then the *Romans* accounted the Man to have *plenam Maturitatem*; and the *Lombards* counted the Age of Eighteen to be Full Age, 1 *Inſt*. 78. *b*. Full Age.

At Fourteen Years in our Law is accounted the Age of Diſcretion, and in ſeveral Caſes at that Age an Infant ſhall be priviledged, puniſhed or chargeable, as you will find in this Treatiſe. Age of Diſcretion.

As for the Age of Conſent to Marry, I ſhall be more particular in that, becauſe 'tis ſometimes a Thing of Conſideration in great Families, where ſuch Eſpouſals are frequent.

Now

When Marriage *infra Annos nubiles* shall be ratified by Agreement, or defeated by Disagreement.

Now when they marry *infra Annos nubiles*, the Time of Agreement or Disagreement for the Woman is at Twelve, or after; and for the Man at Fourteen, or after; and there needs be no new Marriage, if they so agree; but disagree they cannot before the said Ages; but then they may disagree and marry themselves to others without any Divorce; and if once they give Consent, they can never disagree after, 1 *Inst.* 79. *a. b.* 2 *Rep.* 46, 62.

Information for seducing a young Girl to marry.

Information, for that the Defendants used to come and be entertained at the House of *T.* and seducing his Daughter, being Heir apparent to a good Estate, to marry him; and that the Defendant *T.* and the others, without the Assent of the Father, brought the Daughter from the Father's House and married her. It appeared on the Trial at Bar, That the Defendant being a Kinsman remote, and of small Fortune, made Love to the Daughter; but no Proof was of any Seducements but ordinary Compliments between the young People, and the Daughter, by Agreement between her and the Defendants, went from her Father's House to the Place appointed, and there met the Defendant. The Court directed the Jury, that the Daughter being of tender Years, *viz.* about Sixteen, and a great Fortune, that this was an Offence in the Defendants within the Information, and that they ought to find them guilty, which they did; but *hesitantur*: And it was agreed before any Fine imposed, 1 *Lev.* 257.

If a Man at Fourteen marry a Woman at the Age of Ten, at her Age of Twelve he may disagree as well as she may, tho' he were of the Age of Consent; because in Contracts of Matrimony both must be bound, or equal Election of Disagreement given to both: So it is *è converso*, if the Woman be of the Age of Consent, and the Man under.

If a Man marry a Woman which is within the Age of Twelve Years, and after the Wife disagrees to the Marriage within the Age of Twelve Years also, and after the Age of Twelve Years marry with another: Now the first Marriage is absolutely defeated, so that he may take another Wife; for altho' the Disagreement within the Age of Consent was not sufficient, yet her taking another Husband after the Age of Consent, affirms the Disagreement, and so the Marriage is void *ab Initio*, as it was adjudged in the Case of *Babington*. But if a Man marry a Woman within the Age of Twelve Years, and after the Wife at Eleven Years of Age disagrees to the Marriage, and after the Husband takes another Wife, and has Issue by her, this is a Bastard; for the first continues notwithstanding the Disagreement of the Woman; for she may not disagree within the Age of Twelve Years, and so her Disagreement was void, 1 *Roll. Abr.* 341.

If

Baron and *Feme de Facto.*

If a Man within the Age of Fourteen takes a Wife of Twelve, or more, this is a Marriage, and they are *Baron & Feme de Facto*; so that the Husband may have Trespass *de Muliere abducta cum Bonis Viri. Trin.* 12 *Jac. B. Bradshaw* and *Fletcher*. And if the Man come to the Age of Fourteen, and make any Continuance of the Action, this shall be a good Agreement to the Marriage, so as it shall not afterwards be defeated.

What amounts to an Agreement.

If Disagreement be before the Ordinary, then they can never after agree to make it a good Marriage, though within the Age of Consent. *Quære.*

The Heir of an Heir in Socage, and what he may then do.

The Age of an Heir in Socage is Fourteen, and then he shall have Account of his Guardian, and shall, if he please, chuse a new one.

At what Age a Woman is Dowable.

A Woman is Dowable when she is above Nine Years of Age; for then she is able *promereri Dotem, & Virum sustinere.* Now this, though but an inchoate Marriage, to which either of the Parties at the Age of Consent may disagree, after the Death of the Husband shall give Dower to the Wife, and *quoad Dotem*, it is accounted in Law *Legitimum Matrimonium.*

If a Man taketh a Wife of the Age of Seven Years, and after aliens his Lands, and after Alienation his Wife attains to Nine Years, and after the Husband dies, the Wife shall be endow'd; for tho' she was not absolutely Dowable at the Time of the Marriage, yet she was conditionally Dowable, *(viz.)* if she attain'd the Age of Nine Years before

the

the Death of her Husband: And the Bishop upon Issue join'd in a Writ of *Dower*, *Quod nunquam fuer' copulat' in legitimo Matrimonio*, ought to certify that they were coupled in lawful Marriage, albeit the Man were under Fourteen, and the Wife above Nine and under Twelve, 1 *Inst*. 33. *a*.

By the Old Law, at the Age of Fifteen Years a Man ought to be sworn to keep the Peace, 34 *Ed*. 3. *Stat*. 3. At Twelve Years he may take the Oath of Allegiance in the *Leet*. The Age of Twelve Years binds to Appearance before the Sheriffs and Coroner for Enquiry after Robberies, 52 *H*. 3. *cap*. 24. The Age of Fourteen Years enables to enter into Orders of Religion without Consent of Parents, 4 *H*. 7. *c*. 15.

When Infant may make a Will of Goods and Chattels, and Lands.

An Infant of the Age of Eighteen may make a Will as to Goods and Chattels, but not as to Lands till One and twenty; and at the Age of Seventeen Years he is able to act as Executor, and Administration *dur' minori Ætate* ceaseth. A Will made the Day a Man comes to Age is good. A Man makes a Will under the Age of Twenty one Years, and publisheth it the same Day he comes to Age, it is good, 1 *Keb*. 589. *Herbert*'s Case.

The Time of Full Age by Computation.

Now, when a Man shall be said to be of Full Age, or as to the Time of Full Age by Computation, it is agreed in *Herbert* and *Turball*'s Case, 14 *Car*. 2. *Br*. That if *H*. is born on the 16th of *February*, *Anno Dom*. 1608. he is at Full Age the 16th of *February*, *Anno Domini* 1629. and at whatever Hour he was

 born,

born, is not material, there being no Fractions of Days in our Law. *Vide ante.*

Infant under the Age of Seven Years shall not be said to be a Wanderer within the Statute of 39 *Eliz.* *cap.* 4. for the *Punishment of Rogues*, 2 *Bulstr.* 352.

CHAP.

CHAP. IV.

Of Guardian *and* Prochein amy.

Four Ways by which a Man may Sue. The Difference between a Guardian and Prochein amy. *Guardian to be assigned by the Court, and why. Regularly Infant must sue by Guardian, and why.* Stat. 12 Car. 2. c. 24. *Of the Disposition of the Custody of Infants by their Fathers, by Deed or Last Will, explained. In what Cases the Infant shall sue by* Prochein amy. *Of Admittance by a Guardian. Record of the Admittance different in* B. C. *and in* B. R. *Where the Infants Appearance by Attorney is Error, or not. That one of the Avowants was an Infant not assignable for Error, and why. The manner of advancing Infants Moneys on publick Funds, and how to be disposed and allowed by Acts of Parliament. How the Infants Appearance by Attorney shall be tried. Infant Executor must appear by Guardian, and why. Infant Executor may sue by Attorney, and why; but he must defend by Guardian. Error to be assigned by a Guardian, not by Attorney. Of Judgment against an Infant on Default. Of a Guardian being made by the King's Letters Patents.* Baron *and* Feme, *the* Feme *being within Age are vouched, the* Feme *ought to appear by Guardian. The Form of the Entry of the Guardian. To prosecute Three manner of Guardianships. Guardian in Socage, the Nature of him. All Possibility of Discent excluded. Guardian of Copyhold. The Guardian in Socage, and by Nature the Difference. Guardianship not to survive to the Husband. A further Explication of* Stat. 12 Car. 2. c. 24. *Guardianship by that Statute not transferrable over. The Power of a Guardian, or not. He cannot present to a Benefice, and why. Shall have a* Quare Impedit *in his own Name. He may hold Courts, and grant Copies of Leases for Years made by him. Guardian* pro Nurture. *Of Admission of Heirs to Copyhold, by* Prochein amy. *Remedy by Infant against his Guardian, and how and what. Guardian in Socage; how to be charged after the Infants Age of* 14. *Wast. Infants Estates in the Guardians Hands to be employed in the Payment of his Debts.*

Note: BY *Roll's Ch. J.* one cannot answer for an Infant, either in *Chancery*, or in any other Court, unless he be assigned Guardian by the Court; for if he might, that were to make himself Guardian, which might prove Damage to the Infant; but an Infant may sue by *Prochein amy*, though his *Prochein amy* cannot answer for him. *Stiles* 369.

Guardian must be assigned by the Court; and therefore, if an Infant is sued, the Plaintiff must move the Court to assign a Guardian to answer, 1 *Roll. Rep.* 203.

In

In a Writ of Error by Infant, the Assignment of Errors ought to be by the Guardian.

Before I come to treat of Actions and Suits, brought by or against Infants, it will be proper to shew the Nature and Office of a *Guardian* and *Prochein amy*; because by them he must Sue and Defend, Appear and Prosecute.

Now there are but Four Ways by which any Man may Sue. Four Ways by which any Man may sue.

1. *In propria Persona.*
2. *Per Attornatum.*
3. *Per Guardianum.*
4. *Per Prochein amy*, or *Proximum amicum.*

An Infant cannot sue *in propria Persona*, for that he is not supposed of Ability to manage his Causes to the best Advantage: Neither can he sue by Attorney, for he cannot make an Attorney.

But I shall only treat of a *Guardian in Socage*, or by Nurture and Nature, the other Guardians being now useless, their Power and Court being taken away by Act of Parliament. And I shall not only treat of Guardians, in respect of Suits, but also of his Office and Power, in respect of his other Management of the Infant's Person, Estate and Education.

In our Books we find a *Guardian* and a *Prochein amy* have been promiscuously used the one for the other; but in Truth they are several, and ought to be distinguished, or or else the Judgments may be erroneous: And as to that, the Difference lies here; Infant may be admitted to sue by *Guardian* or *Prochein amy*, where he is to demand or gain any Thing; but when he is to defend a Suit in an Action Real or Personal, he ought to be admitted by his Guardian, and the Guardian ought to be admitted by the Court. And the Reason why an Infant shall (in any Action brought against him) appear and defend by his Guardian, and not by his Attorney, is (as I said) because he is not presumed to have Conusance of his own Matters, or to have Intelligence to chuse a fit Man to plead for him; and therefore the Court chooseth one for him, against whom Infant shall have his Action, if he misplead or misbehave himself. And if one has occasion to sue an Infant, he must move the Court, that a Guardian may be assigned for him, if one be not agreed upon by Consent, *Cro. Jac.* 640. *Simpson* and *Jackson.*

The true Difference between a *Guardian* and a *Prochein amy.*

Court moved to assign a Guardian.

By *Stat.* 12 *Car.* 2. *c.* 24. *Sect.* 8. Where any Person hath, or shall have, any Child or Children under the Age of 21 Years, and not married at the Time of his Death, it shall and may be lawful to and for the Father of such Child or Children, whether born at the Time of the Decease of the Father, or at that Time in *ventre sa mere*; or whether such Father be within the Age of 21 Years, or of full Age; by his Deed executed in his Life-time, or by his Last Will and Testament in Writing, in the

Of the Disposition of the Custody of Infants by their Fathers, by Deed or Will.

Pre-

Presence of Two or more credible Witnesses, in such Manner, and from Time to Time as he shall respectively think fit to dispose of the Custody and Tuition of such Child, or Children, for and during such Time as he or they shall respectively remain under the Age of 21 Years, or any lesser Time, to any Person or Persons in Possession or Remainder, other than Popish Recusants; and such Disposition of the Custody of such Child or Children thereafter to be made, shall be good and effectual against all and every other Person or Persons claiming the Custody or Tuition of such Child or Children, as *Guardian in Socage*, or otherwise; and such Person and Persons to whom the Custody of such Child or Children hath been, or shall be so disposed or devised as aforesaid, shall and may maintain an Action of Ravishment of Ward or Trespass against any Person or Persons who shall wrongfully take away or detain such Child or Children, for recovery of such Child or Children; and shall and may recover Damages for the same in the said Action, for the Use and Benefit of such Child or Children, *Sect.* 9. And it was thereby further enacted, That such Person or Persons to whom the Custody of such Child or Children hath been, or shall be so disposed or devised, shall and may take into his or their Custody, to the Use of such Child or Children, the Profits of all Lands, Tenements and Hereditaments of such Child or Children; and also the Custody, Tui-

And of such Guardian, Receipt and Management of the Personal Estate.

 tion

tion and Management of the Goods, Chattels, and Personal Estate of such Child or Children, till their respective Age of 21 Years, or any lesser Time, according to such Disposition aforesaid, and may bring such Action or Actions in relation thereunto, as by Law a Guardian in common Socage might do; provided, That this Act shall not extend to alter or prejudice the Custom of *London*, or any other City or Town-Corporate, concerning Orphans; nor to discharge any Apprentice from his Apprentiship. *Per Stat. W.* 2. *cap.* 15. in every Case where such as are within Age may sue, it is ordained, That if such Infants are eloigned, so that they cannot sue Personally, their *Prochein amy* shall be admitted to sue for them, if the Surmise, that the Plaintiff is within Age, be untrue, and that the Plaintiff is of full Age, his Admittance by *Prochein amy* is Error. This Act extends not to an Ideot. This Act extends not to the Custom, nor controls the Manor, whereby the Lord may grant the Custody of Infant Copyholder, *Lut.* 1189. *Vide* this Statute fully explained in *Bedel* and *Constable*'s Case.

Infant Def. to appear by *Guardian*, and not by *Prochein amy*.

The Defendant ought always to appear by *Guardian*, and not by *Prochein amy*; and the Admittance of the Infant Defendant by *Prochein amy*, hath been adjudged to be Erroneous.

Now the first News we hear of a *Prochein amy*, is in the Statute of *Westm.* 2. *c.* 15. and he is appointed in these Cases:

1. Where

1. Where an Infant is to sue his Guardian, as for Wast, &c *Prochein amy, in what Cases appointed.*

2. When the Guardian will not sue for him.

3. When the Infant is eloigned; and the Reason of that is, when he is admitted by Guardian, he ought to appear in Person to the View of the Court, which he cannot do when he is eloigned; and therefore the *Prochein amy*, who is Guardian in Socage, or by Nurture, (*viz.* the next of Blood, to whom the Land may not discend) may pray to be received as his *Prochein amy*. The Plaintiff in a Writ of *Right* did appear by *Prochein amy*, and afterwards he came to his full Age, and did prosecute his Suit, and did recover by *Prochein amy*, being of full Age: This is not assignable for Error to reverse Judgment, and he might have his Plea to it, and a Verdict pass'd, and so 'tis aided, 1 *Bulst.* 24. *Stone* and *March*.

And in *Simpson* and *Jackson*'s Case, an Infant Defendant was admitted by *Prochein amy* in an Action of *Ejectment*, and it was adjudged Error. So when one is admitted by *Prochein amy* when he is at full Age, it is Error.

But the Case of *Simpson* and *Jackson* is now fully reported in *Palmer*'s Reports; which, because it was a leading and settling Case, as to this Part, I shall more largely recite *Palm.* 296.

It

It was in this Case resolved, when an Infant is Plaintiff, he may sue by Guardian or *Prochein amy*; but when he is Defendant, in all Cases he must appear by his Guardian: And the Reason of the Diversity is, when the Infant is Plaintiff, and when Defendant, that in one Case he may sue by *Prochein amy*, or *Guardian*, and in the other by *Guardian* only, is this; because, when he is sued, and the *Prochein amy* by his voluntary Love appears for him, there, although he loseth by Default of the *Prochein amy*, this is not a final Conclusion to him, but he may resort to a more high Action. And the Law does not give him any *Action on the Case* against his *Prochein amy*; but when the Court appoints a Guardian where the Infant is Defendant, there this Action shall conclude the Infant; and so in all Cases when he sues as Plaintiff by Guardian, except in the Three Cases above-mentioned, 1 *Cr.* 115. *Goodwin* and Sir *R. Moor*'s Case.

The true Reason of the Difference.

No Action on the Case against *Prochein amy*.

Infant Administrator brought Action by *Prochein amy*, 1 *Lut.* 227. against Attorney, but Judgment was given against the Plaintiff, for that all Actions which are in *B.C.* are brought by Original Writ, or Original Bill, or by Attachment of Priviledge; and the Action here was by Way of *Queritur*.

Covenant in Debt for Infant, *per Prochein amy*. Lut. 368.

The Infant to be viewed in Court before admitted.

The Infant ought to be viewed by the Court before he be admitted; and therefore it was agreed in *Siderfin*, *p.* 69. That an Infant, Plaintiff in *Error* to reverse an Attainder,

tainder, may be admitted by a Guardian, or by *Prochein amy*: But the Infant there not being in Court (only his Mother was there) the Court would not intermeddle, *Siderfin*, *p.* 69.

And in 2 *Leon. p.* 189. the Court refuſed to appoint a Guardian for an Infant retorned Tenant in Dower, unleſs he be in the Court in Perſon.

One cannot anſwer for an Infant as Guardian in *Chancery*, or any other Court, except he be aſſigned Guardian by the Court. The Rule was, That the Defendant ſhould appear and plead by Guardian, and Verdict *pro Quer'*. It was moved in Arreſt of Judgment, becauſe its ſaid, he appeared *per Guardian' admiſſum*, and ſaith not *ſpecialiter admiſſum*, and in Fact there was never any actual Admiſſion. *Per Cur.* A Guardian need not be admitted for the Defendant, be he Infant or Ideot, but for the Plaintiff he muſt, and if he be Guardian by the King's Letters Patents, he need not be admitted by the Court, *Stiles Rep.* 369. 2 *Keb.* 302. *Cumber* and *Walter*.

No Special Admittance need to be for the Defendant.

But Note, If one pray to be admitted to ſue Actions by Guardian, and he had a Guardian appointed by his Father, or *Ex proviſione Legis*, (*viz.*) Guardian in Socage, who acts as Guardian to ſuch Perſon, no other ſhall be admitted to ſue for him, unleſs that ſuch a Perſon miſdemean himſelf. *Per Keeling* Chief Juſtice, *Siderfin p.* 424.

Who to be admitted Guardian.

A Re-

A Record of Admittance is made in *B. C.* but in the *King's-Bench* it is only recited in the Court, *J. S. per A. B. Guardianum suum, ad hoc per Cur', specialiter admissum querit*, &c. 3 *Rep.* 53. 1 *Sid.* 173. 3 *Mod.* 236. 1 *Lev.* 224.

Guardian to render Account.

Guardian in Socage, saving his Cost, shall render an Account at lawful Age of the Infant, and make no Sale, Wast, nor Destruction, 52 *H.* 3. c. 17.

Where the Infants Appearance by Attorney is Error or not.

Where it is said in our Books, that if Infant appear by Attorney, it is Error; it is to be understood with this Difference, where the Tenant or Defendant may not by Law appear by Attorney, and where the Tenant or Defendant may appear by Attorney; but upon some *Process*, by reason of some Default or Contempt, he ought to appear in Person. In the first Case, if the Court admit him by Attorney it is Error, as if Infant appears by Attorney; but in the other Case it shall not be Error, for the Court may dispense with the Contempt, and admit him by Attorney; and this is no Prejudice to the Plaintiff, 8 *Rep.* 58. *Beecher's* Case.

How the Infants Appearance by Attorney shall be tried.

Now the Infants Appearance by Attorney is Error, but shall be tried *per pais*, and not by the Justices; for the making the Warrant of Attorney to appear, is an Act of the Party without Examination of the Judges, 9 *Rep.* 30. *Abbot of Strata Marcella's* Case.

Infant Sole Defendant, as Executor, appears by Attorney, its ill, if Judgment be against him, *Showre* 169, 170. *Aliter*, If several Executors, *sed Qu. in Coan's* Case. *Showre* 165. It was assigned for Error in Replevin after Verdict, That one of the Avowants was Infant *per Cur'*, it's not assignable for Error, because it was a Matter which the Plaintiffs might have taken Exception to; by Plea to the Avowry it might have been pleaded in Abatement to the Avowry, but he admitting him thus to appear and answer, admits the Conisance to be good, and well made. Suppose a Feme Covert brings an Action against a Man as a Fee-Sole, the Defendant pleads in Bar, he shall never assign this for Error: *Dighton* and *Bartholomew's* Case seems against this; but the Case of *Bade* and *Starky* is contrary, *Showre* 165. *Coan versus Bowles*, &c.

That one of the Avowants was an Infant not assignable for Error, and why.

Error of a Judgment in *B.R.* in *Eject' firm'*, because one of the Defendants, at the Time of the Judgment, was within Age, and appeared by Attorney, where it ought to have been by his Guardian; the Judgment being upon a Verdict, it was thereupon demurred: All the Judges and Barons held, in regard the Damages and Costs are entire, that the Judgment is reversible for both, and it was reversed, 2 *Cr.* 303. *King* and *Marlborough*.

Three Executors sue *per Attornat'*, and one of them is within Age, this is not Error, *Pal.* 245.

If

If Infant appear in Person, it shall be tried by Inspection, and he only shall avoid it; but if he appear by Attorney, all Persons shall assign this for Error, and it shall be tried *per pais*, for this is Matter of Fact, and triable *per* a Jury, and not by Inspection, where the Court takes notice of the Party judicial, *vid. p.* 47.

Of advancing of Infants Money on Publick Funds.

Guardian or Trustee may advance 100 *l.* of Infants Money on the Acts of 5 *W. & M. c.* 1. and 6 *W.* 3. *c.* 20. and be discharged.

Guardian or Trustee may advance 70 *l.* on the Stat. 6 & 7 *W.* 3. and be discharged, and Infant Contributor, *per Stat.* 7 & 8 *W.* 3. *c.* 18. *Sect.* 13.

Infants chargeable for the Duties on Houses in this Manner:

Where any Person or Persons, chargeable with any Rate or Assessments by the Act, shall be under the Age of 21 Years, the Parents, Guardians or Tutors, of such Infants respectively, upon Default of Payment by such Infants, shall be, and are hereby made liable to, and charged with, the Payments which such Infant ought to have made: And if such Parents, Guardians or Tutors, shall neglect or refuse to pay, it shall and may be lawful to proceed against them in like Manner as against any other Person or Persons, making Default of Payment. And all Parents, Guardians and

Tutors, making Payment as aforesaid, shall be allowed all and every the Sums paid for such Infants, upon his or their Accounts.

How Infants Money may be disposed on by the Act 2 Ann. c. 3.

It shall and may be lawful for any Guardian or Trustee, having the Disposal of the Money of any Infant under the Age of 21 Years, for the Use or Benefit of such Infant, to advance and pay the Sum of 150 *l.* of such Money for the Purchase of any Annuity upon that Act for the Benefit of such Infant; and the said Guardian or Trustee, for so much, is thereby discharged.

Error is to be assigned by a Guardian, not by Attorney, *No. Ent.* 43.

On the Statute 6 *&* 7 *W.* 3. For granting certain Rates on Marriages, Births and Burials; the Duty thereby charged on the Burial of any Person, who shall at the Time of his or her Death be under the Age of 21 Years, shall be answered and paid by the Father of such Person (if living at the Time of the Death of such Person under Age); and if the Father be then dead, then by the Mother, if she be then living; or otherwise by the Guardian, Trustee, Executor or Administrator, of such Person.

In Trespass against Three, after Judgment it was assigned for Error, That one of the Defendants was an Infant at the Time

Time of the Plea pleaded *per* Attorney. *Per Cur'* It is Error, as *Cr. Jac.* 303. *Marlborough's* Case; but being after a Verdict it had not been Error, if one of the Plaintiffs for whom it was had been an Infant, that being saved by 21 *Jac. c.* ... Judgment was totally reversed, 1 *Keb.* 940. *Topham's* Case.

Infant Executor must appear by Guardian, and why.

If an Action of Debt is brought against an Infant Executor, he may not appear by Attorney, but ought to appear by Guardian, otherwise it is Error; for else it might be great Prejudice, for Assets may be found in his Hands, and so Judgment shall be given to recover the Debt, Damages and Costs against him, *De bonis Testatoris si, &c. & si non,* the Damages and Costs *de bonis propriis,* and peradventure the Infant had a Release or Acquittance to plead, and so he shall be charged *de bonis propriis* by ill Pleading, without Remedy against the Attorney; but if a Guardian misplead so, an Action lies against him, if he have any Loss, and his being Executor does not make him as a Man of full Age; and so is *Cro. Jac.* 441. for if he should plead by Attorney, he may by a false Plea be charged *de bonis propriis*; and although he pleads truly, he shall be charged in Damages *de bonis propriis, Mich.* 15 *Jac. B. R. Westcot* and *Colling, Cr. Jac.* 420, 441. The same Case.

Action lies against a Guardian for Mispleading.

The Appearance must be entered in the Name of the Infant, *scil', præd'* Katherine, *pro* J. S. *Guardian' venit & dicit quod ipsa,* not *ipse,* &c. 3 *Mod.* 230.

The

The Court *B. R.* was moved, in Behalf of an Infant, to discharge a Guardian assigned by the Court, to the Intent to make *R. S.* of this Court Guardian in his room, and that the former Inspection may be discharged, and the Infant to be inspected again; because when the former Inspection was, and the Guardian assigned, there was no Action depending against the Infant. *L. Glyn*: Let it be so for the Cause you have alledged, and give Notice of it to the former Guardian. *Stiles* 456.

Note, An Attorney may plead *non sum informatus*, but a Guardian cannot.

Attorney may plead *non sum informatus*, but a Guardian cannot

If a Clerk of *Chancery* declare there by Bill, by force of his Priviledge, he being within Age, and not *per* Guardian; this is Erroneous. And its more dangerous for an Infant to appear in Person than by Attorney; for if Attorney defrauds him he hath Remedy, but not if he appear in Person, 1 *Rolls Abr*. 766.

But now an Infant Executor may sue by Attorney, though he must defend by Guardian, for an Infant Executor Plaintiff cannot by it draw any Loss to himself, and he represents the Person of the Testator; and it was adjudged in *Foxwist*'s Case, (tho' in that Case *Twisden fuit contra fortiter*) that an Infant Executor under 17 Years of Age may not sue *per* Attorney, because he cannot make an Attorney. And in *Mod. Rep*. the same Case, it was held Error for the Infant to appear otherwise than by

Infant Executor may sue by Attorney, and why. But he must defend by Guardian.

F Guar-

Guardian, and this Error was not holpen by the Statute of *Jeofails*, *Mod. Rep.* 298.

Error to reverse a Judgment in a Writ of Entry for the Manor of *W.* against the Earl of *Newport*, where he appeared by his Guardian, wherein they vouched the Common Vouchee; and Judgment given upon his Default after Appearance, and the Error assign'd, for that Judgment is given by Default, he being an Infant. *Per Car.* It is not Error, for that Judgment is not given on the Default of the Infant, but upon the Departure of the Vouchee, in Despight of the Court, *Cro. Car.* 302. Earl of *Newport* against Sir *H. Mildmay.*

Judgment against Infant on Default.

An Infant may appear by Guardian, and when he comes of full Age, he may make Attorney in the same Suit, and it shall not be Error, *Moor* 665.

Now *per Stat.* 21 *Jac. c.* 13. After Verdict given in any Court of Record, Judgment shall not be stay'd nor revers'd by reason the Plaintiff in Ejectment, or other personal Action, (being under Age) did appear by Attorney, and the Verdict pass for him.

And in 1 *Rolls Rep.* 288. it's said, an Infant Administrator may bring an Action of Debt and make an Attorney, and this shall not be Error, if Judgment pass against him; for he is at no Prejudice by it, but only is barred of the Debt of the Testator. And it was adjudg'd in the Time of Q. *Eliz.* That if an Infant and a Man of full Age are made Executors, they may bring an Action as Executor, and the Infant may sue by Attorney with-

without making any *Prochein amy*, because he sues in the Right of the Testator, and not in his own Right, *Trin.* 38 *Eliz. B R.*

If Judgment be given against an Infant, and the Infant being within Age, brings a Writ of Error to reverse the Judgment, he ought to assign the Error by Guardian, and not by Attorney, *Nov. Ent.* 289.

Error to be assigned by Guardian, and not by Attorney.

If a Common Recovery be suffered, and the Baron and Feme (as in the Right of the Wife, the Wife being within Age) are vouched, and they appear by Attorney and Vouch-over, and so a Common Recovery is had, this is Error; for tho' the Husband be of full Age, yet the Wife being within Age, ought to appear by Guardian, 1 *Rolls Abr.* 288. *Holland* and *Lee.*

Baron and Feme (the Feme being within Age) are vouched, the Feme ought to appear by Guardian.

Error was brought of a Judgment in *Assumpsit* against Baron and Feme, and the Error assigned was, That the Feme was an Infant, and appear'd by Attorney, whereas the Court ought to have admitted her by Guardian. But if the Wife be of Age, then the Husband may make an Attorney for her and himself, and the Entry is *per Attornat'* of the Baron and Feme, and not of the Husband only, and for this Cause the Judgment was reversed. And *Hale* said, the Husband could not disavow the Guardian made by the Court for his Wife, 1 *Vent.* 185. *Freeman* and *Boddington.*

Baron and Feme, Feme an Infant admitted by Guardian.

Baron cannot disavow the Guardian

Error was brought to reverse a Judgment in *B. R.* against the Heir. Error assigned was, because the Infant appeared by *J. S.* his Guardian generally, and had not entred any Admiſſion upon the Roll, as he ought. *Vide Rawlins's* Caſe, 4 *Rep.* the Want of which in *B. R.* is Error: And it ſeems there is Difference between *B. C.* and *B. R.* upon comparing 4 *Rep.* 5. 3. *b.* with *Yelv.* 58. *Sid.* 173. *Swift* and *Nott.*

But *Note,* Stat. of 21 *Jac. c.* 13. aids the Appearance by Attorney, where it ought to be by Guardian after Verdict.

Guardian made by the King's Letters Patents.

The King by his Letters Patent may make a general Guardian for the Infant, to anſwer for him in all Actions and Suits taken or to take, and in all Manors and Courts; or may make two or three Guardians jointly or ſeverally to anſwer for him, or to proſecute Action for him; and may grant by the ſame Letter Patent other Guardians jointly or ſeverally in their Places to ſue or defend for the ſame Infant in all Actions and Suits which are taken or ſued, or that ſhall be ſued after, *Fitz. N. B.* 6. 27 *L.*

And the Infant ſhall have a Writ in the *Chancery* to remove his Guardian directed to the Juſtices, and to receive another; or the Court may by their Diſcretion remove the Guardian, and make another, *Fitz. N. B.* 27. *M.*

Having ſhewn how the Law ſtands to *Guardian* and *Prochein amy* as to Infants ſuing and being ſued, I ſhall ſpeak ſomething of the Manner of admitting *per Gardianum,* and the Form of the Entry, in which there is ſome Nicety.

The

The Form of the Entry of a Guardian to prosecute, is this: The Infant must be admitted before a Judge of that Court wherein he intends to prosecute; and the Form is, *Concessum est per Cur' hic, quod (Petens) sequatur per* J. S. *Gardianum suum in placito, &c.* Now in *Young* and *Young's* Case, it was entred on the Plea Roll, *quod concessum est per Curiam*, that the Plaintiff by such a one his Guardian should prosecute, *&c.* and so it was entred in the Remembrance; and the Philazers Roll is, *Quod J. V.* by *J. S.* his Guardian, *ad hoc admissus per Cur' obtulit se 4 Die, &c.* but there was no Entry in the Philazers Roll, as is usual in such Cases, *Quod concessum est per Cur' quod Petens sequatur*, by *J. S.* his Guardian. But by the Court it may be amended, though after a Writ of Error brought, and the Record removed; because it appears by the several Entries, that he sued by his Guardian, and it is only the Omission of the Clerk, *Cr. Car.* 86. *Young* and *Young*.

The Form of the Entry of a Guardian to prosecute.

The Court favours the Entries.

An Action brought against an Infant in *Colchester*, who appears by his Guardian, and no Warrant appeareth for Entry in such Cases, *Quod talis admissus est per Curiam*; and this is Error in *fait* by *Coke*. And in the Common Bench the Entry is *per Custodem admiss', &c.* and a Special Entry is kept of it in a Roll, *Crok. l.l. Silbury* and *Bird*.

Another Entry was also favoured by the Court in *Hesketh* and *Lee's* Case, *Pas.* 22 *Car.* 2. The Entry of the Admission in *Lancaster* was in this Manner: *Concessum est per Curiam hic, quod*

quod Johannes M. sequatur pro Tho' Hesketh Arm', qui infra Ætatem existit, ut Gardianus prædict' Thom' versus Thom' Lee Arm', & Alexandrum Rigby Arm', in placito Terræ; and in the Body of the Common Recovery, immediately after the End of the Count, the Entry is in this Manner; *ss. Et præd' Thomas Hesketh, qui infra Ætatem existit, per Johannem M. Arm', qui admissus est per Curiam hic ad sequendum pro eod' Thom' ut Gardianus ipsius Thom' in placito præd', in propria Persona sua venit, & def. Jus suum quando*; and two Exceptions were taken to it:

1. That the Guardian ought to have been entred *ad defendend'* for the Infant, and not *ad sequend'*, because the Infant was Tenant. But *per Cur'* it is good enough; for the Word *ad sequend'* is as significant as the Word *defendend'*, and the Word *sequend'* may be indifferently applied to the Plaintiff or Defendant; for the Suit of the one or the other ought to be followed; (and tho' this be true *lato Sensu*, yet the Forms of Entries in such solemn Things as Recoveries, ought to be closely kept.) *Ideo quære.*

Ad sequendum, how to be expounded.

2. It's said, the Infant *venit in propria Persona: Sed non allocatur.* It's plain by the Record, that the Infant appeareth *per Gardianum suum*, and then the Words *in propria Persona sua* are idle and superfluous. Or it may be thus explain'd (to support it) that the Infant comes *per Gardianum*, which Guardian *venit in propria Persona.*

In

In *Rawlins*'s Case, 4 *Rep.* 54. the Plaintiff being Infant, was admitted *per Gardian'*, and no *Special* Record made of this Admittance, as is usual in *B. C.* but upon View of the Precedents, it was held good, and no Error: If it cannot appear to the Court that there was a Guardian admitted, the Form of the Entry shall not be so severely examined as in *Rawlins*'s Case. As for *Cro. Jac.* 641. there was another Reason for reversing the Judgment. No Special Record of the Admittance.

Assumpsit against Baron and Feme, the Feme being within Age, appears by Attorney, and Judgment is given against them. This is Error, 1 *Rolls Abr.* 288. But if they bring an Action, they may sue by Atttorney, and the Husband shall name an Attorney for both, 2 *Sanders* 213. But in a real Action, the Wife must appear *per Gardian'*.

Now I come to treat of the Nature, and Power, and Office, of a Guardian; and what Acts of his shall be binding to an Infant, or not.

There are Three Manner of Guardianships, *(viz.)* By Common Law, by Statute Law, and by Custom. Three Manner of Guardianships.

By the Common Law, there are Four Manner of Guardians:

1. Guardian by Chivalry.
2. Guardian by Nature, as the Father of his eldest Son.
3. Guardian in Socage. And,
4. Guardian by Cause of Nurture.

9. Guardian by the Statute, are by *West.* 2. *c.* 5. and by the Statute of 4 & 5 *P.* & *M.* *of Women Children*; and that is in Two Manners, either of the Father or Mother without Assignation, or of any other to whom the Father shall appoint the Custody, either by his last Will, or by any Act in his Lifetime, and by the Statute of 12 *Car.* 2. *c.* 24. *Vide, infra de hoc Statuto.*

Who shall be Guardian in Socage.

Guardian at Common Law. Guardian in Socage, who. The Nature of him.

10. Now Guardian in Socage is he who is the next of Blood, to whom the Inheritance cannot discend, and so Affinity without Blood is excluded. He hath the Profits to the Use of the Heir, till the Heir accomplish the Age of Fourteen Years, and must yield therefore an Account to the Heir.

The Guardian hath nothing to his own Use, but to the Use of the Heir; and therefore he shall not forfeit his Interest by Outlawry, or by Attainder of Felony or Treason.

In *Sadler* and *Draper*'s Case, the Point was; Whether the Brother of the Half-Blood of the Mother of an Infant, shall be Guardian in Socage of Land *per* Descent on Part of the Father, *Cro. El.* 825. *Swan*'s Case, *Jones p.* 17. *Sadler* and *Draper.*

But this being in Ejectment, and it not being found by the Verdict that the Lessor of the Plaintiff, who claims to be Guardian in Socage, *fuit proximus de Sanguine a quel,&c.* the Court shall not intend it; and so no

Title

Title found *pro Quer*; but as to the Point in Law, no Resolution.

In *Moor* 635. the Brother of the Half-Blood shall be Guardian in Socage before the Uncle of the Part of the Mother; yet the Book makes a *Quære*, if the Brother himself be within Fourteen. But that is no *Quære* now; for it is resolved, that one under Fourteen Years shall not be Guardian, *Mo.* 635.

If Three Uncles are in equal Degree, the eldest shall be Guardian in Socage, 1 *Inst.* 88.

If a Copyhold discend to an Infant within the Age of Fourteen Years, the *Prochein amy*, to whom the Land may not descend, shall have the Custody of this, as well as of his Freehold, unless the Custom appoint it to some other, *Hill.* 44 *El. B. R. Eggleton's* Case. Guardian of Copyhold.

If a Man seised of a Rent-charge, Rent-seck, Common of Pasture, *&c.* and such like Inheritance that lies not in Tenure, and dies, his Heir within the Age of Fourteen, may chuse his Guardian, unless he be of very tender Years, 1 *Inst.* 87. *b.*

If there be Three Brethren, and the youngest holdeth Lands in Socage, and hath Issue and dieth, his Issue within the Age of Fourteen Years, both the Uncles are in *æquali Gradu*, yet the Law preferreth the eldest, and he shall be Guardian. If a Man be seised of Lands holden in Socage of the Part of his Father, and of other Lands held in Socage of the Part of his Mother, and dieth, his

his Issue being within the Age of Fourteen Years; in this Case, such of the next of Kin of either Side as first happeth the Body of the Heir, shall have him; but the next of the Blood of the Part of the Father shall enter into the Land on the Part of the Mother, and the next of Kin of the Part of the Mother shall enter into the Lands of the Part of the Father. Now all Possibility of Discent is excluded as to being such Guardian; therefore if a Man hath Issue two Sons by several *Venters*, and having Lands held in Socage of the Nature of Burrough *English*, and dies, the younger Brother within the Age of Fourteen Years, the elder Brother of the Half-Blood shall not have the Custody of the Lands, because by Possibility the elder may inherit the Land; for if the youngest dies *sans* Issue, and the Land discend to an Uncle, the elder Brother of the Half-Blood may be Heir to him.

All Possibility of Discent excluded.

In *Rolls Abr. 2 part, p.* 40. It's said, the Brother of the Half-Blood shall be Guardian in Socage.

Guardian by Nature, and in Socage, the Difference.

There is a Difference between Guardian in Socage, and Guardian by Nature, though one and the same Person is both, as the Father in case of a Tenure in Socage shall be by Law accounted as Guardian in Socage, and not as a Guardian in Nature; because in the Case of a Tenure in Socage, the Father must be accountable to the Son for the Profits of his Lands, which he should not be, if he had the Custody as Father, and by Nature,

ture; and the Act of the Law does no Man Wrong, 1 *Inst.* 88. *b.*

Infant within Age, that is in the Custody of another, cannot be Guardian in Socage, because no Writ of Account lies against an Infant. Infant cannot be Guardian in Socage.

If the Mother be Guardian in Socage, and takes Husband, and dies, the Husband shall not have this Custody by Survivor, because the Wife had it *en auter droit*, and in Right of the Heir. Guardianship not to survive to the Husband.

But the ancient Law, in the Case of Guardians, is in a great Measure altered by the Statute of 12 *Car.* 2. *c.* 24. if the Statute be pursued. It enacts, That where any Person hath, or shall have, any Child or Children under the Age of Twenty one Years, and not married at the Time of his Death, it shall be lawful for the Father of such Child or Children, whether born at the Time of the Decease of the Father, or at that Time *en Ventre sa Mere*, or whether such Children be within the Age of Twenty one Years, or of full Age, by Deed executed in his Life-time, or by his last Will and Testament in Writing, in the Presence of two or more credible Witnesses, to dispose of the Custody and Tuition of such Child or Children, for and during the Time he or they shall remain under Age, or any lesser Time, to any Person or Persons in Possession or Remainder, other than Popish Recusants; and such Disposition shall be good against all Persons claiming such Child as Guardian in Socage, or otherwise. Though all Tenures are now Socage, Stat. 12 *Car.* 2. *c.* 24.

Explained. Socage, and the next of Kin to whom the Land cannot discend, is Guardian until the Heirs Age of Fourteen: Yet the Father by this Act may nominate the Guardian to his Heir, and for any Time until the Heirs Age of One and twenty Years; and such Guardian shall have the like Remedy for the Ward as Guardian at Common Law. The Land follows the Guardianship; such a Special Guardian cannot transfer the Custody of the Ward by Deed or Will, or any other Way: The Trust is only Personal and not assignable, and if such Guardian to whom such Custody is appointed dies before the Heirs Age of 21 Years, it dies with him, *Vaughan* 181, 182.

A Prohibition was prayed to the *Prerogative Court* of *Canterbury*, Sir *Henry Wood* having devised the Guardianship of his Daughter by his Will in Writing, according to this Act, to the Lady *Chester* his Sister; the Dutchess of *Cleveland*, to whose Son this Daughter, being about Eight Years old, was contracted, pretending that Sir *Henry Wood* by Word revoked this Disposition of Guardianship, sued in the *Prerogative Court*, to have this Nuncupative Will proved; and the Court granted a Prohibition, for they are not to prove a Will concerning the Guardianship of a Child, which is a Thing conusable here, and to be judged whether it be devised pursuant to the Statute, 1 *Vent. Rep.* 207. Lady *Chester*'s Case.

In

In the Lord *Anglesey* and the Lord *Ossery*'s Case, 27 *Car.* 2. *B. R. Hale* Chief Justice; and the Court agreed, That this Statute extends to *Ireland*, and that the Guardian appointed by the Will may have Ravishment of Ward, as the Guardian by Knights Service, or Guardian in Socage at Common-Law.

This Act extends to *Ireland*. The Guardian by this Act may have Ravishment of Ward

And a Guard disposed by Will in Writing, is not repealable by *Parol Codicil* in the Spiritual Court.

Of the Power of a Guardian.

Guardian in Socage shall not present to a Benefice in the Right of the Heir, because he cannot be accountable for it, and he can make no Benefit thereof, for that the Law hates Simoniacal Contracts, but the Heir shall present himself, 1 *Inst.* 88, 89.

Not to present to a Benefice, and why.

In some Acts the Heir shall do contrary to the Will of his Guardian. As in Appeal by Infant of the Death of his Father, if the Plaintiff hath Guardians assigned him; and after the Infant, by the Mediation of Friends compoundeth with the Defendant for 1500 *l.* and thereupon the Infant comes into Court, and saith he will relinquish the Suit against the Defendant, and yet notwithstanding the Guardian will prosecute the Suit; the Court in Discretion may discharge the Guardian, and so the Suit will be discontinued, for his Demand by this Suit is but Revenge, and it may be chargeable to him, and perhaps he will leave the Revenge to God, 1 *Rolls Abr.* 288. *h. Slaning* and *Fitz.*

What Acts the Heir may do contrary to the Will of his Guardian.

Han-

Hanbury Armig. & Anna Maria per Hanbery, Prochein amy, contra Hanbury & Walker in Canc. Veneris 16 *Dec.* 22 *Car.* 2.

The Matter of the Plaintiff's Bill, and Demurrer put in thereto: The Scope of the Bill being as the Grandfather, and next Friend of the said Infant, to call the Defendant to Account for her Personal Estate, and of the Rents and Profits of her Real Estate; the Plaintiff in the Bill charging the Real Estate to be about 500 *l. per Annum*, and the Personal Estate to be worth 5000 *l.* That the Defendant, *Theophilus Walker*, who claims to be Guardian by Law to her, as Great Uncle by the Mother's Side, is a Batchelor that failed in his Estate, and is become Journeyman to another, and doth conceal the Infant from her Grandfather, so that he is not a fit Person, *&c.* The Defendant for Demurrer saith, That he by the Law of the Land hath the Right of Guardianship of the Infant during her Minority, he being next of Kin by the Mother's Side, who can have no Benefit by the Death of the Infant; and that the said *John Hanbery* has no Right to the Infant's Real or Personal Estate, or to the Guardianship, he cannot give this Defendant a Discharge, and therefore the Defendant conceived he ought not to be compelled to give any Account to him of the Infant's Estate: His Lordship, on the hearing that the Court ought to take Care of Infants, and of their Education and Estate, and perceiving the Plaintiff the Grandfather of the Infant to be a good *Prochein amy*, the Defendant being charged to be a Mean and Insolvent Person, doth think fit and order, that the Defendant *Walker* to so much of the Plaintiff's Bill as demands Account of the Estate, and where the Infant is, and how she is bred, without Costs; but this to be without Prejudice to the Legal Right: The Defendant hath both to the Custody of the Infant, and the Management of her Estate; and 24 *Feb.* 1670. the Defendant having answered, and confessed he had given over his Trade, and had a Salary from another, and that the Infants Estate was 300 *l. per Annum*; the Court ordered him to account Yearly, but saw no Cause, till a Fault in him, to make him give Security.

Guardian in Socage of a Manor, to which an Advowson is Appendant, if he be disturbed he shall have a *Quare Impedit* in his own Name, although he cannot account for it, 1 *Ed.* 132. — Guardian in Socage shall have a *Quare Impedit.*

But Guardian in Socage may hold Courts in his own Name, and may grant Copies, for he is *Dominus pro tempore*, and hath Interest in the Lands *ex provisione Legis*; but yet so as to be accountable for Fines: And so he may grant a Copyhold in Reversion according to the Custom of the Manor, and this shall be good, although it doth not come in Possession during the Minority of the Heir, *Owen p.* 115 *Shopland* and *Ryder*, 1 *Rolls Abr.* 41. *Messa*'s Case. — May hold Courts and grant Copies.

If the Ward in Socage had a Rent-Charge, or Seck, or such Things which are not held of any Person; yet the Guardian in Socage shall take into his Custody as well these as Lands held in Socage, 1 *Inst*. 88.

Guardian in Socage may make a Lease for Years of the Land of the Ward, and the Lessee shall have *Ejectione firmæ*, 2 *Rolls Abr*. 41.

If Guardian by Nurture make a Lease by Indenture to one, being under the Title of the Infant, rendering Rent to himself, which is paid accordingly; yet this is not any Disseisin to the Infant, *Pasch*. 3 *Jac. B. R. per Tanfield*.

It was a Question, if *A*. seised in Fee of Lands in Socage, and let the same to *J. S*. for Years, and died, his Heir within the Age of 14 Years; the Wife of *A*. being Guardian in Socage, let the same to *J. S*. for Years; whether this Lease was surrendred or determined. *Per Cur'*, It is determined by Operation of Law, for surrendred it cannot be, for the Guardian hath not any Reversion capable of a Surrender, but only Authority in Law to take the Profits to the Use of the Heir. Guardian in Socage has such Estate in the Reversion, that he may enter for Condition broken, yet that is in Right of the Heir, 1 *Leon p*. 322. *Wilers* and *Whitewood*.

Surrender determined.

If Lessee for Years take another Lease from Guardian in Socage, the same is a Surrender of the first Lease.

4 *Note*,

Note, The Second Leaſe was made in the Name of the Guardian, 4 *Leon.* p. 7.

Tenant in Socage makes a Leaſe for Four Years, and dies, his Heir within the Age of Eight Years, the Mother being Guardian in Socage leaſeth by Indenture to the ſame Leſſee for Fourteen Years, the Firſt Leaſe is ſurrendred. *Aliter* of a Leaſe made by Guardian *per Nurture*, 4 *Leon.* p. 161. But it's reported differently in 4 *Leon.*

If Guardian by Nature make a Leaſe by Indenture to a Stranger, being in under the Title of the Infant, rendering Rent to himſelf, which is paid accordingly, yet this is not any Diſſeiſin to the Infant, *Paſch.* 3 *Jac. B. R. per Tanfeild.* Guardian by Nature.

A Leaſe made by a Guardian in Socage ends by his Death, 1 *Brownl.* 79. Leaſe by Guardian ends by his Death.

The *Prochein amy* may make Partition with the other *Parcener*, and this ſhall bind the Infant if it be equal, 9 *H.* 6. 5.

The Admiſſion of Heirs to Copyhold *per Prochein amy*, 1 *Siderfin* 37. is not good, for he muſt do Corporal Service. *Quære*, For ſome ſay it is good, the Heir conſenting, 4 *Rep.*

The Guardian recovers in Debt on Bond made to an Infant, and the Defendant paid the Principal, and prays that the Guardian be ordered to acknowledge Satisfaction. *Per Cur.* The Guardian may not acknowledge Satisfaction for more than he receives, and for ſo much they ordered him to acknowledge, and that no Execution ſhould issue out for the Residue, *Moo.* 852. *White* and *Hull*.

If the Guardian takes Bond in his own Name for Arrears of Rent due from the Infants Tenants; by this the Guardian hath made it his own Debt, 26 *Car.* 2. *Beale* and *Buckley in Chancery*.

Remedy against the Guardian by Infant.

The Guardian to answer the Issues of the Infants Lands.

By the Statute of *Marlbridge* it is provided, *Quod cum* the Infant *ad Legitimam ætatem pervenerit*, the Guardian shall answer the Issues of his Land, *per Legalem computationem salvis rationalibus misis suis, &c. Legitima ætas*: Here must be intended *Secundum subjectam materiam, viz.* Fourteen when he is out of the Custody of the Guardian, *Rolls* 1 *Abr.* 117. *Cok. Litt.* 89. a. *contra Fitzh. Account* 120.

When and how.

If the Guardian in Socage occupies the Lands of the Heir after he comes to Fourteen, for this Occupation he may at any Time be charged as Bailiff, *Cok. Litt.* 90. a.

Infants Estates in the Guardians Hands to be applied to the Payment of his Debts.

Sir *Tho. Badd* was Guardian to *Ed. Dennis*, (whose Sister and Heir, *Bridget Dennis*, the Plaintiff is) and at Fifteen Years of Age married him to the Defendant *Frances*, his Daughter; Sir *Robert Dillington* had a Mortgage of 200*l.* of Part of the Infant's Estate, which Mortgage Sir *Tho. Badd* paid off, and took the same assigned to other Persons: The Infant after at Seventeen Years of Age made his Will, and the Defendant

Frances,

Frances, his Wife, Executrix: The Bill was, That though Sir *Tho. Badd* had paid off the Mortgage with the Infant's own Money, yet he now pretends it was not for the Benefit of the Infant, but that he paid it with his own Money; and for what Money he had of the Infant's, he was accountable to his own Daughter, the Executrix, and so would leave the whole Mortgage-Money still on the Mortgaged Lands, which belong to the Plaintiff, as Sister and Heir to the Infant.

The Defendant, Sir *Tho. Badd*, by Answer said, That the Money he had paid Sir *Robert Dillington* was his own Money, and that he had not near enough of the Infant's to pay the same; and that if he had enough of the Infant's Money, yet he could not justify the disposing of it.

It was proved, that when Sir *Tho. Badd* paid off the Mortgage, he called in about 100 *l.* of the Infant's Money, and that it was applied that Way.

In this Case the Master of the Rolls declared, That Sir *Tho. Badd* ought to employ what he had of the Estate of the Infant, as far as it would go to pay his Debts, and did Decree a Redemption of the Mortgage, and that Sir *Tho. Badd* should account; and that what he had of the Infant's in his Hands when the Mortgage was paid off, should be applied in Discount of Mortgage-Money, and upon Payment of what was more due to the Plaintiff to redeem, *Cases in Chancery* 156. *Bridget Dennis* by Sir *A. F.* her Committee,

Redemption of a Mortgage.

mittee, against Sir *Tho. Badd*, *Frances Dennis* his Daughter, and others.

Account. The Heir, after the Age of 14 Years, shall have an Action of Account against the Guardian in Socage, when he will at his Pleasure; but no *Capias* lies against the Guardian in Socage, neither doth the Statute of *W.* 2. *c.* 11. of Imprisonment for Account to Guardians in Socage, neither are they within the Word *Servientes*, 1 *Inst.* 89.

No *Capias* against him.

Allowance for reasonable Costs and Expence. But Guardian in Socage on Account shall have Allowance of all his reasonable Costs and Expences.

Guardian in Socage, how to be charged after Fourteen Years. He shall be charged as Bailiff after the Age of 14 Years. If Guardian recovers the Rents and Profits of the Infant's Lands, and be robbed of the same, if he be robbed without his own Default or Negligence, he shall be discharged thereof. 2 *Cr.* 219.

Wast.

In what Cases to be discharged of the Rents and Profits. Some Books say, Action lies against the Guardian by the Infant, for not praying his Age.

No Action of *Wast* lies against a Guardian, but an Account or Trespass doth, nor against Tenant by Stat. *Staple*, *Elegit*, *&c.* 1 *Inst.* 54.

CHAP.

CHAP. V.

Of Actions by Infants.

Account by Infant against his Guardian, when and how. He may have a Dum fuit infra ætatem, *and in what Cases. Surrender of a Copyhold makes no Discontinuance. Assize* port *by Infant; where the Assize shall be taken at large, or not. Of a Statute being extended against Infant. When he shall bring a* Quare Impedit *upon an* Usurpation. W. 2. c. 15. *explained. Of his Action in reference to reciprocal Contracts.* Audita Querela, *in what Cases, and when to be brought by him.* Error *brought by him. The Condition of a Recognizance on Error for an Infant. How far the Statute of* 21 Jac. Of Limitations, *extends to Infants bringing Actions, or not. Precedents. Admission to sue* per Guardian. *Appeal by Infant. Infant replies his Infancy to a Plea of* Non assumpsit infra sex annos. *His Admission to sue by* Prochein amy. *How Wrongs done to Infants shall be punished. Of stealing them away.*

HAving shewed how an Infant must sue and be sued, as Plaintiff or Demandant, Tenant or Defendant; and having discoursed of the Nature, Power and Office of a Guardian, I shall proceed to the Actions themselves, and shew where and

 in

in what Cases what Special Actions may be brought by Infants; and what Actions, and for what Causes, may be brought against them.

And First, of Actions that may be brought by Infants.

Account against the Guardian, and how brought.

You may in the Close of the precedent Chapter observe, how that an Heir, after Fourteen Years of Age, may have an Action of *Account* against his Guardian; and as to that observe further, That it was resolved in *Cro. Jac.* 219. in Case *Anonymous*, that an Infant was admitted by his Guardian (or rather *Prochein amy)* to sue *Account* against his Guardian in Socage, for the Profit received after the Infant had accomplish'd his Age of Fourteen Years; and the Action was brought against him as against his Bailiff, and so it ought to be, *Cro. Jac.* 219.

Executors of the Heir shall have Account against the Guardian, and when.

And where the Heir in Socage dies before the Age of Fourteen, his Executors or Administrators shall have an Action of *Account* presently, and yet the Heir himself should not have an Action before Fourteen; but the Reason is, because the Statute of *W.* 2. *c.* 23. saith, *Eandem Actionem habeant Executores*, and not *ad idem tempus*, 2 Inst. 204.

In *Hughe*'s Case, *Godb.* 214. it was agreed *per Cur.* That if an Infant brings an Action against his Guardian for Money, and recovereth, and he bringeth the Money into Court and there deposeth it; that the same is a good Discharge against the Infant, and he he ſhall not anſwer the Suit again in Account.

Dum fuit infra ætatem, is a Writ lying where an Infant within Age alieneth his Land, which he hath in Fee Simple, Fee Tail, or for Life. In this Caſe, when he comes of Age, (or if he die, his Heir when he comes of full Age) may have this Writ to recover the Land again. *Dum fuit infra ætatem*, what.

Infant may have an Action in Nature of a *Dum fuit infra ætatem* upon a Surrender of Copyhold Land, 1 *Leon.* 95. and he may enter: For the Surrender of a Copyhold Eſtate doth not make a Diſcontinuance. The Caſe was, *M.* had Iſſue Two Sons, *Richard* and *Thomas*, and ſurrendered Copyhold Lands to the Uſe of *Richard* for Life, and after to the Uſe of *Thomas* in Fee, they both (*Thomas* being within Age) ſurrender to the Uſe of *Robert* in Fee, who is admitted; *Richard* dies, *Thomas* dies, having Iſſue *A.* who is alſo admitted, and enters into the Land; and it was adjudged his Entry was congeable, and he need not be put to his Plaint in Nature of a *Dum fuit infra ætatem*, 1 *Leon. p.* 225. *Knight* and *Foreman*. Surrender of a Copyhold makes no Diſcontinuance.

Two Jointenants make a Feoffment, they ſhall have ſeveral Writs of *Dum fuit infra ætatem*, as upon ſeveral Feoffments, 19 *H.* 6. 43.

But *Note*, in a *Dum fuit infra ætatem*, the Plaintiff need not ſhew the Time when the Alienation was made.

Assize, in case of Infants, where Assize shall be taken at large.

In the Case of Infants bringing an Assize, it's commonly reported in our Books, That the Assize shall be taken at large; that is, without any respect to the Bar. As, where an Infant brings an Assize at Fifteen Years of Age of Gavelkind Land, where the Custom was that he might alien at that Age as well as a Man at full Age, and the Tenant pleads in Bar, the Assize shall be taken at large; it shall be enquired of the Bar, and if that be found against the Infant, it shall be enquired whether he had other Title, although he was of full Age to alien, 32 *Ass.* 4.

But where an Infant is put to answer a Plea in Bar, there it shall never be enquired at large, or of the Circumstances of the Bar, 22 *H.* 6. 51. *b.*

As in Assize brought by an Infant, if the Defendant pleads a Release of the Ancestor of the Plaintiff by Fine with Warranty, the Assize shall not be taken to enquire of the Circumstances, for that this is a Matter of Record, to which the Infant of Necessity ought to answer. *Id. ibid.*

And it's said in 12 *H.* 4. 22. If the Warranty of the Ancestor be pleaded in Bar against an Infant, because the Infant cannot answer to the Deed without Enquiry of the Bar; if the Bar be found, it shall be enquired of all Things which may avoid or destroy the Warranty, if he had other Title: But if Infant bring an Assize, and upon *Nul Tort nul Disseisin* pleaded, it be found against the Plaintiff, this by Intendment shall be an

Enquiry

Enquiry of the Circumstances; for upon this Issue they may enquire of any Right, 12 *H.*4. 22. *b.*

In an Assize brought by Infant in *B. R.* if the Tenant pleads a Matter of Record in Bar, (*viz.*) a Recovery by him against the Plaintiff in another *Assize* brought by him in *B. C.* To which the Plaintiff replies, He is yet *deins Age*, and that his Writ was purchased and bore Date before the Writ brought in *B. C.* Upon which the Tenant demurs. This was adjudged a good Replication, and the Assize shall be taken only in the Right of Damages; for by the Demurrer, the *Ouster* of the Plaintiff is acknowledged, and the *Disseisin*, *Cro. Jac.* 468. *Holford* and *Platt.*

Though *M.* had once extended his Statute upon an Infant, which was void, yet the Extent being void, it was relievable in *Chancery*.

Also agreed *per Cur.* though for a great Part of the Time there was Infancy in the Case, so that he could not extend the Statute; yet he might have sued in Equity, during the Infancy, to have Relief, tho' he could not extend the Statute at Common Law; but in as much as he had not done it, but sat still Fifty Years without seeking Relief in Equity, he was not relieved. *An.* 43 *Eliz.* *Shelley*'s Case.

Statute extended upon an Infant.

But enough of this ancient Learning in this Point, in favour of an *Assize* brought by Infant, the then most usual Action to recover Possessions.

As

Quare Impedit. Stat. W. 2. c. 15. explained.

As to *Quare Impedit* upon the Statute of *W. 2. c. 15.* it is to be known, that that Statute extends to none but those who are Heirs, or in Degree of Heirs, and are in by Discent: For at Common Law Infant Heirs were by an Usurpation driven to a Writ of *Right*; and no Purchasor, though an Infant, is relieved by that Statute, *Hob. p.* 238. Lord *Stanhope*'s Case.

Now if an Infant Heir suffers an Usurpation, and another Avoidance falls during his Nonage, he may have a *Quare Impedit* presently, though the Statute saith, *post quam ad ætatem pervenerit.* And if a Guardian in Socage, or his Ward, after Fourteen Years of Age, suffer an Usurpation, he shall have a *Quare Impedit* at any other Turn before One and twenty: But if the Infant comes to Age within six Months after the Usurpation, and remove not the Incumbent by Suit, he is out of the Statute.

Vide Hetly 159. Sir *Wollaston Dixey* against the Burgesses of *Darby*.

Infant *habeat eandem actionem possessionam qualiter Antecessor.*

But it would be in vain to enumerate particular Personal Actions; for an Infant may have as much a Remedy for any Debt or Duty, as a Man of full Age, if he pursue his Remedy as he ought. Yet I shall mention a particular Resolution as to Considerations, (which will be more at large handled when I speak of *Contracts.*)

In

In Consideration of such an Act to be done by an Infant, the Defendant assumes to pay him so much Money; the Infant may maintain no Action for the Money before the Act done. And yet (in other Persons the precedent Act is to be done first) as the Consideration is upon the Infant's paying a Sum of Money; and it was urged that this is void, and so wants a Consideration. And *per Cur'*, though the Money is not paid, yet the Action well lies; for it is only in the Election of Infant to make his own Promise void, and not in the Election of the other Party, *Siderf. p.* 38, 41. *Forest*'s Case. Consideration reciprocal.

But more of this, *vide postea, sub tit. Acts, Contracts.*

Of Audita Querela *brought by Infant.*

If an Infant acknowledgeth a Recognizance, Statute-Merchant or Staple, he cannot avoid this without *Audita Querela* be brought before his full Age, because in such Cases of Record his Nonage ought to be tried by Inspection, and these concern but Personal Duties: But if an Infant bargain and sell Land by Deed indented and inrolled, he may avoid this when he pleaseth without *Audita Querela*, because it is real, *Vid supra & infra.* *Audita Querela.*

Of Error brought by Infant to reverse Judgment, Fine and Recovery, *Vide infra, tit. Fine, Recovery, &c.* Error.

In

The Condition of a Recognizance on Error for an Infant.

An Infant in Execution on Condemnation in Debt sued a Writ of Error, and Two bailed him. *Per Cur'*, the Recognizance shall be by them Two only, That the Infant shall appear, and if the Judgment be affirmed, that they pay the Money, and not that they shall render his Body to Prison; for when he is once discharged out of Execution, he shall never be in Execution again, 4 *Leon.* 6. *Tucker* and *Norton*.

In Trespass by Infant *per* Guardian, the Defendant pleads, the Plaintiff was above 16 Years old, and agreed for 6 *d.* in Hand paid, that the Defendant have Licence to take Four Ounces of her Hair. The Plaintiff demurred: And *per Cur'*, its no Plea, for the Infant cannot Licence, though she may agree with the Barber to be trimmed, 3 *Keb.* 389. *Scroggan* vers. *Stewardson*.

Statute of *Limitations*, how it extends to Infants.

It has been a Question, Whether the Statute of 21 *Jac. c.* 16. *Of Limitations*, extends for to save the Rights of Infants to Actions on the Case: And in *Chandler* and *Violet's* Case, *P.* 22 *Car.* 2. *B. R.* it was held that it did, and that the said Action is within the Equity of the saving Clause of it, tho' it be named in the limiting Clause only. Infant by his Guardian declares upon Two Promises, that the Defendant was indebted to him in 50 *l.* and 12 *l.* for Moneys by the Defendant to the Use of the Plaintiff, *ante tempus illud habit' & recept'*; and being so indebted, he promised to pay these Monies. The Defendant pleads in Bar, *Non assumpsit infra sex annos*. The Plaintiff replies, That at at the Time of the Promise, and also of the Bill exhibited, he was, and yet is, an Infant of the Age of 21 Years. Defendant demurs, and adjudged *pro Quer'*. For the Intention of the Act was not to preserve a Petty Action on the Case for Slanderous Words, in respect of Infancy, and not to save an Action for an Infant for a Real Duty, as here was. And the Court was of Opinion, That this Saving extends to all Actions on the Case; for there is a Saving of Trespasses generally, and all Actions on the Case are Trespasses, *scilicet*, Trespass on the Case; and the Infant may pursue his Action at any Time within Age, though the Years limited by the Statute are elapsed during his Nonage, *Siderf.* 453. 2 *Saund.* 121. *Chamber* and *Violet*.

Appeal was brought by Infant *per* Guardian, and at the Day in Court the Guardian was demanded; and though he was sick, the Court would not give Day over, for that may not be in Appeal, *Latch*, *p.* 173. Appeal.

Note, If an Infant declare by Guardian or *Prochein amy*, the Defendant is not compellable to plead until the Plaintiff shews a Rule of Court for his Admittance, *per Magn' Livesey* and others, *Pas.* 21 *Car.* 2. *B. R.*

Precedents.

Infant Suing by Guardian.

Admission to sue *per Gardianum*

ss. T. B. qui infra etatem viginti & unius annorum existit per B. R. Gardianum suum p. Curiam Dom Regis hic specialiter admissus Queritur de, &c.

Infant replies his Infancy to a Plea of *Non Assumpsit infra sex annos.*

Infancy replied to a Plea of *Non assumpsit infra sex annos.*

ET pd Thomas dicit qd ipse p aliqua, &c. precludi non debet, Quia dicit quod ipse idem Thomas tempore confectionis seperalium pmission & assumpcon pd necnon die exhibitionis Bille ipsius Thome pd scilt pd 23 die Octob Anno vicesimo primo supradict fuit infra etatem viginti & unius annorum videlt apud H in Com. pdict', Et hoc paratus est verificare, &c.

E. Saunders.

Admission to sue *per Prochein amy.*

ADmisso querent infra etatem existen ad psequend p proximos amicos suos versus M. H. gen in partitione facienda. Browol. Rediv. 391.

How Wrongs done by Infants shall be punished.

Per Stat. 4 *&* 5 *P. & M. c.* 8. If any take or convey away any Maid, under Sixteen Years of Age, out of the Custody of her Parents, Guardians or Overseers, against their Wills, they are to be imprisoned Two Years without Bail or Mainprize. *Stat. eod.*

If any take and marry any such young Woman, against the Will of them that have the Government of her, they are to be imprisoned Five Years without Bail or Mainprize, *eod. Stat.*

To lie with an Infant Maid, though with her Consent; this Abuse of her is Felony.

By Force or Fraud to steal, or cause to be stolen or taken away, any Person under the Age of 21 Years, with Intent to marry the same Person; for this, a Man shall forfeit his whole Estate, and he is to be imprisoned in the House of Correction during his Life: All that are aiding and abetting, are to be imprisoned and kept at hard Labour for Seven Years.

Such Marriage, so made by Force or Fraud, to be void.

There was a good Law made the 24th of *August*, 1653, That if any Guardian or Overseer shall betray his Trust, touching

ing any Child, by seducing, selling, or otherwise wilfully putting such Child into the Hands or Power of any Person who shall marry her without his or her free Consent, he shall forfeit double the Portion which of Right did belong to such Person, the one half to the Child, the other to the Commonwealth.

CHAP.

CHAP. VI.
Actions brought against Infants.

Action of Wast *lies against him, being Tenant for Life or Years.* Cessavit *lies against him. How Debt lies.* Insimul computasset *in no Case lies against him. Action on* Disceit *lies not against him. Torts* Vi & armis *lie against him. He is punishable for judicial Perjury. Diversity as to* Torts. *If* Trover *and* Conversion *lies against an Infant. Trespass lies against an Infant: So Action on the Case for Words. Action of* Debt *for Rent, how it lies against him, or not. How Infant may avoid Lease and Rent. Action lies against him for Necessaries.* Audita Querela, *in what Cases it lies against an Infant. Appeal of Felony lies against an Infant.*

IN Actions brought against Infants, how he ought to appear by Guardian, and not by Attorney, or *Prochein amy. Vide supra.*

Yet if an Infant appears by Attorney in *Trespass* or *Ejectment*, and had a Verdict, Judgment was reversed, 1 *Keb.* 184. *Whitacre* and *Pellington.*

Quære, If it be holpen by the Statute of 12 *Jac. Of Jeofails. Vide Stat. Car.* 2.

If Infant or Feme Covert Lessee for Life commit Wast, this shall bind the Infant and Feme Covert, for the Statute gives Action to recover the Land. If Infant be a Gaoler

 and

and ſuffer an Eſcape, Actions lies, 8 *Rep.* 44. *b.*

Diſſeiſor. Infant at the Age of Diſcretion may be a Diſſeiſſor by his actual Entry, *Perk.* 106. 3 *H.* 4. 17.

Agreement to a Diſſeiſin doth not make the Infant a Diſſeiſſor, *Ibid.*

Waſt. Infant being Tenant for Life, or Years, ſhall be puniſhed for doing or ſuffering Waſt.

Ceſſavit. Where Infant claims by Purchaſe, a *Ceſſavit* lies againſt him, if he pay not his Rent by Two Years; and if he have the Tenancy by Diſcent, and he himſelf ceſs, a *Ceſſavit* lies; *Plow. Com. Stowel*'s Caſe, 1 *Inſt.* 380, 381.

Debt. Action of Debt lies not againſt Infant, without ſhewing how it aroſe, (as ſuppoſe for Neceſſaries) an *Inſimul computaſſet* in no Caſe lies againſt him, 2 *Keb.* 581. *Mod. Rep.*

Torts. The Court, in *Siderfin, p.* 258. in *Johnſon* and *Pye*'s Caſe, made this Difference: Though Infants ſhall be bound for their actual Torts, as Treſpaſs, *&c.* which are *vi & contra pacem*, yet they ſhall not be bound

Diſceit. by thoſe which ſound in Diſceit; and therefore Action on the Caſe lies not againſt an Infant on his Affirmance that he is within Age, 1 *Keb.* 908. 1 *Lev.* 169. *Johnſon* and *Pye.* In *Grove* and *Nevil*'s Caſe, in *B. R. Paſ.* 16 *Car.* 2. *Rot.* 400. in caſe againſt Infant for ſelling a Faux Jewel, affirming it to be a true one, Action lies not.

Treſpaſs

Treſpaſs lies againſt Infant, *Doct. & Stud.* 149, and by *Wangford*. Treſpaſs lies againſt an Infant of Four Years, 35 *H.* 6. 11. *b.* but *Br. Cor.* 6. makes a Quære of this. Treſpaſs.

Per Cur', On Evidence to a Jury, Action on the Caſe for Words lies againſt an Infant of 17 Years of Age for *Malitia ſupplet Ætatem*, *Noy* 129. and ſo for a Nuſance, *March* 42.

The Infant ſealed a Deed of Mortgage to the Plaintiff, (he was 20 Years and an half old, and appeared to be of full Age,) and affirmed himſelf to be of full Age; and he after avoided this for Infancy to the Plaintiff's Damage, *&c.* and *Not guilty* was pleaded. *Per Keeling*, The Judgment will ſtay for ever, or elſe the whole Foundation of the Common Law will be ſhaken; for this was but a Slip, and he might have pleaded his Minority, 1 *Keb.* 778. *Johnſon* and *Pye*'s Caſe.

And *George* and *Nevill*'s Caſe, cited in *Siderfin*, *p.* 258. is to the ſame Purpoſe. Which was, Action on the Caſe was brought againſt an Infant for affirming a Jewel to be his own, which was not; and the Defendant pleaded Infancy, and the Plaintiff demurs, and it was adjudged for the Defendant; for be the Jewel his own or not, the Plaintiff was not bound by his Affirmation, *Sid.* 258. *George* and *Nevill*'s Caſe.

But it was there agreed, That if Infant judicially perjure himſelf in Point of Age, or otherwiſe, he ſhall be puniſhed for the Perjury. Judicial Perjury.

So you may observe a Difference between Torts *Vi & armis*, and Torts *Ex causa contractus*.

It seems to me, if *A.* sells Wares to *B.* an Infant, for 10 *l.* *B.* receives the Wares, and pays not the Money there because the Contract was void, Trover lies for *A.* against *B.* for the said Wares.

Contract.

Indeb. ass. against Executor of an Infant, as well for Money lent as laid out for the Testator, *&c.* Defendant pleaded, That the Testator was an Infant. Plaintiff *protestando*, That the Testator was not at that Time an Infant. *Pro placito*, That he laid out Money for Lodging and for Meat and Drink, and that it was laid out so for Necessaries; on Demurrer to the Replication Judgment was given for the Defendant, for though the Plaintiff had made a good Answer concerning the Money laid out, yet he said nothing to maintain his Declaration for the Money lent, 5 *Mod.* 368. *Ellis*'s Case.

Replication ill.

Trover and Conversion.

If one delivers Goods to an Infant by Contract, *&c.* knowing him to be an Infant, the Infant shall not be charged in Trover and Conversion for them. *Aliter*, If Goods be delivered to an Infant, not knowing him to be an Infant, *Sid.* 129. *Manby* and *Scot.*

Sed Quære of this; for if he be an Infant, the knowing him, or not knowing him to be so, alters not the Case.

It was the Opinion of some, That an Infant is chargeable for a Tort; and therefore Trover and Conversion being a Tort, an Infant is chargeable with it, and that therefore

fore Trover lies against him, and he cannot plead *deins age*.

But we must distinguish of Torts; for as to such which are *Vi & armis*, an Action lies against Infant; but such Torts which concern Contract, Lending, Finding and Conversion, the Original Cause whereof is not *Vi & armis*, or such as sound in Deceit, no Action lies against him. But, Torts, Diversity.

In an Action on the Case, and a Trover brought against an Infant, as against a common Carrier (as they may be joined in one Action, for *Not guilty* answers both, but Trover and *Assumpsit* cannot be joined) and the Defendant pleads, He was an Infant at the Time of the Conversion: To which the Plaintiff demurred. This Plea prevents a Discontinuance, but is not good as to the Trover; and therefore Judgment for the Plaintiff in the Action on the Case. It's pleaded, the Defendant was an Infant at the Time of the Conversion; which being pleaded in Bar to the whole, prevents any Discontinuance, 3 *Keb.* 59. *Owen* and *Lewis*. *Qu.* *Action sur le Case.* Discontinuance in Pleading.

It hath been controverted, whether and how Action of *Debt* lies against an Infant for Rent? As to that, *Ketly's* Case was this: Debt for Rent.

Action of *Debt* was brought for Rent on a Lease for Years. The Defendant pleads in Bar, That at the Time of the Lease made he was within Age. Plaintiff demurs. *Per Cur'*, A Lease to an Infant is not void, but voidable; for if it be for the Infant's Benefit, be that Benefit apparent or implied, it shall be void in no Case *Primâ facie*, 21 *H.* 6. 31. *b.*

How an Infant may make a Lease void. But the Infant may make it void at his Election; for he may, before the Rent-Day come, refuse and wave the Land, for otherwise such Lease would be more strong than a Fine on Record; and if more Rent be reserved than the Value of the Land, he ought to have set it forth: But in the principal Case it was not shewed, that the Rent was of greater Value. And, Secondly, the Defendant was of full Age before the Rent-Day came. And it's clear, if Infant doth not enter and manure the Land, no Action of *Debt* lies against him, 1 *Brownl.* 120. *Ketley*'s Case. 11 *Jac.*

Statute. A Statute is not extendable against an Infant, but *Chancery* will relieve against an Infant, 1 *Lev.* 198. And how, *vide infra.*

Infant may wave his Demurrer, and plead to Issue. Debt was brought against an Infant for Rent arrear on a Lease made to him: The Defendant demurs to the Declaration, and afterwards waved his Demurrer, and pleads to Issue. *Per Cur'*, Infant may wave his Demurrer at another Day, after he hath demurred, and plead to Issue: But this ought to be in the same Term; and agreed, that the Infant shall be chargeable with the Rent.

As for the Law in Actions against Infants, for Necessaries, *Vide infra, tit. Contracts.*

Infant not charged as Bailiff, or Receiver. One under the Age of 21 Years shall not be charged as Bailiff or Receiver to any Man; because by Intendment of Law, before

fore his full Age, he has not Skill or Ability to raiſe or make any Improvement of Lands, Goods or Chattels, 1 *Inſt.* 172.

If a Statute is acknowledged to Two, whereof One is an Infant, and they make a Defeaſance, and after ſue Execution againſt it, the *Audita Querela* ſhall be brought againſt them both: For it doth not appear within the Deed that he is an Infant, (alſo the Deed of the Infant is not void) and peradventure he will affirm it, 48 *Ed.* 3. 12. *b.* *Audita Querela* againſt two, whereof one is Infant.

An Appeal of Felony lies againſt an Infant. *Stamf.* 62. *a.* So of any other Appeal. *Hale*'s *Pleas of the Crown* 185. Appeal againſt Infant.

An Infant having entered into a Statute, brought an *Aud' Querela.* To avoid it, he was brought into Court, and Two Witneſſes were ſworn to prove his Age, and then his Appearance and Inſpection were recorded. He was bound in this Caſe with Two other Perſons for 1600 *l.* and had no more than 200 *l.* for his Share, 3 *Mod.* 229. Statute.

CHAP. VII.

Of Fines levied by Infants.

Where Infant ſhall be bound by a Fine, & è contra. *Diverſity between Matters of Record done or ſuffered by an Infant, and Matters in Fact. How, and in what Manner, and when he ſhall avoid a Fine. Of Inſpection, and the Reaſon of it. Of his Declaration of Uſes upon a Fine, where good, and where not. Where the Heir ſhall avoid the Fine for the Nonage of the Anceſtor, or not. Where Infant ſhall not have a Writ of Error during his Nonage, and where he ſhall. Infant levies a Fine to the King,* quid operatur. *Where Infant ſhall be bound by Fine and Non-claim, or not; and how the Five Years ſhall be accounted. What Act ſhall bar an Infant from reverſing a Fine during Nonage. Where the Infant's Heir may reverſe a Fine after his Death. Of a Fine being reverſed for the Nonage of the Wife, and whether the Coniſee ſhall retain it during the Coverture. Where a Fine levied by Infant is vacated by Writ of Error. Of Commiſſioners taking a Fine of an Infant, how puniſhable, or not. What Act or Thing ſhall bar an Infant to reverſe a Fine. The Manner of reverſing a Fine by a* Feme Covert *within Age. How it ſhall be done, when Infant and one of full Age join in a Fine, and the Operation of Law thereon. The Husband not admitted to diſavow the Guardian, aſſigned for his Wife in Error,* to *to reverse a Fine.* Quære, *If he can release the Error; And what is to be done if the Husband will not suffer Proceedings in a Writ of* Error?

IT is agreed by all, that where an Infant levies a Fine, it shall bind him, (that is, till it be judicially reversed;) and as to the Reason and Manner of their being so bound, tho' they have a natural Disability, my Lord *Hobart*'s Notion is very fine: 'The Reason '(saith he) why Infants are bound by their 'Fines, is, not because the Law binds such 'Persons, but because the Law finds them 'Persons not so disabled; neither does it ad'mit the Averment of such Disability, for 'that it is certified by the indisputable Credit 'of the Judge, that they were perfect and 'able Persons: And so here is a Law of Po'licy, that doth not cancel the Law of Na'ture, but doth only bound it in Point of 'Form and Circumstance, it being better to 'admit a Mischief in particular, even against 'the Law of Nature, than an Inconvenience 'in general; and it is not the Law of Na'ture to admit any improbable Surmise a'gainst Authentick Record or Evidence. Reason why Infant is bound by his Fine.

So that a Fine levied by an Infant is not void, but voidable. But an Infant shall not be received to aver that he was within Age; for this would be against the Record of the Court. Fine by Infant not void, but voidable. No Averment that he was within Age.

To

Diversity between Matters of Record done or suffered by Infant, and Matters *en fait.*

To this Purpose is the known Diversity between Matters of Record done or suffered by an Infant, and Matter *en fait*: For Matters *en fait* he shall avoid either within Age, or at full Age; but Matters of Record, as Statutes-Merchant, and of the Staple, Recognizances acknowledged by him, and Fine levied by him, and Recovery against him by Default in Real Actions (saving in Dower) must be avoided by him; (that is to say) Statutes, and other Obligations on Record, by *Audita Querela*, and the Fine and Recovery by Writ of *Error*, during his Minority. And the Reason thereof is, because they are Judicial Acts, and taken by a Court or Judge; and therefore the Nonage of the Party to avoid the same, shall be tried by the Inspection of the Judges, and not by the Country; and because his Nonage must be tried by Inspection, this cannot be done after his full Age.

What voidable by *Audita Querela*, and when.

The Reason of Inspection.

And so is *Moor*, *fol.* 75. *Worley*'s Case: If Infant acknowledges a Recognizance, or levy a Fine, he shall not have *Audita Querela*, nor a Writ of *Error*, at his full Age, unless he reverse it during his Minority; for when he is of full Age, the Court cannot judge by Inspection of what Age he was at the Time of the Conisance; and by his Surmise only, the Law will not suffer that to be reversed, which was so solemnly and lawfully done: But if he still continue within Age, so as the Court may compare the Time of the Action brought with the Time of the Acknowledgment, if they judge him within Age by Inspection,

ſpection, they will reverſe the Fine, and ſo alſo the Statute, *Moor, fol.* 75. *Worley*'s Caſe.

And there is not any Means to reverſe a Fine but by Inſpection; and therefore it's uſual at this Day to take a Fine of Infants a little before their full Age, for that then they have not any Time to reverſe it; but by Inſpection the Court may inform themſelves, and by other Teſtimonies alſo, 1 *Bulſtr.* 206. *Butts* and *Jenning*'s Caſe. *Vide infra, Titulo Trial.*

Now if the Age be inſpected by the Judges, and it be recorded that he is within Age, albeit he come of full Age before the Reverſal, yet may it be reverſed after his full Age, as is *Kechwiche*'s Caſe, cited 1 *Inſt.* 380. *b.* Fine may be reverſed after full Age, if it be recorded that he was within Age.

And as it is in the Caſe of a Fine, ſo it is in a Judgment. If the Infant bring a Writ of *Error* to reverſe a Judgment againſt him in an Action of *Debt*, becauſe he then was, and ſtill is an Infant: In this Caſe he muſt be inſpected by the Court. He muſt be inſpected to reverſe a Judgment.

As to Error brought to reverſe a Fine during Infancy, the Infancy was aſſigned, and here ſhe was inſpected, *i. e.* in *B. R.* and on *Scire facias* againſt the Defendant, he pleads *In nullo eſt erratum*, and the Fine was reverſed. Now it is not uſual to reply *In nullo eſt erratum*, but to leave it to the Court, *Mich.* 25 *Car.* 2. *B. R. Oakover*'s Caſe. Error brought to reverſe a Fine during Infancy and Pleading.

By *Hales*, If Error be well aſſigned in Fact, *In nullo eſt erratum*, confeſſeth it; but if it be Matter in Law, there muſt be a Demurrer, and *In nullo eſt erratum* is ill. But if if the Error in Fact be not well assigned, (as that in Fact he did not appear at such a Day, which being against the Record, is not well assigned) and so confessed; but this Matter of Fact being well assigned, the Fine was reversed.

The bringing a Writ of *Error* to reverse a Fine by Infant during his Nonage, is not sufficient; but the Fine by Judgment in the Writ of *Error* must be reversed during his Nonage, *Godb.* 120. 1 *Inst.* 380.

Where Infant shall not have a Writ of Error during his Nonage.

Infant levies a Fine *sur Grant*, and Remainder in Tail or for Life, he shall not have a Writ of Error during his Nonage, because he himself is Tenant of the Land, and he may not have a Writ of Error against himself, and so the Infant is without Remedy. *Per Catlyn* Ch. J. *Crompton Jurisd. of Courts*, 37. *a.*

If Infant grant a Rent by Fine, this Grant is voidable by himself, during his Nonage, by Writ of Error, *Perk.* 4. *b.* So of Land, 1 *Inst.* 380. *b.* But if he doth not avoid it during his Nonage, it's good for ever; and tho' he die during his Nonage, before he had avoided it, yet his Heir shall not avoid it, for that it must be avoided by Inspection, *Bridgm. Rep.* 122, 123, 125.

The Law which allows a Fine by Infant, allows him also to declare the Use, *Hob.* 234.

Infant die before the Reversal, his Heirs are bound by it.

If the Infant die before the Reversal, his Heir shall be bound by it, and he cannot reverse it, because this ought to be by Inspection,

ſpection, which cannot be when he is dead, *Winch*, p. 104.

So by *Hales*, in *Parker* and *Primate*'s Caſe, 27 *Car*. 2. *B. R.* a Fine is levied by Infant, and ſhe lived to full Age, it is unavoidable; and if ſhe die within Age, it is alſo unavoidable, it not being avoidable but by Error during her Minority; and till the Fine be reverſed, it's not avoided by Evidence of Miſdemeanor.

So is *Co.* 12 *Rep. Ann Hungate*'s Caſe expreſs. If the Fine be not reverſed during the Minority of the Heir, the Fine is unavoidable in Law, and the Heirs of the Infant have not any Remedy by the Law to reverſe it, becauſe it muſt be tried by Inſpection of his Perſon. Fine muſt be reverſed during Minority.

But there is another Diverſity to be obſerved as to Matters of Record; that is, between a Statute, *&c.* and a Deed inrolled; for he may avoid a Deed inrolled at his full Age; for in this Caſe nothing paſſeth by the Inrolment, but all by the Deed before, 2 *Inſt*. 673. Difference between a Statute and a Deed inrolled.

Now the Law which allows the Fine levied by the Infant, allows him likewiſe to declare the Uſes by his Deed, as being a Part of the Operation of the Fine; and this Declaration ſhall bind ſo long as the Fine remains in Force. So of a Man of *Non ſane memorie*, 2 *Rep*. 58. *Beckwith*'s Caſe, 1 *Roll. Rep*. 730. *Spring* and Sir *Julius Cæſar*. Infants declaring Uſes upon a Fine.

And if an Infant levy a Fine, and declares the Uſes when he comes of full Age, (the Fine not being reverſed) he ſhall be bound

bound by the Deed that leads the Uſes of the Fine, as well as by the Fine it ſelf, for they make but one Aſſurance.

But it has been queſtioned, when Infant makes an Indenture to declare the Uſes of a ſubſequent Fine, and after *A.* levies another Fine generally, whether he may avoid it? I conceive it's all but one Aſſurance, and ſo ſhall bind, as in the other Caſe of a ſubſequent Declaration, *Mod. Rep.* 252.

If Infant covenant by Indenture to levy a Fine, and that this ſhall be to certain Uſes and dies within Age, the Limitation of the Uſes ſhall bind the Heir of the Infant, as well as the Infant himſelf, ſo long as the Fine continues not reverſed, 1 *Roll. Rep.* 730.

And ſo it was reſolved in the *Star-Chamber*, That an Infant having levied a Fine, may declare the Uſes upon it; and ſuch Declaration is good notwithſtanding his Nonage, 2 *Leon.* 159.

And Mr. *Plowden* affirmed it was ſo adjudged in his own Caſe, by which he loſt Lands of the Yearly Value of 40 *l.*

If Infant levies a Fine to the King, and declares the Uſes of it by his Deed, it ſhall bind him, *Hob.* 224.

Where a Fine ſhall be reverſed by the Heir of the Infant after his Death.

Now, where it may be reverſed by his Heir after his Death, we muſt know: If the Infant is inſpected and dies before the Fine is reverſed, yet after his Age adjudged and recorded, his Heir in that Caſe ſhall reverſe the Fine for the Nonage of the Anceſtor, *ut ſupra. Mo.* 844. *Keckwith*'s Caſe.

As to the Infant's being bound by the Fine of their Anceſtor; though the Iſſue be an Infant, yet foraſmuch as he is Privy, and out of all the Savings of 4 *H.* 7. he is bound by the Fine of his Anceſtor.

But as to the Infant's being bound by Fine and Non-claim, or not, the Caſe of *Stowel* and *Zouch* is a *Leading Caſe.* The Caſe was:

Zouch diſſeiſed the Grandfather of *Stowel*, of Lands in Fee, and levies a Fine with Proclamations, and *Stowel* the Grandfather lives Three Years after, and dies; *Stowel* his Grandſon and Heir being then Six Years old, who enters at his full Age. And the Queſtion was, Whether he ought not to have entered during the firſt Five Years from the levying the Fine, Part of which was attached in the Grandfather; or whether he has Time to enter at his full Age? And it was reſolved in the *Exchequer Chamber*, That notwithſtanding his Infancy, yet he ought to have entered within the Five Years after the Fine levied; which he not doing, but ſtaying till he came of Age, is barred by the Statute of 4 *H.* 7. *c.* 24. For the Exception is of ſuch Infants or Perſons as had Right at the Time of the Fine levied, and no others; and *Stowel* the Grandſon had no Right at the Time of the Fine levied; but the Grandfather had the Right then, againſt whom the Statute takes Place: And the Heir within Age is bound to purſue his Right before his full Age, becauſe he had no preſent Right at the Time of the Fine

How Infant bound by Fine and Non-claim, or not.

Fine levied; so that he shall not have a new Five Years after his full Age, but the Five Years commenced in the Time of *Stowel* the Grandfather ought to be continued without Interruption. By the first Saving, the Heirs shall be as general as the Saving, and shall comprehend Heirs within Age. And in this Case the Grandson is not within the second Saving, because it is saving to others. Now the Word [*Others*] is exclusive of those comprised in the Exception. And old *Stowel* his Heirs were comprised in the first Saving, because he had Right at the Time of the Fine ingrossed; which Right is saved to him and his Heirs, upon Condition, that they pursue their Right within Five Years, which was not done: And by the Word [*Prierment*] *Stowel* the Grandson had no Right first came to him, for any Cause or Title, before the Fine levied, as the Law-makers intended it: For they intended a Special Cause, which was the Cause efficient to have the Right, and such Right was not in any other, but first in him; and the Disseisin which was before the Fine, was no Matter or Cause to make *Stowel* to have the Right: For if the Disseisin had not been, he had had the Right and Possession by discent. And the Reason why *Walsh* changed his Mind, who was of the contrary Opinion at first, is to our Purpose; for that the Act which had limited the Time, had made a Condition to the Right of *Stowel* the Grandson, (*viz.*) That he ought to pursue his Claim within the Five

Years attached first in the Grandfather; of which his Nonage shall not discharge him, no more than if a Man make a Feoffment in Fee upon Condition on the Part of the Feoffee and his Heirs to be performed; if the Feoffee dies, his Heir within Age, he is bound to perform the Condition during his Nonage, as well as if he had been of full Age. And this Construction was made in this Case, for the quieting and Repose of Men's Estates, which Universal Benefit the Law prefers before the Priviledge of Infancy; which though it may in some few Cases be a Prejudice to the Infant, yet the other is more to be favoured, *Plowd.* 354. *Zouch* and *Stowel.*

But in *Dyer* 133. Tenant in Tail, Remainder in Fee to a Stranger; Tenant in Tail levies a Fine with Proclamations; he in the Remainder dies, his Heir within Age; and afterwards Tenant in Tail dies without Issue; so as a Title to have a *Formedon* in Remainder accrues to the Infant, who suffers Five Years to pass after his Title accrued; yet he may bring his Action after Five Years, because the Statute of 4 *H.* 7. *Of Fines*, saves his Claim till of full Age, and then he shall have Five Years, *Dyer* 133.

What Acts shall bar an Infant from reversing a Fine during his Nonage.

But in some Cases an Infant may do such Acts as shall bar him to reverse a Fine during his Nonage: As if Infant bring a Writ of *Error* to reverse a Fine, levied by himself during his Nonage, and is inspected by the Court and found within Age; which is recorded by the Court, and afterwards (before Fine reversed) he levies another Fine to another; this shall bar him to have the Fine reversed. But it was adjudged *contra*, because the second Fine was not pleaded. *Mich.* 28 & 29 *El. B. R. Hart's* Case.

If Infant levy a Fine, and take back an Estate in Life or in Tail by Render, he shall not have a Writ of *Error* to adnul the Fine; because he himself is seized of the Land, and so without Remedy. *Mo. p.* 44.

Note, Infant levied a Fine, acknowledged before the Chief Justice, and the Conisees would not demand the Fine to be ingrossed until his full Age: And now the Infant comes with the Note of the Conisance, and prays that he may be admitted to a Writ of *Error*, and to the Examination of his Age; and the Judges agreed to it, and made Entry of it, and by this they would save the Advantage to him. *Mo.* 189.

If the Queen's Silver be paid before the Death of the Fee-Heir, shall be barred.

Husband and Wife, in the Vacation after *Hill.* Term, by *Ded. pot.* acknowledged a Fine of the Wife's Land, the Wife being then but of 14 Years of Age. The Writ of Covenant bore Date in *January* before, retornable *Cras. Pur.* and the *Dedimus* bears Date Three Days after the Original, and the

the Queen's Silver was entered, *viz. Die Veneris in Septimana Paschæ*, which was Four Days before the Death of the Wife, but the Fine was not ingrossed till afterwards. The Heir of the Wife in *Easter* Term prayed, That the Fine might not be recorded nor delivered to the Party; but because the Queen's Silver was entered, notwithstanding the Under-practice of the Husband, the Fine was ingrossed, and so did bind the Heir, though the Wife was within Age at the Time of the Acknowledgment. *Dier* 220. *Carell*'s Case.

I shall now consider how the Law stands when an Infant and one of full Age join in a Fine; how the Reversal of the Fine shall operate: And also when Baron and Feme levy a Fine, and one is within Age, and how the Conisee shall detain or make Restition.

Infant and one of full Age join in a Fine; how the Reversal shall operate.

It is adjudged in the Case of one *English*, cited in 1 *Rep. Bredon*'s Case: Tenant for Life, Remainder in Fee to an Infant, they both join in a Fine, and they both bring a Writ of *Error*: It shall be reversed as to the Infant, and stand good as to the other, and the Conisee shall have the Land for the Life of the Tenant for Life, *English*'s Case, 1 *Rep. Bredon*'s Case. *Aliter* in the Case of *Baron* and *Feme*.

And to this Purpose is *Pigot* and *Russel's* Case; Lessee for Life, and he in Reversion, join in a Fine to a Stranger, and he in Reversion reverseth the Fine for Nonage. Two Points were adjudged:

First, That he shall not enter for the Forfeiture, because he joined in the Fine and consented to it.

Secondly, He alone may bring his Writ of *Error* to reverse it, for it's brought of an Error in Fact (*viz.*) his Nonage, *Cro. El.* 115, 124. *Pigot* and *Russel.*

Two Infants levy a Fine, how reversable.

And so it was adjudged in *Pigot* and *Harington's* Case; and it's there agreed, That if Two Infants levy a Fine, they may sue several Writs of *Error*, or join in one Writ; but they ought to assign Errors severally, 1 *Leon.* 317.

Fine by *Baron* and *Feme*, the *Feme* being within Age, how reversed, and the Consequence.

If a Fine be levied by *Baron* and *Feme*, the *Feme* being within Age, and in Error brought the Fine is reversed for the Nonage of the Wife, the *Baron* and *Feme* shall have Restitution presently, and the Conisee shall not detain it during the Coverture; for all the Estate passeth from the Wife. *Worsley* and *Charnock's* Case, cited 2 *Rep.* 77. *Lord Cromwell's* Case.

But this Case is more fully reported in 1 *Leon.* 114. And the Question was, If the Fine

Fine ſhould be utterly reverſed, or ſhould be reverſed only as to his Wife, and ſhould ſtand good againſt the Husband? And Two great Precedents were cited, one contrary to the other. They that argued that the Fine ſhould be reverſed for the whole, cited *Ely* and *Ford*'s Caſe, P. B. H. 8. A Fine was levied between *R. Ely* Plaintiff, and *N. Ford*, and *Jane* his Wife, Deforceants, the Wife being within Age: And Judgment was given, *quod Finis præd' adnulletur* and *pro nullo penitus habeatur*, and that the *Baron* and *Feme* ſhould be reſtored; and thereupon a Writ iſſued to the *Cuſtos brevium*, to bring into Court the Foot of the Fine, and it was preſently cancelled in Court.

The other Precedent cited contrary to this, was 7 *Eliz. Baron* and *Feme* levied a Fine, the Husband died, the Wife being within Age; the Wife took another Husband, and they brought a Writ of *Error*, and the Wife by Inſpection was adjudged within Age, and the Fine was reverſed as to her and her Heirs only. But indeed the ſecond Husband was a Stranger to the Fine, and ſo it might ſeem abſurd to reverſe it as to him; but in the principal Caſe it was adjudged, that the Fine ſhould be reverſed as to both, for the whole Eſtate moved from the Wife, and all paſſeth out of her; and Judgment was given *quod Finis præd' reverſetur*. And by *Gawdy*: We cannot by this Reverſal make the Coniſee to have a particular Eſtate

 during

during the Life of the Wife. *Ideò penitus reverſetur.* 1 *Leon.* 114. *Worſley* and *Charnock.*

The Huſband not permitted to diſavow the Guardian aſſigned for his Wife, to reverſe a Fine. *Quære*, Of a Releaſe by the Huſband.

A *Feme Covert* Infant levied a Fine, and her Friends got a Writ of *Error* in her and her Huſband's Name, yet the Court would not ſuffer her Huſband to releaſe; by *Twiſden*: But by *Hales*, I cannot ſee how that can be avoided; but (he ſaid) he had known in ſuch Caſe, that the Court would not permit the Huſband to diſown the Guardian, which they admitted for his Wife, 1 *Ventr.* 209.

Full Age of a *Feme Covert*, as to a Fine tried by a Jury, and ill.

A *Feme Covert* levied a Fine within Age; ſhe was inſpected by the Court, and adjudged within Age; whereupon a *Scire facias* iſſued to the Tertenants, who pleaded ſhe was of full Age at the Time of the Fine levied. Upon which Plea Iſſue was joined, and a Trial had at the Aſſizes, and a Verdict for the Plaintiff, who came into Court, and now prayed Judgment. *Per Glyn*, The Court is to judge of her Infancy, and not the Jury; and tho' the Proceedings are not duly, yet they do no Hurt. And the Fine was reverſed, *Stiles* 472. *Vidian* and *Fletcher.* *Vide Trial infra.*

Of Commiſſioners taking a Fine of an Infant.

The Fine not to be ſet aſide.

If Commiſſioners do take a Fine of an Infant, yet the Court will not ſet it aſide. It was *Herbert Parrot*'s Caſe. A *Feme Covert* (his

(his Wife) at 20 Years of Age levied a Fine before Commiſſioners in the Country, and the Wife dies without Iſſue; ſhe had ſettled the Eſtate upon her and her Husband, and the Heirs of their Two Bodies. The Court was moved to ſet it aſide; but they agreed they could not meddle with it: But if the Wife had been alive, and under Age, they might bring her in by *Habeas Corpus* and inſpect her, and ſet aſide the Fine upon Motion; for perhaps the Husband would not ſuffer the bringing or Proceedings in a Writ of *Error*. And the Commiſſioners in this Caſe were not fined, becauſe they could not diſcern whether ſhe was of Age by the View, ſhe being 20 Years of Age; but if it had been apparent by Inſpection that ſhe was within Age, then they ought to have been fined, 2 *Vent. pag.* 30. *Perrot*'s Caſe, *Mod. Rep.* 246.

What is to be done, if the Husband will not ſuffer Proceedings in a Writ of Error.

H. and his Wife, ſhe being Infant of Sixteen Years of Age, levy a Fine of the Lands of the Wife, and pay the King's Silver, and have the Fine finiſhed and exemplified; but upon the Complaint of him in Remainder in Fee depending on the Eſtate Tail of the Wife, the Husband and Wife were brought into Court by Rule and examined, and upon Examination the levying the Fine and Infancy appear. But *per Cur'*, and Prothonotaries, ſuch Fines have been vacated notwithſtanding the King's Silver paid, and the Fines perfected. It was ordered to vacate this Fine, and to cauſe the Exemplifica-

Fine levied by Infant vacated without Writ of Error.

tion to be brought into Court and delivered up, and ordered him in Reversion to prosecute Information against the Commissioners who took the Conisance of the Fine; but the Note of the Vacate was entered, *quoad* the Wife only, 3 *Lev.* 36. *Hutchinson*'s Case.

Information against Commissioners that took the Caption.

To this Purpose is a notable Case in *Coke*'s 12 *Rep.* *Anne Hungate*'s Case in the *Star-Chamber*; and in that Case, forasmuch as no Corruption and Circumvention was proved in the Commissioners, the Fine stood good, and it was not there apparent to the Commissioners that he was within Age, he wanting but Six Weeks of his Age: But if the Commissioners had had Knowledge he had been within Age, it had been a Misdemeanor in them.

Commissioners, in what Cases fineable.

And so was *Cavendish*'s Case, cited there: The Commissioners did perfectly know that the *Feme Covert*, who levied the Fine, was within Age; and for this Cause every one of them was fined. But the Fine stood good, and not reversed, 12 *Rep.* 122. *Anne Hungate*'s Case, & 1 *Roll. Rep.* 112. *Mesme Case.*

It was the Opinion of *Coke*, in 2 *Brownl.* 271. If Commissioners by force of a *Dedimus potestatem* take a Fine of an Infant, they are fineable and ransomable to the Value of the Lands.

But in *Requish*'s Case, 2 *Bulstr.* 320. and *Moor* 840. the Court was more favourable to the Commissioners, and to the Infant.

Requish,

Requish, of whom the Fine was taken, was an Infant of the Age of Twenty Years and Three Quarters: The Commissioners had no Notice that he was within Age, and by Inspection they could not perceive. *Per Cur. in Camera-Stell*, This was a Fault in them, but not a Crime; and they were not punished. *Requish*, upon Proof made by the Church-Book, was adjudged within Age, and the Fine was avoided; and the Court *ex assensu partium* did take upon them the setting and disposing of his Lands in such Manner as he should not sell them, but to his youngest Brother, because of his Simplicity, 2 *Bulstr.* 320. *& Moor* 844. *Requish*'s Case.

And because this is a Matter of great Weight, (*viz.*) the passing of Lands away by a Fine, many Times to the subversion and alienation of fair Estates from ancient Families; and yet the Solemnity of a Fine is so great, that I shall cite One Case more, which is in *Dyer* 220. *b. Carel*'s Case, but more fully reported in *Co.* 12 *Rep.* 124.

Undue Means in gaining a Fine.

A *Feme Covert*, of the Age of Nineteen Years, acknowledged a Fine before Commissioners (several Judges being in Town who might have examined her). She died on *Friday* in *Easter-Week*, but the Fine and Queen's Silver was entered as of last Term, (*viz. Hillary,*) Four Days before the Death of the Wife; and the Original Writ of *Covenant* bore Date the 15th of *January*, retornable *Crast. Purificat'*, and

and the *Dedimus potestatem* the 18th Day of *January*, 12 *Rep*. 124. *Carryl's* Case.

In *Dyer* it seems, that the ingrossing this Fine was stop'd for undue Means in gaining it: But in the Twelfth *Report*, before the Judges in the *Star-Chamber*, the Husband, who perswaded the Wife, was not punished, though he knew his Wife was within Age. And *per Cur'*, the said Fine is good, and orderly sued out, and available and effectual in the Law, *Dyer* 220.

CHAP.

CHAP. VIII.

Of Common Recovery, and other Matters of Record suffered by Infants.

Recovery against Infant by Vertue of a Privy Seal. Infants permitted to suffer Recoveries by the Court: And the Reasons thereof. The manner of passing such Recoveries. Recovery suffered by Infant of Four Years of Age. If Infant appear by his Guardian, and suffer a common Recovery, it cannot be reversed for Error: But if in such Case he appear by Attorney, it may be reversed after his full Age, and why. And if he appear in Person it may be reversed within Age, but not after full Age, and why. Difference where Infant comes in on single Voucher, and where on double Voucher. Recovery by Infant in Person, may be avoided in Error before full Age, but at full Age he cannot avoid it by Entry. Judgments in Courts not to be subverted by Matters in Pais. *If Infant suffered a Recovery by Attorney, he in Remainder may vouch it for Error, and why. The Appearance by a* Feme Covert *within Age in a Recovery by Attorney is Error.* Regula *as to* Baron *and* Feme, *as in respect of the Inheritance of the Wife, being impeached by the Husband. Difference between Matters of Record, and Matters of Fait as to their being void or voidable for Infancy, and how*

how and when to be avoided. Infants shall avoid Matters in Fait within Age, or at full Age. Statutes and Recognizances are avoided by Audita Querela. *Fines, Recoveries and Judgments are avoided by Error. By* Audita Querela *during Minority.* Audita Querela, *where brought in* B. C. *or in* B. R. Audita Quer. *by Infant, to cancel a Recognizance how to be brought. In* Audita Querela, *Judgment was reversed for Error in Proceedings; no new* Audita Querela *lies at full Age, and the Reason. Reinspection not of Force, but in the same Court where the first Inspection was.* Audita Querela *lies upon Judgment against Infant-Bail upon a Recognizance. If the Recognizance is avoided by* Audita Querela, *Judgment upon it is avoided also. Infant cannot enter into a Recognizance to discharge himself of Execution. Judgment by Default cannot be avoided by Infant at his full Age. Infant confesseth a Judgment: How to be avoided. Who shall take Advantage of Infancy.*

A Recovery was suffered by an Infant, by Vertue of a Privy Seal for that Purpose, directed to the Lord Chief Justice, *Hob.* 196. *Vide.*

An Infant may suffer a common Recovery at the Discretion of the Court, as is resolved in *Mountjoy Blunt*'s Case, before the Lord Chief Justice *Hobart*, it being adjudged convenient by himself (he being at the Age of Ten Years) and his Trustees; and

and divers Precedents are there cited of the like Nature, *Hob.* 196, 197.

So was the Case in 1 *Leon.* 211. In Covenant for further Assurance, it was devised, That for further Assurance and cutting off a Remainder, a common Recovery should be suffered, in which an Infant should be Tenant to the *Præcipe*, and should vouch the Vendor; and because the Recovery was intended to be to the Use of the Infant and his Heirs, it was prayed, That such a Recovery might be received and allowed. At the first the Justices were doubtful what to do; but at last, upon Affidavit made, That the said intended Recovery was to the Use of the Infant, and upon Appearance of a good and sufficient Guardian for the Infant in the Recovery, who was of Ability to answer to the Infant, if he should be deceived in the passing the Recovery, the Recovery was received and allowed. And as to the Manner of passing such Recoveries, *Stapleton*'s Case, in *Cro. Eliz. p.* 471. speaks fully. The Case was, 1 *Leon.* 211.

Infant permitted to suffer a Recovery by the Court, and why.

Tenant in Tail, in Consideration of the Marriage of his eldest Son, covenanted to stand seized to the Use of himself for Life, and after to the Use of his eldest Son for Life, and after to the Use of the first Son of his eldest Son in Tail; the Grandfather afterwards would sell Part of the Land, and the Purchaser would not take any Assurance, unless the Infant, who was but Four Years of Age, would suffer a common Recovery: And yet it was conceived that that Covenant

The Manner of passing such Recoveries.

Recovery suffered by Infant of Four Years of Age.

nant did not alter any Estate; but to satisfy the Purchaser, he prayed a Guardian might be allowed to the Infant, that a Recovery might be suffered against him as Vouchee, whereto the Court agreed; and therefore admitted a Gentleman there present (the Infant being brought into Court) to be Guardian for him; and then a Recovery was had of that Land at the Bar, wherein the Infant was vouched, and he by his Guardian appeared and vouched the common Vouchee.

I find in a Manuscript, That if an Infant by his Guardian suffer a common Recovery, he being Tenant to the Præcipe, this shall bind him; so that he shall not avoid it by a Writ of Error, for by Intendment he shall have Recompence in Value; and if it be not for the Good of the Infant, he may have his Recompence against his Guardian, and there are divers Precedents of such common Recoveries suffered by an Infant, and much Land depends upon such Recovery; as may be seen by Precedents in the Time of *Ed.* 4. *H.* 7. *H.* 8. Q. *Mary*, Q. *Eliz.* and King *James*, *Sed vide* the Cases following as to this.

It was a great Question in *Raby* and *Robinson*'s Case, *Sid.* 321. Whether when an Infant suffers a Common Recovery in Person, he may avoid it for Error after his full Age. For it was agreed, That if Infant appear by his Guardian, and suffers a Common Recovery, that this is good, and shall not be reversed for Error, according to the Lord *Newport's*

If Infant appear by his Guardian and suffer a Recovery, it cannot be reversed for Error.

port's Case, *Cr. Car.* 301. *Hob.* 196. For the Judgment is not given upon Default of the Infant, but upon Departure of the Vouchee in despight of the Court. So that *Mary Portington*'s Case seems in this Point not to be Law, though the Report in *Rolls* seems to confound it self, *Cr. Car.* 301. 1 *Rolls Abr.* 751. Lord *Newport*'s Case.

If the Infant appears by Attorney and suffers a Common Recovery, it was agreed in *Raby* and *Robinson*'s Case, That this may be reversed for Error after his full Age, because it shall be tried *per Pais*, Whether the Warrant of Attorney was made by him when he was an Infant; and so is *Aylet*'s Case, *Stiles* 246. And this is the true Reason why Judgment so obtained against Infants may be reversed after his full Age, (*Scilicet*) because the Trial is here not by Inspection, but by *Pais*. Tho' in such Case it is worse for the Purchasers than a Fine levied by an Infant; for 40 Years after this it may be alledged for Error, that he that gave the Warrant of Attorney was an Infant, 2 *Keb.* 40. *Stiles* 246. *Aylet*'s Case, *Cr. Eliz.* 569. *Moor* 46. 1 *Inst.* 380.

If Infant appear by Attorney and suffers a Common Recovery, it may be reversed after his full Age, and why.

But now where the Infant appears in Person, and cannot be tried but by Inspection, the Party being at full Age, the Trial fails; and therefore it was resolved, that this cannot be assigned for Error, because he ought to be tried by Inspection; and it is no greater a Mischief than if a Fine had been levied by Infant, that after his full Age it is unavoidable.

But if he appear in Person it cannot be reversed after full Age, and why.

The

The principal Case of *Raby* and *Robinson* was this: Error was brought of a Common Recovery on a Writ of Entry, by *Præcipe* against *R.* of Lands in *G.* who vouched *E.* the Plaintiff in a Writ of *Error*, who enters in the Warranty and voucheth *H.* and so a Recovery passed, *G.* being an Infant.

And so was *Darcy* and *Jackson*'s Case: Error was brought of a Recovery against a Feme Infant who appeared by Attorney. And it was adjudged, That it being by Attorney she might reverse it; but *contra*, if it had been in Person. *In the Case of *Raby* and *Robinson*, there was a Distinction started; where the Infant comes in upon single Voucher that shall bind him, because he comes in upon the Warranty of his Ancestor; but if an Infant come in upon double Voucher, that shall not bind him, because he comes in upon his own Warranty, but this Difference was not allowed.

*Difference where Infant comes in on single Voucher, and where upon double.

But *Note*, Though such Recovery wherein Infant Vouchee comes *in propria Persona* (and not by Attorney or Guardian) does not bind him, but that he may avoid it in a Writ of *Error*; for that it is Error in Law; yet at his full Age he may not enter into the Land and avoid it by his Entry, before he has revers'd it by a Writ of *Error*; because he himself is privy to the Judgment, and may not reverse it by such Means. For Judgments are not to be subverted by Matters *en Pais*, without Matter of Record; as Recognizance or Fine by an Infant, nor any Judgment in other

Recovery by Infant in Person may be avoided in Error before full Age, but at full Age he cannot avoid it by Entry.

Judgment not to be subverted by Matters *en Pais*.

Action given against Infant, where he appears by Attorney, and not by Guardian, 1 *Rol. Abr.* 742. *Aylet's* Case.

If Tenant in Tail within Age is vouched, who appears by his Attorney, he in Remainder may assign this for Error; for that he is privy to the Judgment in regard of his Interest, and the Appearance by the Infant by Attorney is void, 1 *Rol. Abr.* 755. *Holland* and *Lee.*

If Infant suffer a Recovery by Attorney, he in Remainder may vouch it for Error.

The Appearance by a *Feme Covert* (in a Recovery) within Age by Attorney, is Error: And tho' it may be objected, That the Husband is of full Age, and therefore he may make Attorney for himself and his Wife, the Law is not so; for the Rule of it is, That the Husband cannot give away or lose the Inheritance of his Wife; but it must be given or lost by her self, or her own Act; and she ought to appear by Guardian, notwithstanding the full Age of the Husband, who is to be join'd for Conformity with her. But *quære*, if it be void, or voidable, *Sid.* 322. *Bridgm.* 75. *Holland* and *Jackson.*

The Appearance by a *Feme Covert* (in a Recovery) within Age by Attorney, is Error.

Regula as to *Baron* and *Feme*.

A Writ of Error was brought to reverse a Common Recovery, and a *Scire facias* against the Tertenants, who are summoned to appear, and the Sheriff hath retorned there are no other Tenants. The Error assigned, was, That the Vouchee was a Feme Covert, and under Age, and appear'd by Attorney. If she had vouched in Person, or by Guardian, such a Recovery should not be reversed for Error after full Age, because a Guardian is made by the

Court, who will not admit of any one but such as ſhall be anſwerable for the Loſs that the Infant may ſuſtain; but an Attorney is made by the Party, and an Infant may not have Diſcretion enough to chuſe an Attorney who will be faithful to him.

Therefore ſhe appearing by Attorney, and ſuffering a Recovery, it ſhall be reverſed for the ſame Reaſon after the Party comes of Age, becauſe it ſhall be tried by the Country, whether the Warrant of Attorney was made when under Age, or not.

Neither can the Husband, though of full Age, make an Attorney for himſelf and his Wife (under Age) to bind the Inheritance of the Wife; but ſhe being the principal, muſt be barred by her own Act; and therefore ſhe muſt appear in Court in ſuch Manner as the Law hath directed by reaſon of her Infancy.

It may be a Queſtion, Whether ſhe can be barred by any Act of her own, for ſhe is not examined upon a Common Recovery? But this is not like the Caſe of a Fine levied by an Infant, for that cannot be reverſed but by the Infant himſelf during his Nonage; for it being the Act of the Court to ſuffer ſuch a one to levy a Fine, the Court muſt therefore reform the ſame by Inſpection, which cannot be after full Age. For this Reaſon the Recovery was reverſed, 5 *Mod.* 209. *Stokes* and *Oliver*. In this Caſe, *Cr. Car.* 307. 1 *Rol. Abr.* 731, 751, 752. *Sid.* 322. *Raby* and *Robinſon*, were cited.

The

The Form of the Entry of the Suit, or of the Defence by a Guardian in a Recovery, *Vide supra, Tit. Guardian.*

In the next Place, I shall consider of other Matters of Record done or suffered by Infants, and where they are void or voidable; and if they are voidable, how to be avoided, and where.

And as to this, take this Diversity as a General Rule, as it is set down, 1 *Inst.* 380. *b.* which is this:

The Difference is betwixt Matters of Record done or suffered by Infants, and Matter *en fait*: For Matters *en fait* he shall avoid within Age, or at full Age; but Matters of Record, as Statutes Merchant, and of the Staple, Recognizances acknowledged, or Fines levied by him, Recovery against him by Default in all real Actions (except Dower), must be avoided by him during his Minority, *viz.* Statutes by *Audita Querela*, and Fines and Recoveries by Writ of *Error*; for there it must be tried by Inspection, 1 *Inst.* 380. *b.* 2 *Inst.* 673.

So is *Mary Portington*'s Case, 10 *Rep.* 43. If Infant acknowledge a Statute or Recognizance, this is not void, but voidable by *Audita Querela* during his Minority; for in this Case Judges may know by Inspection whether he be within Age, 10 *Rep.* 43. *Portington*'s Case.

H. was bound to *W.* in a Statute Staple of 600 *l.* *H.* then being under the Age of Twenty one Years. *H.* at Twenty three Years of Age brings *Audita Querela* upon this

Difference between Matters of Record and Matters of Fact.

Infant shall avoid Matters of *fait* within Age, or at full Age.

Statutes, Recognizances, *&c.* avoided by *Audita Querela*; Fines, Recoveries, Judgment, by Error.

By *Audita Querela* during his Minority.

Matter. But *per Cur', Nil capiat per Breve*; for now he cannot be tried by Inspection whether he be within Age or not. And this is the Rule; notwithstanding in *Fitzherbert* it seems to the contrary, 1 *Anderson* 104. *Harison* and *Wirley*.

Infant may have *Audita Querela* upon a Statute Staple, notwithstanding the Statute is not certified or retorned into any Court; else the Certificate may not be retorned till after he comes of Age, and then he cannot be aided, 1 *Anders.* 228.

Now that the Writ of *Audita Querela* must be sued whilst the Infant is within Age, appears by the Words of the Writ:

Mandamus, &c. Quod si vobis legitime constare poterit ipsum T. &c. Tempore Recognitionis praed' infra etatem extitisse, & adhuc existere, tunc Audita Querela ipsius T. in Premissis faciatis fieri, quod de Jure & secundum Legem, &c. fuerit faciend', 1 Anders. 158.

An Infant shall avoid an Extent upon a Statute of his Ancestor by *Audita Querela*. The Case was,

A Feoffment in Fee by Deed indented, rendring Rent, with a Clause of Distress, and after was bound in a Statute; and the Day being incurred, Execution was awarded to the Conisee; and upon the Extent, the Sheriff retorned, That the Party was dead, and that he had extended the said Rent, the Heir of the Conisor being within Age, be-

cause

cause the Rent was extended during his Nonage, brought *Audita Querela*. *Per Dyer*, The Writ is well maintainable, for that there is an Exception in the Writ of *Extent*; yet if the Lands are discended to an Infant, that he shall surcease to extend, *Mo. p.* 37.

Extent upon a Statute is made by the Conisees during the Heir's Minority, the Writ being [*Nisi alicui Hæredi infra Ætatem existent' Jure Hereditarii descenderint*] Whether this be totally void, not only against the Heir who did consent, but against all others? *Per Cur.* This Extent upon the Infant is totally void, so void that any Stranger may take Advantage of it. The Sheriff had no Power to extend these Lands discended to the Heir, and Action of Trespass lies against the Sheriff for extending; and the Infant might bring Action for the mean Profits, and he that hath a subsequent Judgment, shall extend, *Carter* 19, 20. *Kerl* and *Clopton*. Extent upon an Infant totally void.

Audita Querela was brought in the *Common Pleas*, for that the Cognizor was within Age at the Acknowledgment; and it was adjudged to be well brought there, 1 *Leon.* 303. and so it is in the *King's-Bench*, *Cro. El.* 308. *Audita Querela* well brought in B. C. or in B. R.

Infant enters into a Recognizance, and brought *Audita Querela* within Age in the *Common Pleas*, and upon Inspection was adjudged within Age, and a *Scire fac'* awarded against the Conisee; and upon one *Nihil* only retorned, the Judgment was, That the Recognizance should be cancelled. The Conisee brought Error in the *King's Bench*; for *Aud. Quer.* by Infant to cancel a Recognizance, how to be brought.

Two *Nibils* amount to a Garnishment.

there ought to be two *Nihils* retorned; for two *Nihils* amount to a Garnishment, and without Garnishment, and *Oyer* of the Conisee, it ought not to be adjudged to be cancelled; and it was reversed for this Error. Whereupon the Conisor, when he was at full Age, brought another *Audita Querela* in the *King's Bench*, and shews how only the first Judgment was reversed for Error in the Proceedings, and not in the principal Matter. The Conisee hereupon demurs.

Per Cur.

In *Audita Quer.* Judgment was reversed for Error in Process, no new *Aud. Quer.* lies at full Age, and the Reason.

1. The *Audita Querela* lies not; for the Judgment of the Reversal is general, and not for any special Cause; but the Party shall be restored to all that he lost by the former Judgment, and so the Recognizance set on Foot again.

Inspection not of Force but in the same Court where it was.

2. The Judgment of Inspection, tho' it is not but an Award, yet it is not of Force but in the same Court where the Proof by *Testes* and Inspection was; and this shall not conclude the Judges in the *King's Bench*, but that they ought to have a Re-inspection, which cannot be in this Case, because the Plaintiff in the *Audita Querela* is of full Age.

And further, If in this Case, upon the first Judgment reversed, the Conisee being within Age, had brought a new *Audita Querela* in the *Common Pleas*, he ought to be newly inspected, because this is a new Original, and all the former Proceedings are dissolved by by the Reversal of the Judgment, *Yelv.* 88. *Randal* and *Wale*, *Winch* 106. This Case cited, and misreported.

Aud. Quer. lies upon Judgment against Infant Bail upon a Recognizance.

But *Audita Querela* lies upon Judgment against the Bail within Age on a Recognizance. The Case was, *M.* was Bail for *S.* in Debt brought by *T.* and *M.* was within Age. Judgment pass'd against *S.* and he did not render his Body; and upon two *Scire facias's* and *Nihil* retorned against *M.* (the Infant Bail) Judgment was given against him, and he brought *Audita Querela*, because he was within Age. *Williams* Justice was against it, and said, He ought first to have Error to reverse the Judgment; for during the Judgment is in Force, the Recognizance is affirmed. But *per Cur.* Then *M.* is without Remedy, and at great Mischief, if he may not have *Audita Querela*; for it may be the Judgment had no Error in it, and upon the *Scire facias*, *M.* the Bail could not have pleaded his Infancy; for this Suit goes in Affirmance of the Recognizance, and demands Execution of it, but yet the Error of the Infancy remains; and here, by the *Audita Querela*, the Recognizance being avoided for Infancy by Inspection, the Judgment upon it is avoided also, *Yelv.* 155. *Markam* and *Turner*.

If the Recognizance is avoided by *Aud. Qu* Judgment upon it is avoided also.

Infant cannot enter into a Recognizance to discharge himself of Execution.

Infant being in Execution upon Condemnation in Debt, brought a Writ of *Error*: His Father and his Brother were his Bail. *Per Cur.* They two shall only enter into the Recognizance that the Infant shall appear; and yet if the Judgment be affirmed, that they shall pay the Money, and not that they shall render the Body of the Infant again to Prison; for when once he is discharged of the Execution, he shall never be in Execution again, 3 *Leon. pag.* 113. *Tucker* and *Norton.*

Judgment by Default cannot be avoided by Infant at full Age.

Judgment by Default cannot be avoided by him at full Age, for the Reverence due to Records; and the same Ground is laid, 9 *Rep.* 30. *b.* But

Judgment by Default in a *Formedon* against an Infant in *B. R.* was reversed by Inspection, *Pasch.* 36 *H.* 8. *Rot.* 22.

If a Judge takes a Recognizance of an Infant, or Infant levies a Fine there, because it is an Act Judicial, there the Infant must reverse it during Nonage; but where it is not tried by Inspection, there it may be tried after his Death, or at any Time, being Matter *en fait.*

Formedon brought against Infant in *B. C.* and he confesseth the Action, and he brought Error in *B. R.* after which he comes of full Age. Because his Confession was made judicially, and recorded by the Court upon his Appearance, it ought to be reversed during his Nonage; but if it were on Default, he may reverse it, because he never came into Court by reason of the Default, so as the Court may view him, *Palm.* 247. *Darcy* and *Jackson.*

As

As to Infants entring into Judgments, and avoiding them, he shall not have *Audita Querela*. The Case was, Infant confesseth a Judgment, how to be avoided.

Randal had married the Daughter of Justice *Clench*; he being an Infant, confess'd a Judgment in Action of Debt brought against him in *B. R.* and now he brought *Audita Querela* during his Nonage. *Per Cur.* It lies not in this Court, as it should upon a Statute or Recognizance, because he never was view'd; but the Party shall have Error, but not in *B. R.* but in the *Exchequer Chamber*, by the Statute of 27 *Eliz.* *Mo.* 460. *Randal*'s Case.

Who shall take Advantage of Infancy.

He in Remainder may assign the Infancy of Tenant in Tail for Error; for tho' they in Remainder are not Privies in Blood nor Estate, yet they are Parties to the Record, and that is sufficient.

The Rule in *Whittingham*'s Case, 8 *Rep.* is, That none shall take Advantage of Infancy but Privies in Blood. But this Rule admits of Exception.

If two Jointenants, Infants, make a Feoffment, the one dies, the other shall avoid the whole by Entry (tho' not by Action); for the Estate was joint in Right, and the entire Right survives.

Tenant in Tail within Age makes a Feoffment, and dies without Issue, the Donor may enter, and good Reason; for the Feoffment of the Infant shall not put him to a *Formedon* by by Discontinuance; and then if he should not enter, he should be without Remedy. And the Opinion of *Coke* in 8 *Rep.* is denied for Law; but the Lord by Escheat may not enter for Infancy, *Palm.* 254. *Darcy* and *Jackson.*

If Infant appear in Person, he shall be tried by Inspection, and he only shall avoid it; but if he appear by Attorney, all Persons shall assign this for Error, and it shall be tried *per Pais*, *Palm.* 247.

CHAP.

CHAP. IX

Of Conveyances and Specialties.

Feoffment by Infants, what are void or voidable; and the Time of avoiding such Feoffment. His Heir shall avoid it, though a Special Heir. Baron, *within Age, makes a Feoffment of the Wife's Land, and dies; she may enter, but the Entry of the Heir is taken away by Corruption of Blood.* Baron *and* Feme, *within Age, make a Feoffment, and* Baron *dies; what Remedy for the Wife. Two Jointenants, within Age, make a Feoffment in Fee, and one dies; Entry into the whole accrueth to the Survivor; But if one had only made a Feoffment in Fee, the Right shall not survive, and why. What Privies shall avoid a Feoffment of the Infant-Ancestor. Bargain and Sale may be avoided by Entry at any Time. The Nature of a Bargain and Sale inrolled. Of Exchanges by Infants. What shall be said an Affirmance or an Agreement to an Exchange. Attornment by Infant good, and why. Infant shall be compelled to Attorn. How Infants are bound by Partition, or not. By what Acts a voidable Partition shall be made good. Leases made by Infants voidable: If without any Rent or Recompence, void. Lease made by one Jointenant within Age, who dies, is void, and the other shall avoid it. Lease made by Infant, to try a Title,*

Title, void Ne granta pas, *where a good Plea. Where Infant's Lease is void for want of Privity; but his Confirmation shall be good. Whether a Lease made to an Infant is void. The actual Surrender of an* Interesse termini *by an Infant, is void. His Surrender by acceptance of Second Lease, is void. Copyholds granted by Infants good, and why. Infant surrenders his Copyhold Land, he may enter at his full Age. Release by Infant, how void, or not. What Obligations by Infants are voidable, and what void. How Infant bound by Covenant, or not. Of Conveyances, Leases, Bonds,* &c. *made to Infant. Infant may purchase. Grant to a reputed Son, good; but not to an illegitimate Issue before Birth. Lease to an Infant is voidable, and how.* Per Stat. 7 Ann. *Infants seized or possessed of Estates in Trust, or by Way of Mortgage, may make Conveyances of such Estates. What Grants made to an Infant are good, or not.*

IN the next Place, I shall consider of Matters *en fait* done by an Infant, and how he shall be bound by them or not, and whether they are void or voidable. And herein I shall first treat of such Acts done by him in reference to Lands or Tenements; as Feoffment, Bargain and Sale, Exchange, Surrender, Leases, *&c.* or in respect of Specialties.

Feoffment by Infant voidable or void, with a Diversity.

If an Infant make a Feoffment, it is voidable, but not *ipso facto* void; yet note, some Books take this Difference:

If

If Infant make a Feoffment in Fee, and delivers it with his own Hands, this is but voidable; but if it be executed by Letter of Attorney it is void, as being a Diſſeiſin to him; and the Feoffee is a Diſſeiſor, 2 *Brownl.* 248.

All Gifts, Grants or Deeds, made by an Infant, which do not take Effect by Delivery of his own Hand, are void; but ſuch Gifts, Grants or Deeds, made by an Infant, by Matter in Deed or Writing, which takes Effect by Delivery of his own Hand, are voidable by himſelf, and his Heirs, and thoſe which ſhall have the Eſtate. *Perk. tit. Grants.*

If an Infant deliver Money with his own Hands, it is but voidable, and to be recovered by Action of Account. *Hob.* 77.

So it is agreed in 9 *H.* 6. 6. and in ſuch Caſe of a Feoffment, it is not material of what Age the Infant is that makes it; for be he within the Age of Diſcretion, as Ten Years, or Five Years; or above the Age of Diſcretion, as Sixteen, or more; the Feoffment is not void, but voidable. 9 *H.* 6. 6.

If Infant make a Deed, he may not plead *Non eſt factum*, but the Special Matter, and conclude Judgment, *ſi Actio.* 5 *Rep.* 119.

Infant enrolls a Deed to the King, this is good when he comes of full Age, for it is not void, but voidable, *Kellow* 13. *a.*

It's a Rule, *If the firſt Delivery of a Deed be not void, but the Deed only voidable, a ſecond Delivery ſhall not make it good.*

As

As if an Infant make and deliver a Deed, and after at full Age deliver it again; this second Delivery is void, because the Deed was voidable by Plea, and not void, 8 *H.*6.7.

But by 1 *Roll. Abr.* 730. it seems, if it be made by Letter of Attorney it is good: But I conceive it is meant, That it is not void.

The Time of avoiding a Feoffment.

Now for his Time of avoiding it, the Law is: If an Infant make a Feoffment, *&c.* he may enter within Age, or at any Time after his full Age; and so may his Heir, 1 *Inst.* 248. *a.*

The Infants Heir shall avoid it.

And it shall be avoided by a Special Heir.

And to the Avoidance by the Heir of the Infant; Note, a Special Heir shall take Advantage of the Infancy of the Ancestor. As if Tenant in Tail of an Acre of Borough-*English* makes a Feoffment in Fee within Age, and dies, the youngest Son shall avoid it; for he is privy in Blood, and claimeth by Discent from the Infant. So if Tenant in Tail to him, and the Heirs Females of his Body, makes a Feoffment in Fee, and dies within Age, having Issue a Son and a Daughter; the Daughter shall avoid the Feoffment. Whereupon we may observe, that a Cause to enter by reason of Infancy, is not like to Conditions, Warranties and Estoppels, which ever discend to the Heir at the Common Law, 1 *Inst.* 337. *b.*

Contrary of Warranties, Estoppels, Conditions, *&c.*

Baron within Age makes a Feoffment of the Wife's Land, and then dies; the Wife may enter.

If a Woman Inheritrix taketh an Husband who is within Age, and he being within Age makes a Feoffment of the Tenements of his Wife in Fee, and dies, the Entry of the Wife is congeable; for the Husband might well enter notwithstanding such Feoffment during the Coverture, and he could not enter but in Right of the Wife, and this Right of Entry remaineth to his Wife after his Decease.

But the Entry of the Infant is only in respect of the Right that he hath; for if an Infant is Tenant *pur auter vie*, and makes a Feoffment in Fee, and *cestuy que vie* dies, the Infant himself shall not enter; for now he hath no Right at all. And, The Entry of the Infant is only in respect of the Right.

If Tenant in Tail within the Age of 21 Years makes a Feoffment in Fee, and after is attainted of Felony, and dies, the Entry of Issue is not lawful; for his Entry is not lawful in respect of his Estate only, but of his Blood also, which is corrupted; and therefore in that Case he is driven to his *Formedon*. Entry of the Heir taken away for Corruption of Blood.

If the Husband and Wife be both within Age, and they by Deed indented join in a Feoffment, reserving a Rent; the Husband dieth, the Wife may enter or have a *Dum fuit infra ætatem*: But if she were of full Age, she shall not have a *Dum fuit infra ætatem* for the Nonage of the Husband, although they be both one Person in the Law. *Baron* and *Feme* within Age make a Feoffment, and *Baron* dies, what Remedy for the *Feme*.

If Two Jointenants within Age make a Feoffment in Fee, and one of the Infants dies and the other surviveth, the Right of Entry accrueth to him that surviveth, and he may enter into the whole; and because they might join in a Writ of *Right*, the Right shall survive: But they shall not join in a *Dum fuit infra ætatem*; for the Nonage of the one is not the Nonage of the other. Two Jointenants within Age make a Feoffment in Fee, and one dies, Entry into the whole accrueth to the Survivor.

And

If one had made a Feoffment in Fee, the Right should not survive, and why.

And in this Case, if one Jointenant had made a Feoffment in Fee, the Right should not have survived, for the Jointure was severed for a Time; but if Two Jointenants be, and one is of full Age, and the other within Age, and they both make a Feoffment in Fee, and he of full Age dieth, the Infant shall enter, or have a *Dum fuit infra ætatem* for the Moiety.

What Privies shall avoid a Feoffment of the Infant Ancestor.

Note, None shall avoid the Feoffment of the Infant, when Livery is made with his own Hands; but only he himself, or his Heirs, which are Privies in Blood inheritable, and neither Privies in Law, nor Privies in Estate.

Lease made by Two Jointenants, and one dies, the survivor shall avoid it.

And therefore if Two Jointenants are within Age, and one makes a Lease for Years and dieth, the other shall avoid it; for the Lease is utterly void, of which every Stranger shall take Advantage: But if there are Two Infants Jointenants, and the one leaseth for Life and makes Livery in Person and dieth, the other shall not avoid it. Two Jointenants, the one maketh a Feoffment upon Condition and dieth, the other shall not take Benefit of the Condition, 2 *Leon. p.* 218.

Feoffment by Infant no Forfeiture. *Aliter* of a Fine.

Infant, Tenant for Life or Years, makes a Feoffment in Fee, it's no Forfeiture; for if the Lessor entereth, Infant may enter upon him again. *Aliter*, if it be by Matter of Record. If Infant be Lessee for Life, and levies a Fine, it is a Forfeiture, and if Lessor enters, Infant shall not enter again. So if

Infant commit Wast, which is against a Statute, it's a Forfeiture; and if Lessor recovers the Places wasted, Infant shall not enter again, 8 *Rep. Whittingham's* Case, *Godb.* 365.

A Bargain and Sale of Lands by an Infant may be avoided when he will by his Entry, for a Bargain and Sale inrolled is no Record, nor *Nul tiel Record* pleadable to it, it's only a Deed inrolled for better Evidence. But my Lord *Coke* gives another Reason in 2 *Inst.* 673. If Infant bargain and sells Lands, which are in the Realty, by Deed indented and inrolled, he may avoid it when he will, for the Deed was of no effect to raise an Use, and the Statute of Inrolments of Bargains and Sales is intended of lawful and effectual Bargains and Sales, and such as would have raised a Use at Common Law, and doth only restrain the Execution of them that be of effect, except the Deed be inrolled, 2 *Inst.* 671. Bargain and Sale may be avoided by Entry at any Time.

Per totam Curiam: If Infant by Indenture bargain and sell his Land for Money, and after levies a Fine *Come ceo, &c.* this Indenture is not void, but voidable, and the Use shall pass by the Bargain, and then the Fine being levied, by this the Bargain is irrevocable, unless by Error, *Moo. p.* 22. Bargain and Sale by Infant, and a Fine thereupon

If Infant makes Exchange of Land for less Value than his own Land that he gave in exchange, it shall not bind him; but at his full Age he may make it good by Agreement, 12 *H.* 4. 12. But an Exchange by Infant is good until he defeats it, 12 *H.* 4. 13. Exchange by Infant

What ſhall be ſaid an Affirmance or Agreement to an Exchange.

Now as to what ſhall be ſaid an Affirmance or Agreement to the Exchange, you muſt know, That if an Infant exchange Land with another, if he continue in the Land given in exchange at his full Age, he hath affirmed the Exchange, and ſhall never avoid it afterwards, 16 *Ed.* 3. 2.

So is 1 *Inſt.* 51. *b.* If the Infant exchange Land, and at full Age occupy the Land taken in exchange, the Exchange is become perfect by this; for the Exchange at firſt was not void, becauſe this amounts to a Livery, and alſo in reſpect of the Recompence, but it is only voidable.

If a Man make a Deed of Feoffment to an Infant, and Infant makes a Letter of Attorney to another to take Livery for him; this is good, becauſe it is for his Avail. 1 *Rol. Abr.* 73. *a.*

Attornment by Infant good, and why.

Attornment by an Infant to a Grant by Deed is good, and ſhall bind him:

1. Becauſe it is a lawful Act.

2. He gives away no Intereſt from himſelf.

3. It is to perfect a Thing; though he is not upon the Grant by Deed compelled to attorn.

Where Infant ſhall be compelled to attorn.

Yet if Infant hold Lands by Purchaſe or Diſcent, he ſhall be compelled to Attorn in a *Per quæ ſervitia*, and this is no Miſchief to the Infant; for when he comes of full Age, he he may disclaim to hold of him, or he may say, he holds of him by lesser Services. But it would be a greater Mischief to the Lord, to lose his Services in the mean Time: And if Infant be Lessee, he shall be compelled to atttorn in a *Quid juris clamat*, 1 *Inst.* 315. *a.*

Lord and Tenant by Fealty and Rent: The Lord made a Feoffment of the Manor, the Tenant being an Infant, having Lands by Discent attorned, *per Cur'*, the Attornment was good; and in that Case it was resolved, 1. That in a *Per quæ servitia* against Infant, who hath the Tenure by Discent, he shall not have his Age; because the Lord, at the First, deputed with the Land, in Consideration that the Tenant should hold of him, and pay to him the Rent; and it is presumed, that the Tenant hath a Benefit above his Services which he doth, and the Rent which he payeth; and the Tenant shall be distreined for his Rent during his Nonage, because the Law gives him Remedy, during his Nonage, to have an Acquittal. 2. That though the Tenant Infant in the principal Case was not compelled to attorn, yet because he was by a Mean compelled to have attorned, if a Fine had been levied; the Attornment of the Infant was good, and an Attornment is but a bare Assent, and doth not give an Interest; and therefore it shall bind an Infant, 9 *Rep.* 85. *Conny*'s Case.

How Infants are bound by Partition, or not.

Now as to an Infant's being bound by Partition, or not, and by what Acts it shall be made good, the Law stands thus:

If the Partition be equal at the Time of the Allotment, it shall bind the Infant for ever, because he is compellable by Law to make Partition; neither shall he have his Age in a *Partitione facienda*. And tho' the Partition be unequal, and the Infant hath the lesser Part, yet is not the Partition void, but voidable, by his Entry; for if he takes the whole Profits of the unequal Part after his full Age, the Partition is made good for ever, 1 *Inst*. 171.

By what Acts a voidable Partition shall be made good.

A Partition made by the King's Writ [*De Partitione facienda*] by the Sheriff, by the Oath of twelve Men, and Judgment thereupon given, shall bind the Infant, tho' his Part be unequal; for the Judgment is, that the Partition shall remain *firma & stabilis*.

But a Partition in *Chancery* shall not bind an Infant.

What Leases, Releases or Surrenders, made by Infants, are void, or voidable only.

Leases made by Infants voidable.

Grants of Infant where himself hath Benefit *(viz. quid pro quo)* are only voidable, as, if he lets Land for Years, reserving a Rent.

Vide infra in Fine hujus Capitis, *Kelsey*'s Case.

Infant leaseth for Years, and Lessee enters, the Infant may have Trespass against him, 18 *Ed*. 4. 14. *b*.

In-

Infant lets Lands to another for Twenty one Years, and after the Grantee granteth Lands to another for Ten Years, if the Tenant at his Age releaseth to the Grantee of the Lessee, it is void, because there is no Privity: But if in this he confirms his Estate, it is good; but if the Infant had granted all his Estate to another, his Release had been good, 1 *Inst*. 300. *Lit. sect*. 547. Where Infant's Release is void for Want of Privity. But his Confirmation shall be good.

If a Lease be made by an Infant without Rent, Profit, or other Recompence, the same is utterly void: As, if he grant a Rent or Advowson, *&c*. he may say, That he did not grant, *&c*. for the Thing included in the Deed doth not pass, although he delivereth the Deed of Grant with his own Hand. *Aliter* of a Feoffment. Lease by Infant, without any Rent or Recompence, void. *Ne grant a pas*, where a good Plea.

2 *Bulstr*. *Kirton* and *Eliot*, 2 *Cr*. 310. *Kelsey's* Case. In Debt for Arrearages of Rent upon a Lease made to an Infant, he pleads Infancy at the Time of the Lease made. The Question was, Whether a Lease made to an Infant was void, because it might be prejudicial to him, and he had not Discretion to manage it? *Per Cur*. It's voidable only by him at his Election; for if it was for his Benefit, it's no ways void: But the Infant, at his Election, may make it void by refusing and waving the Land before the Rent-Day incurs, and then no Debt will lie against him. But in this Case, because it's not shew'd that the Rent was of greater Value than the Land, and the Defendant was of full Age before the Rent-Day, Judgment *pro Quer*.

If Infant lease for Years, rendring Rent, it is at his Election to affirm it, or to have Trespass against Lessee for the Occupation, 18 *Ed.* 4. 2.

Custom. Infant, Tenant in Socage, may by Custom make a Lease for Years at his Age of Fifteen, 1 *Inst.* 45. *b.*

Infant at Fifteen may make a Feoffment by the Custom of Gavelkind in Kent, 21 *Ed.* 4. 24. *a.*

So Infant, Lord of a Manor, may grant by Copy, 4 *Rep.*

But a Custom that Infant may make a Grant or Feoffment when he can tell 12 *d.* is ill, because uncertain, 13 *Ed.* 3. *dum fuit infra Ætat.* 3.

Surrender. If an Infant surrender a Lease for Years to him in Reversion, this is void, and may not be made good by any Agreement at full Age, 1 *Rol. Abr.* 728. *Fludd* and *Gregory.*

Custom. Custom that Infant at Fifteen may devise his Inheritance, *Com.* 97. *b.*

Lease made by one Jointenant *deins age,* who dies, is void; and the other shall avoid. *Regula.* If two Jointenants are within Age, and one makes a Lease for Years, and dieth, the other shall avoid it; for the Lease is utterly void, of which every Stranger shall take Advantage. But of Acts voidable, it is otherwise: As, two Infant Jointenants, the one leaseth for Life, and makes Livery in Person, and dieth, the other shall not avoid it, 2 *Leon.* 217, 218. *Humfreston's* Case.

Lease made by Infant to try a Title. Infant of the Age of Six Years entreth into the Land, and leased the same to the Plaintiff for Years, to try a Title in Ejectment; and tho' it was made upon the Land to to try a Title, which is a good Considera-tion, and Profit to the Infant, yet it is void. *Quære.* 2 *Leon.* 218.

I find in the Case of *Raines vers. Machin*, in *Noy*'s *Rep.* 130. *in Ejectione Firmæ per Cur.* A Lease for Years by Infant to try a Title, is good enough, because it is for his Advantage. And it's there said, *Note*, 21 *H.* 6. 31. Letter of Attorney *per* an Infant to re-ceive Livery and Seisin for him, *Noy* 130. is good; *per Ascue* Just. *contra Paston* Just. 21 *H.* 6. 31. *Br. Faits* 31.

Infant made a Lease for Years, rendring Rent, and when he came to his full Age, he said to his Lessee, *God give you Joy of it.* It was held by *Mead* Justice, That the Lease was affirmed and made good; because the Law saith, he hath a Recompence, 4 *Leon. pag.* 4. Lease affirmed.

Lease for Years, Remainder for Years, ren-dring Rent, by Infant, and at full Age he ac-cepts the Rent of the particular Tenant, it's a good Confirmation of the Estate of him in Remainder, so that such Lease is not void; for if it were, it is not good, *Com.* 545.

It was a Question in *Ashfield* and *Ashfield*'s Case, Infant, Copyholder in Fee, makes a Lease without License, not warranted by the Custom, rendring Rent, at full Age he ac-cepts the Rent, and after ousts the Lessee; Lessor brings Ejectment; Whether this Lease is affirmed by Acceptance? Which is doubt-ed in *Godb.* but in *Noy* 92. resolved, it is af-firmed by Acceptance, and that such a Forfeiture ſhall not bind the Infant, *Noy* 92. *Aſhfield*'s Caſe, *Godb.* 456.

Infant cannot take Surrender, and why.

Infant not capable to take a Surrender, becauſe he cannot give his Aſſent, which is an eſſential Requiſite to a Surrender; but an Infant may take the Land by way of Feoffment, or grant any Conveyance of like Nature, 3 *Mod.* 299.

The actual Surrender of an *Intereſſe Termini* by Infant is void.

The actual Surrender of a future Intereſt, or *Intereſſe Termini*, by an Infant, is void; and a Surrender of an Infant cannot be by Deed, but it is actually void; and a Surrender by Acceptance of a ſecond Leaſe is void, becauſe it is without Increaſe of his Term, or Decreaſe of his Rent. The Caſe was:

Surrender by Acceptance of a ſecond Leaſe is void.

A Leaſe for 99 Years was made by a Dean and Chapter, 1 *Ed.* 6. to begin at the Feaſt of the *Annunciation*, after the End of a Leaſe of 50 made *Anno* 35 *H.* 8. This Leaſe being aſſigned to *J. S.* and *W. S.* Infants of Eleven Years of Age, they, 29 *Eliz.* (which was before the End of the Term of 50 Years) take a new Leaſe of the ſame Lands from the Dean and Chapter for the ſame Term, and for the ſame Rent, and upon the ſame Condition; and after the End of the ſaid Term of 50 Years, the Infants being of full Age, enter, and hold by the ſecond Leaſe, and pay the Rent accordingly to the Dean and Chapter, which they accept for divers Years; and afterwards a new Dean and Chapter cauſe

cause an Entry to be made to avoid this Lease. And it was adjudged, That the Surrender and Acceptance by the second Lease is void, *Causa qua supra*, *Cro Car.* 502. *Lloyd* and *Gregory*. 3 *Mod.* 304. 1 *Rol. Abr.* 728.

As to the Infants Grants of Copyhold Estates, &c.

If Infant, Lord of a Manor, grants Copyholds, it shall be good, and shall bind him, 4 *Rep.* 23. 8 *Rep.* 63. for neither Infancy, nor *Non sane Memorie*, nor Coverture, nor other such Disabilities of Person; neither in respect of the Exility or Uncertainty of the Estates of the Lords, as at Will, or upon Condition, *&c.* shall avoid Grants by Copy: And the Reason is, for that the Estate of the Copyholder is not derived out of the Estate of the Lord of the Manor, for he is but an Instrument to make the Grant; but the Custom of the Manor, after the Grant made, establisheth it to the Grantee. And tho' the Grant be now the Title of the Copyholder, yet the Custom of the Manor is the main Foundation on which is built the whole Fabrick of the Copyhold Estate, which the Custom doth confirm to the Copyholder, and the Law will ever allow and support it, notwithstanding any such Imperfections in the Grantor's Person, as Infancy, Outlawry, *&c.* And by *Noy*, such Grants by Infants shall be good, as well as Presentation to a Benefice,

Copyholds granted by Infants are good, and why.

fice, 4 *Rep.* 23. 8 *Rep.* 63. 1 *Inst.* 58. *b.* 8 *Rep.* *Swain*'s Case, *Noy* 21, 41.

Grants made before his Entry into a Manor not to be avoided.

If the Infant enfeoff me of a Manor, tho' he may enter upon me at his Pleasure, yet Grants made before his Entry shall not be avoided by any subsequent Entry: Nay, such Grants are so favoured in Law, that if a Man espouseth the Lady of a Manor under the Age of Consent, and after she disagreeth, tho' the Marriage by Relation is void *ab Initio*, yet Copyholds granted before Disagreement shall never be avoided, *Owen* 28. *Rouse*'s Case.

Infant surrenders his Copyhold Land, may enter at full Age.

If Infant surrender his Copyhold Land within Age, he may enter at his full Age without being put to any Suit for it, *Winch*, *p.* 39.

Copyhold.

Infant not obliged to be admitted during his Infancy, or to tender the Fine in order to his Admittance, 1 *Levin.* 100. 3 *Leon.* 221. 3 *Mod.* 223.

Now for Specialties made by Infants, what are void or voidable, is in the next Place to be considered.

Release by Infant void.

A Release by Infant without Consideration is void; so is *Cro. El.* 671. *Knot* and *Barton*'s Case. Debt on Bond made to the Testator. Defendant pleads a Release made by one of the Plaintiffs (Executors). Plaintiff replies, this Release was made without any Consideration, and he who released, was within Age at the Time of the Release made; and upon Demurrer, it was adjudged for the

Plain-

Plaintiff, and that it was a void Releaſe, 5 *Rep. Ruſſel's* Caſe, *Cro. Eliz.* 671. *Knot's* Caſe.

If Infant maketh an Obligation, it is not void, but voidable. *Vide infra tit. Pleading,* and *Non eſt factum.* Obligation by Infant is not void, but voidable.

If Infant make a Bond, and after he is ſued upon it, and the Attorney without Warrant ſuffers a Judgment by *Non ſum Informatus*, this is no Cauſe to grant an *Audita Querela*, for he ſhall have a Writ of *Error* if he were within Age; and if he was not, then he ſhall have a Writ of *Diſceit* againſt the Attorney, *Winch*, *p.* 114. *Aſhley* and *Collins.*

Bond to perform Covenant in Indenture by Infant.

Infant makes an Indenture, and at full Age binds himſelf in a Bond to perform all the Covenants in the Indenture, he ſhall not avoid this Indenture in a Writ of Debt upon the Bond, 14 *H.* 8. 28. *a. Quær.*

The Bond beareth Date when the Defendant (Infant) was within Age, but ſealed and delivered when he was of full Age; the Time of making the Bond ſhall be adjudged when the Bond is ſealed and delivered, and not when it bears Date, 1 *Brownl.* 31.

If one pays Money for the Neceſſaries of the Infant, and took Bond of him in double the Sum, it's void; but if he had taken Bond for the very Sum, it had been good. And ſo the Infant may bind himſelf to pay for Ne- If Infant bind himſelf in a Bond with a Penalty to pay for Neceſſaries, it's void.

Necessaries; yet if it be by Bond, or other Writing, with a Penalty, it shall not bind him, *per tot' Cur'*. And if Infant avoid such a Bond with a Penalty for his Infancy, as he may, it seems that the Contract is not revived, 1 *Rol. Abr.* 604. Nay, such a Bond from an Infant doth so extinct the Contract, that it is not made good by *Assumpsit* at his full Age, 1 *Inst.* 172. *Cro. Eliz.* 920. *Ayliff* and *Archdale*, *Godb.* 6. 219. 1 *Rol. Abr.* 729. *Mo.* 679. 3 *Keb.*

And the Contract is not revived, nor can be made good by *Assumpsit* at full Age.

Debt on Bond dated 10 *June*, and delivered the 18th Day of the same Month; the Defendant pleads by Protestation, That it was delivered the 18th Day, although that at that Time he was of full Age, *Noy* p. 32. *Qu.*

Presentation.

Infant at the Age of 14 Years may present to an Advowson, which belonged to his Father, and it shall be good, *Perk.* 4. Guardian in Socage of a Manor to which Advowson belongs, the Heir shall present, and not the Guardian, because he cannot account for it. *Fitz. N.* 13. 33.

Attorney *sans* Warrant suffers a Judgment by *Non sum Informat'* on Bond by Infant, what Remedy.

If an Infant make an Obligation, and being sued thereupon, an Attorney without Warrant suffers a Judgment by *Non sum informatus*; if he were within Age, he shall have a Writ of *Error*; if he were not, he shall have a Writ of *Disceit* against the Attorney; but no *Audita Querela*, *Winch*, 114. *Ashly*, and *Collings*.

Vide infra tit. Pleadings.

Infant

Infant shall not be bound by his Covenant, unless for Necessaries. How Infant bound Covenant, or not.

Infant may voluntarily bind himself an Apprentice, and he is compellable by the Statute of 5 *Eliz.* to be bound out Apprentice; yet neither by the Common Law, or by any Words of the Statute of 5 *Eliz.* a Covenant or Obligation of an Infant may bind him; but by the Custom of *London* it shall. *Cro. Car.* 179. Covenant in Indenture of Apprentiship.

And how far Infants are bound by Covenants, and Apprentices bound, *vide infra tit. Apprentice.*

Feme (who was the Mistress) was to teach the Infant to Sing and to Dance, and to find with Meat, *&c.* and the Infant covenants to serve her. The Infant brought Covenant, and assigns for Breach, That the Defendant did not find Meat, *&c. Per Cur.* Though the Covenant of the Infant doth not bind her, yet the Covenant of the Mistress, who is of full Age, shall bind her self; and an Action well lies, *Sid. p.* 446. *Farnham* and *Atkyns. Vid. infra, tit. Contracts.*

Stat. 7 Annæ Reginæ, *enables Infants, who are seized or possessed of Estates in Fee in Trust, or by Way of Mortgage, to make Conveyances of such Estates.*

It shall and may be lawful for any Person or Persons, who have Estates in Lands, Tenements or Hereditaments, only in Trust for others, or by Way of Mortgage, being under the Age of 21 Years, by the Direction

rection of the High Court of *Chancery*, or the Court of *Exchequer*; signified by an Order, made upon a Hearing of all Parties concerned, on the Petition of the Person or Persons for whom such Infant or Infants shall be seized or possessed in Trust; or of the Mortgagor or Mortgagors, or Guardian or Guardians, of such Infant, or Person or Persons entitled to the Money secured, by or upon any Lands, Tenements, or Hereditaments; whereof any Infant or Infants are, or shall be, seized or possessed by Way of Mortgage, or of the Person or Persons entitled to the Redemption thereof; to convey and assure any such Lands or Tenements, in such Manner as the said Court of *Chancery* or *Exchequer* shall (by such Order so to be obtained) direct, to any other Person and Persons: And such Conveyance or Assurance, so to be had and made, as aforesaid, shall be as effectual in the Law to all Intents and Purposes whatsoever, as if the said Infant or Infants were, at the Time of making such Conveyances, of the full Age of 21 Years.

And that all and every such Infant or Infants, being only Trustee or Trustees, Mortgagee or Mortgagees, shall and may be compelled by such Order, so as aforesaid to be obtained, to make such Conveyances and Assurances as aforesaid, in like Manner as Trustees or Mortgagees of full Age, are compellable to convey or assign their Trust, Estates or Mortgages.

Of Conveyances, Leases, Bonds, &c. made to Infants.

An Infant hath, without Consent of any other, Capacity to purchase; for it shall be intended for his Benefit, and at his full Age he may either agree to it and so perfect it, or without any Cause alledged, wave or disagree to it; and so may his Heir after him, if he agree not thereunto after his full Age, 1 *Inst.* 2. *b.* Infant may purchase.

Of Estates; how they may be limited to Illegitimate Infants, and by what Names or Description good.

If a Man be baptized by one Name, and confirmed by another Name, he may be Grantee by the Name confirmed. Name of Confirmation.

If a Remainder is limited to *J. S.* Son of *W. S.* although he be a meer Bastard, and no *Mulier* by the Spiritual Law; yet if he be reputed for his Son, it's a good Remainder, *Blodwel* and *Edwards*'s Case. To Bastard Reputation.

If *A.* makes a Feoffment in Fee to the Use of himself for Life, the Remainder to the Issue Male of one *Mary Lloyd*, of her Body begotten by *A.* the Feoffor; whether he be lawfully begotten or not, so that he be the reputed Son of *A.* it is sufficient for him to entitle himself to say, That he is the Son of the said *A.* begotten on the Body of the said *Mary Lloyd*, and that he is so reputed in the common Reputation of the Country, Reputed Son.

altho'

altho' he was not born, nor *in esse*, at the Time of the Remainder granted; and although there are lawful Issues between them, which are *Puisne* to the Bastard; for the Person who is to Take is certainly described. For the Bastard of a Woman is certainly known to be her Issue; and this is limited to the eldest Issue, *Mich.* 38 & 39 *Eliz. Blodwell* and *Edwards*.

What Grants made to an Infant are good, or not.

Judicial Offices may not be granted to an Infant, 1 *Inst.* 3. *b.*

Ministerial Offices, which concern Administration of Justice, may not be granted immediately to an Infant; as to be Steward of a Manor, *March* 43. but if granted to an Infant in Reversion, may be good, if he be of full Age when it falls; and accordingly it was adjudged, in the Case of Registership of the Bishop of *Rochester*, in *Young* and *Fowler*'s Case, *March* 38, 39. And Justice *Jones* there, *p.* 43. said, That *Scantler*'s Case, cited *in* 1 *Inst.* 3. *b.* was adjudged contrary, That Infant was capable of a Stewardship in Reversion; and it was adjudged a good Grant against 1 *Inst.* 3. *b.*

One may not be an Attorney within Age, because he cannot be Sworn, *March* 92. and because an Attorney may not make a Deputy.

Infant may be Prebend, *Br. Ag.* 80.

Infant may be Executor, 5 *Rep.* 27.

Infant may be Mayor, 21 *Ed.* 4. 13, 14. 13 *H.* 8. 12. *b.* *Br. Corpor.* 63, 74.

Grant of Parkership to an Infant is good, *March* 41.

Infant before the Statute of 10 *Eliz.* might have been presented to a Benefice, and he was Parson *de facto*, *March Rep.* 43. But this is intended of an Infant which was of the Age of Discretion.

A *Prebendary* was granted to *Prideux* at the Age of Three Years, and it was adjudged void, because he was not of the Age of Discretion, *ib.*

Infant may be an Abbot without Disability.

Infant may be a Bishop without Disability, *Brook Court* 54.

Per Stat. 13 *Eliz. cap.* 12. None shall be a Minister, or be admitted to preach or administer the Sacraments before 24 Years of Age.

It has been continually seen, that Prebends were given to Infants, and yet they are not Priests, nor have they any Orders; but it is for that they have not the Cure of Souls, *Per Conisby.* 21 *H.* 7. 2. *a. b.*

If an Estate for Life be made, the Remainder to the Issue of the Body of *J. S.* or of him begotten on the Body of *A. S.* if he hath afterwards an illegitimate Issue, yet this Issue shall never take this Remainder; for that he cannot have the Reputation of Issue before his Birth, 1 *Inst.* 3. 6. But a Remainder to an illegitimate Issue (before Birth,) is void.

But if a Man has a Baſtard, and after by continuance of Time he is known for his reputed Son, then a Remainder limited to him, by the Name of his reputed Son, is good, *id. ibid.*

Leaſe to an Infant is voidable.

Debt is brought upon Leaſe for Years, for Arrears of Rent againſt *R.* The Defendant pleads in Bar Infancy at the Time of the Leaſe made. Plaintiff demurs. The Queſtion was, Whether a Leaſe made to an Infant was void? It was ſaid, It ſhould be void; for the Rent may be greater than the Value of the Land. But *per Cur'*, it is voidable only at Election; for if it were for his Benefit, it ſhall no Way be void; but the Infant at his Election may make it void, by refuſing and waving the Land before the Rent-Day comes. But in the principal Caſe it was not ſhewed that the Rent was of greater Value, and the Defendant was at full Age before the Rent-Day came. Judgment *pro Quer. Cro. Jac.* 320. *Kelſey's* Caſe.

Bound by Covenants, Conditions in Leaſes.

Infants are bound to Performance of Covenants in Leaſes, and to Conditions *en fait* or Law, as a Man at full Age. If Feoffment be upon Condition; if the Feoffor or his Heirs pay at ſuch a Day, *&c.* an Heir within Age ought to pay at the Day. Feoffment to Infant, on Condition that he ſhall not enfeoff *J. S.* Infant within Age enfeoffs *J. S.* and re-enters; yet the Feoffor may enter upon the Infant, *Com.* 357. Covenant or Proviſo, That his Bargainee ſhall renew his Leaſe, Aſſignment is made to Infant,

Infant, Infant is bound by this Covenant and Assignment, 2 *Rol. Rep.* 403. *Ascue* and *Belt.*

If a Lease for Years be made to an Infant, rendering Rent, the Rent is Arrear; and after the Infant comes to full Age, and continues the Occupation of the Land; this shall make him chargeable with the Arrears incurred during the Infancy, *Pasch.* 11 *Jac. B. R. Ketle* and *Ellyot.*

CHAP. X.

Of Contracts, Promises, and other Acts of Infants.

Infants bound by Contract for Necessaries, but a Bond with a Penalty for them is void. The Case of Rainsford *and* Fenwick, *about Wedding Apparel, being Necessaries, or not. What are Necessaries, or not. And pleading his buying Necessaries to maintain his Trade, not binding. As to this, no Relief in* Chancery. *Debt lies on Promise to pay for Necessaries.* Insimul computasset *lies not against Infant. What Averments are needful in Declaration against Infants for Necessaries. Demurrer is a Confession they were for Necessaries. Of Reciprocal Considerations and Promises made for and on the Behalf of an Infant. Infant sells an Horse; where he may take him again, or sue for him. Promise by Infant at full Age to pay, if he forbear to arrest him on a Bond given under Age, not good. Infants other Acts, what are binding, or not, stated in some Rules. Infant buys Necessaries for his Houshold, it shall bind him. Vendee of the Goods of an Infant, if he take them, is a Trespasser. Infant bound by Sale in open Market. Of Infants submitting to Arbitrament. Submission of Father, and Son an Infant. Arbitrament*

ment concerning an Infant, set aside in Equity.

IT is a known Rule, That Infants are bound by their Contracts for Necessaries. As *Cro. Jac.* 494. *Whittingham* and *Hill.* But it will be demanded, what are Necessaries; and what Actions may be brought for such Necessaries; and how the Declaration shall be laid: And it will be needful to shew, what shall be a good Consideration to bind Infants, or not, though the Considerations be Mutual and Reciprocal: And then at last to shew, by what Acts of his own he shall be bound. *Cro. Jac.* 494. *Whittingham* and *Hill.* Infants bound by Contracts, for Necessaries.

The Case of Rainsford *and* Fenwick, *in* Carter's *Reports, will much illustrate many Subsequent Cases.*

Quantum meruit, for divers Wares and Merchandizes; as Cloaths, Laces for himself and his Servants; and also *Indebitatus assumpsit*, and mentions the Wares in particular. Defendant pleads, *infra ætatem.* The Plaintiff replies, and confesseth the Minority, but saith at that Time he was Son and Heir Apparent of Sir *R. F.* and by Consent of his Father was in Treaty of a Marriage with the Earl of .... Daughter, and these Things were for Wedding Clothes. Defendant demurs.

Sise, Serjeant for the Plaintiff.

Such Contracts as are made for Infants Advantage, as Leases for Years, and such as are for Necessaries, the Law holds good; and yet Contracts for Necessaries the Law will not allow with a Penalty. Those Things of Necessaries have been referred to the Judges, and not to the Jury; and so the Law distinguishes of Persons, and Times of Infancy. 1 *Rol. Abr.* 729. *Delavall* and *Clare*'s Case, *Cr. Jac.* 560. *Ive* and *Chester*.

Brown Serjeant, *contra.*

1. It appears not how many Servants he had.

2. It appears not that these Servants he had were necessary for his Attendance.

3. It appears not what was for himself, and what for his Servants.

It appears by his own Pleadings his own Father was alive, and it may be for more than he would allow him.

Wild, J. You declare upon a *Quantum meruit*, and upon *Indeb. assumpsit*, and you have made Particulars of the Things, but no Prizes set upon the Things, which should have been done.

Vaughan, J. I remembred the Case of the Earl of *Essex*'s Valet de Chambre. The Valet de Chambre might have been as good a Man as a Knight's Son, and the Books are against you. Balls and Serenadoes at Night must not be accounted Necessaries, *North* and *Tompson*'s Case, *Coke. Ent.* 125. a Nobleman's Case.

Tir-

Tirrel, J. I think something must be given to the Plaintiff for Necessaries.

Wild, J. It is upon Demurrer, and Damages are entire, and we cannot sever.

Tirrel, J. Something must be given to the Plaintiff for Necessaries, we being Judges; and as the Jury, *in Coke*'s *Entr. Tomson*'s Case, were Judges, and did sever Damages, so may we in this Case.

Wild, *Archer* and *Vaughan*, for the Defendant; one being Judges of the Necessaries, is to the Nature of the Thing, not the Particulars; that indeed must be tried by a Jury, for there may be Difference from 1 *s.* to 20 *s.* in Laces.

The Case of the Earl of *Essex*'s Valet de Chambre was this: The Plaintiff delivered to the Defendant divers Suits of Apparel, *viz.* Sattin Doublet and Hose, with Silver and Gold Lace; a Velvet Jerkin; and the Defendant promised to pay 40 *l.* when required. Defendant pleads, *Tempore assumptionis* he was within Age. Plaintiff replied, That at the same Time the Defendant was Servant, and attending on the Earl of *Essex* in his Bedchamber, and that this Apparel was delivered to him for his necessary Apparel during the Time of his said Service. Defendant demurs. The Court caused the Declaration to be read in open Court, to see of what Degree the Defendant was, of his Addition, and he was written Gentleman. *Per Cur'*, That Sattin, with Silver and Gold Lace, &c. are not necessary Apparel for a Gentleman. But

 there

there was also for a Fustian Doublet and Hose of Cloth, and the Action lies for them, for the Prices are severally set down in the Declaration. *Popham*; the Plaintiff, in his Declaration, hath confessed he is satisfied of Part of his Contract, but *non constat* for what Part of the Clothes the Money received was paid, *viz.* Whether for the necessary or unnecessary. *Gaudy*; it shall be intended for the necessary Apparel. *Goldsb.* 168. *Mackerell* and *Batchelor*.

Debt upon a single Bill. Defendant pleads within Age; Plaintiff replies, it was for Victuals and Clothes necessary, and delivered to him, and suitable to his Quality. Defendant demurs. *Per Cur'*, a single Bill is good, but Obligation with a Penalty void; it was excepted, that they were delivered to him to his own Use, but disallowed; for when the Things are delivered to him, and suitable to his Quality, it cannot be intended but they were for his own Use, 1 *Levints*, *Russel* and *Lea*.

If an Infant make a Contract for his Table, he may be charged in an Action on this Contract, 18 *Ed.* 4. 2.

In *Tillet* and *Buck*'s Case, *Tr.* 15 *Jac. B. R.* adjudged, That Action on the Case lies against Infant, upon a Promise of Payment, for Beer and Billets. *Delaval* and *Clare*, 1 *Rol. Abr.* 729.

Ayloff brought Debt on Bond of 20 *l.* made 14 *May*, 41 *Eliz.* against *Archdale*; and the Condition was, That whereas he had paid 10 *l.* for the Meat, Drink and Apparel of of *Archdale*, if he repay him the said 10 *l.* upon the Feast of, *&c.* and he said he was within Age. Plaintiff replies, The said Obligation was made for Security of Payment of 10 *l.* by him paid for the Meat, *&c.* Defendant demurs. *Per Cur'*, *absente Anderson*, the Obligation shall not bind the Infant; *aliter*, of a Bill for the said Sum; and they said, *Revera*, the first Contract was determined by the taking the said Obligation, *Hill.* 45 *Eliz.* but entered *M.* 44 *&* 45 *Eliz.* *Rot.* 1560. in a private Manuscript, and *Vide Crok.* 1 *Rep.* *p.* 920.

Infant of 20 Years and an Half makes a Contract for good Consideration; this doth not bind him, and the other shall not be relieved in *Chancery*, for this would be to subvert a Rule of the Common Law; and for this the Cause was dismiss'd out of *Chancery*, by *Phillips* Master of the Rolls, *M.* 9 *Jac.* in a private Report. No Relief in *Chancery*.

We take it for a Rule in general, That if the Contract have but a Mixture of Prejudice to the Infant, it shall be void.

5 *Jac.* *B. R.* *Bendloe* and *Holiday*'s Case, An Obligation was made by an Infant, with Condition to pay so much for his Apparel; because the Bond was with a Penalty, it was adjudged void: But Obligation or Bill for the very Sum laid out, is good enough, *Cro. Eliz.* *ult.* *Case Ayliff*, 5 *Jac.* *B. R.* *Bendloe* and *Holiday*'s Case. Bond with a Penalty for Necessaries void, but for the very Sum good.

And the Opinion of *Paston*, 26 *H.* 8. 2. was always taken for Obligation with a Condition; nay, Bond with Penalty so far

far extinguished the Contract that it can never be revived; and if he promise at full Age to pay it, it shall not be good. *Vide supra.*

What are accounted Necessaries.

Now an Infant shall not be bound by his Contract or Bargain for any Thing, but for his Necessity, (*viz.*) Diet, Apparel, Learning, and necessary Physick.

Therefore it was adjudged in *Dale* and *Copping*'s Case, The Promise of an Infant to pay Money for the curing him of the *Falling Sickness* is good, and shall bind him, 1 *Bulst.* 39. *Vide* the Book, if the Plea in Bar, that at the Time of the Promise he was within Age, is good.

But an Action doth not lie against an Infant upon an *Insimul computasset* for Diet, because the Infant may be misreckoned; but if the Infant promise a certain Sum for his Diet, there need not be an Averment, it was worth so much, *Palm.* p 528.

Per Haughton in *Tirrel*'s Case, 2 *Rol. Rep.* 271. If Infant have Houses, it is necessary for him to have them in Repair; and yet Contract to repair them, doth not bind him. No Contract binds him, but what concerns his own Person.

If Infant promiseth another, That he will find him Meat and Drink, and pay for his Learning, that he will pay him 7 *l. per Annum.* Action on the Case lies on this Promise. And although it is not mentioned what Learning it is, yet it shall be intended that that is fit for him, until it be shewed to the contrary of the other Part; although he he to whom the Promiſe is made does not intruſt him himſelf, but pays another for it, the Promiſe of Repayment is good, 1 *Rol. Abr.* 729. *Pickering*'s Caſe.

Learning, though it be not neceſſary *de eſſe*, yet it is ſo *de bene eſſe*; and *omne quod eſt utile eſt aliquando neceſſarium*, 1 *Inſt*. 172. *Palm*. 528. *Pickering* and *Gunning*.

But Contract for Dancing, *&c.* is not binding, *Sid. p.*

It's ſaid in 3 *Keb*. 387. That an Infant, as Houſekeeper, may contract for Neceſſaries, (*viz.*) clear Neceſſaries, *convenientia*; though they are not neceſſary *quoad eſſe*, yet that for ſuch Proviſion he ſhall be chargeable: And *Hill* and *Blackſtone*'s Caſe is cited there, *Hill*. 15 *Jac.* and ſo was the Reſolution in *Whittingham* and *Hill*'s Caſe.

His buying of Neceſſaries to maintain his Trade, not binding.

Error of a Judgment was brought in *Shrewsbury*, in *Aſſumpſit*, to pay ſuch a Sum for Wares ſold. The Defendant pleads, he was within Age at the Time of the Wares being ſold. The Plaintiff *proteſtando* that he was not within Age, *pro Placito* ſaith he bought them *pro neceſſario victu & apparatu, & ad manutenentiam familiæ ſuæ*. The Defendant rejoins, That he kept a Mercer's Shop at *Salop*, and bought theſe Wares to ſell again; and traverſeth, that he bought them *pro neceſſario victu & apparatu*. The Plaintiff demurs, and adjudged for the Plaintiff; and the Error was aſſigned in Point of Law, That ſuch Buying ſhall not bind an Infant. And *per Cur'*, his buying to maintain his Trade, though he gain his Living thereby,

thereby, shall not bind him, *Hill* and *Blackstone's* Case, 2 *Rol. Rep.* 49. *Cro. Jac.* 494. *Whittingham* and *Hill's* Case.

Debt lies on Promise to pay for Necessaries.

Action of Debt lies against an Infant on his Promise to pay for Necessaries; as Meat, Drink, Lodging and Apparel: But if the Infant and the Party, from whom he had these Necessaries, do come to an Account, and reduce the Debt to a certain Sum, *&c.* And upon this Account the Party brought an Action against the Infant for the Money stated to be due by the Account. This Action will not lie against the Infant, for the Account on which the Action is grounded is void; for Infants cannot agree to any such Account, and so *Insimul computasset* lies not against him, for the *Assumpsit* is upon Account, *Trin.* 24 *Car. B. R.* 2 *Roll. Rep.* 271. *Tirrel's* Case.

Insimul computasset lies not against Infant.

Infant may bind himself in *Assumpsit* for the Payment of Necessaries, and Action on the Case lies upon the Promise, 15 *Jac. B. R. Tillet* and *Buckston*.

By *Wild*, in *Rainsford* and *Fenwick's* Case, *Carter's Rep.* 216. *Indebit. assumpsit*, the Defendant pleads under Age; the Defendant replies, Wares sold for necessary Apparel, suitable to his Degree. Defendant demurs. By his Demurrer, he hath confess'd them to be Necessaries. The Defendant should have come and rejoined, they were not for Necessaries; and so upon the Issue the Jury should have tried it.

What is confess'd by Demurrer.

Now

Now in Action brought against an Infant, it must appear in the Declaration that the Apparel was for the Infant himself; and if it be averred, that they were for himself and his own Wearing, yet it must be averred that they were necessary and convenient for him to wear, according to his Estate and Degree. And therefore where Executor brought an *Assumpsit* against C. for that the Defendant in Consideration would buy and pay for the Defendant these Wares, (*viz.*) Twenty four Yards of Lace, Eleven Yards of Velvet, Three Yards of Broad-Cloth, and would make a Cloak for him; promised not only to pay him such Sums as he should expend for the said Wares, but would pay to him as much as he deserved for making the said Cloak; and alledgeth *in facto*, That he bought the said Wares, and laid out for them 21 *l.* and that he made the said Cloak, and deserved for it 6 *s.* And also he declares, That the Defendant was indebted to the said Testator in 27 *l.* for a Doublet and a Pair of Hose of Velvet made for him, and delivered by the Testator; and that he promised Payment, and had not paid it. The Defendant pleads, That at the Time of these several Promises he was within Age. The Plaintiff demurs; and it was adjudged for the Defendant, because it was not averred that they were for his own Wearing, and that they were convenient and necessary. *Vide* more of this *infra, tit. Pleadings.*

What Averments are necessary in Declarations against Infants for Necessaries.

It

It was ſaid *per Coke*, (*arguendo* in *Stone* and *Withypole's* Caſe 1 *Leon.* 113. upon the Book of 19 *Ed.* 4. 2. in Debt againſt Infant in neceſſary Contract) the Plaintiff ought to declare ſpecially, ſo as the whole Certainty may appear: Upon which the Court muſt judge, if the Expences were neceſſary or convenient or not, and alſo upon the Reaſonableneſs of the Price, 1 *Leon.* 113. *Stone* and *Withypole.*

But in *Ruſſel* and *Lacy's* Caſe, 1 *Keb.* 382. the Particulars are needleſs to be ſet forth.

Reciprocal Conſiderations and Promiſes. As to Conſiderations: It is now ſettled, though the Remedy is not reciprocal, yet the Conſideration of the Act or Promiſe to do ſomething of Infant, ſhall be good.

Action on the Caſe was brought by Infant *per* his Guardian, in Conſideration the Defendant did agree to pay 6 *l.* for Permiſſion to have the Plaintiff's Graſs carried off one Acre of Land, and of 6 *l.* Debt owing to him the Defendant promiſed to pay. The Plaintiff was an Infant, and was not bound by his Agreement, yet he had Judgment, *Mod. Rep.* 25. *Smith* and *Bowen.*

And *Twiſden* there cited a Caſe to be adjudged, in Conſideration the Infant would permit the Defendant to enjoy an Houſe, the Defendant promiſed to pay; and it was agreed after Debate, That it was a good Promiſe, and a good Conſideration; albeit the Infant, as to his Part, may avoid it for the Infancy, and the Promiſe is entire, 2 *Keb.* 581. *Smith* and *Bowen.*

And so is *Austin* and *Jervis*'s Case, in *Hob.* 67, 77. If Infant deliver to *B.* 20 *l.* and in Consideration of this, *B.* promiseth to him to make him an House. This is not a good Consideration, because that tho' the 20 *l.* was delivered with the Hand of the Infant, yet this is unavoidable by him, and to be recovered against him in an Action of an Account; and by *Hobart*, the Consideration was not absolutely void, *Hob.* 67, 77. *Austin* and *Jervis*'s Case.

If Infant sell an Horse, or any such-like Thing, for Money, and the Vendee take it of himself, in this Case the Infant may have Action of Trespass for the taking; but if the Infant delivered the Thing with his own Hands, the Vendee is excused from any Action of Trespass, yet the Contract is voidable; and therefore the Infant may take his Horse again, and cannot sue for the Money, but may sue for his Horse, if he be kept from him. Infant sells Horse; where he may take him again, or sue for him.

If Infant buy an Horse, and gives Earnest, and the Seller break with him, he may sue him, because of his Earnest, which only is recoverable in Damages, and may be sued for by Action of Account, *Hob.* 96. 14 *H.* 8. 29. 21 *H.* 7. 29.

Now let us see what Promises and Considerations made for Infants are good, it being, as it were, a Consequence of the former Resolution. Considerations and Promises made for and on the Behalf of Infants.

The Plaintiff comes and demands a Debt of the Executrix for the Apparel of the Testator. The Executrix said to him, *Forbear*

bear till Michaelmas *and I will pay you, or put you in sufficient Security for the Payment of it.* And declared further, That at *Michaelmas* ſhe did not pay or put in Security. The Defendant pleads Infancy in the Teſtator at the Time of the Contract for the ſaid Apparel: And it was adjudged for the Defendant; for the Contract was void, and the Infant may plead in Action brought againſt him *Non debet*, 1 *Leon.* 113. *Stone* and *Withypole*.

Pleading.

This Caſe is abridged in *Rolls* much to the ſame Purpoſe, though the Suit was not brought againſt the Executrix.

If Infant take up certain Commodities of a Mercer in *London* at a certain Price; and after, for Non-payment of the Money, he threatens to ſue him, and the Mother of the Infant promiſeth to pay the Money at a certain Time, if he will not ſue the Infant. This is no Conſideration to maintain the Action; for that the Infant was not chargeable in Law for the Money, 1 *Rol. Abr.* 21. *Latch. p.* 21.

But it is ſaid in this Caſe in 1 *Leon.* 114. If Infant be bound in an Obligation with a Surety, and after at his full Age he in Conſideration thereof promiſeth to keep his Surety harmleſs, that upon that Promiſe Action lies, for the Infant cannot plead *Non eſt factum*, 1 *Leon.* 114. *Mich.* 28 & 29 *Eliz. Edmond*'s Caſe. *Quære.*

1 If

If Infant enter into an Obligation to pay a certain Sum of Money, and after the Obligee brought Debt for the Money, and procures a *Latitat* to arrest him; and the Obligor being now at full Age, and having Conisance of it, comes to the Obligee, and saith to him, *That if he will not arrest him, he will pay the Money to him.* This is not any Consideration to maintain the Action, forasmuch as the Infant might avoid the Obligation by Plea, 1 *Rol. Abr.* 18. *Monneys* and *Knapy.*

Promise by Infant at full Age, if Defendant forbear to arrest him on a Bond given under Age, to pay, it's not good.

Now as to what other Acts of his own an Infant shall be bound, or not, take Two or Three Rules and Resolutions thereupon:

Infants other Acts.

1. Acts which Infant doth out of Necessity shall bind him: As his Presentation to a Benefice shall be good, otherwise Lapse shall incur against him.

1. *Regula.* Acts of Necessity.

So if Infant be Executor, upon Payment of any Debt due to the Testator, he may make an Acquittance, and it shall be good; but in that Case a Release without Payment is void.

2. Acts of Compulsion: Regularly, whatsoever an Infant is bound to do by Law, that shall bind him, albeit he doth it without Suit in Law, 1 *Inst.* 172.

3. It's laid down as a Rule in *Siderfin*: Acts of Ideots, Infants and Masters of Ships, shall bind them and others in case of Necessity.

And our Law allows many Persons to make Contracts in Cases of Necessity, which of themselves are void. And so tho' Contracts of Infants are generally void, yet in Cases of Necessity they shall bind them; and this not only *quoad esse*, but *quoad necessitatem convenientiæ*: As if Infant contracts for so much to instruct him in Writing and Reading, *Sid.* 112. *Scot* and *Manby*.

Infant buys Necessaries for his Houshold; it shall bind him.

And for this Reason, if Infant is House-keeper, and buys Necessaries for his Houshold, it shall bind him, as was adjudged in *Hill* and *Blackston's* Case, *Trin.* 15 *Jac. Rot.* 1374. But not for his Trade. *Vide supra.*

Vendee of the Goods of an Infant a Trespasser.

If an Infant sells Goods for Money, and doth not deliver them, but the Vendee takes them; he is a Trespasser, and the Action lies against him, 1 *Leon.* 114.

Bound by Sale in open Market, and how.

Infant's Right regularly is bound by Sale in open Market: But Sale in Market-Overt by an Infant of such Tenderness of Age, as that it may appear to the Buyer that he is within Age, bindeth not, 2 *Inst.* 713.

Of Infant's submitting to Arbitrament.

Where Infant makes a Trespass, and submits to Arbitrament, it shall bind him at his full Age; because he is chargable for Trespass, and shall pay Damages, *Latch* 21. 207.

Submission of Infant not binding.

If Infant submits a Battery done to himself, and an Award is made thereupon; yet this shall not bind the Infant, 13 *H.* 4. 12. for his Submission is meerly void. *Br. Abr.* 42.

If

If one gives Bond in the Condition, of which it is recited, That an Infant hath submitted to the Award of *J. S.* And it's conditioned, That he shall perform the Award, it is void. *March* 11. 141. *Rudson* and *Yates*.

Obligee conditioned, That if the Father *J. B.* and *J. B.* his Son, and every of them, shall perform the Award of *A.* and *B.* Arbitrators, *&c. ita quod, &c.* Defendant pleads, *J.* his Son was within Age. Plaintiff demurs. It was argued, Submission by Infant is void; and, being void in Part, is void in all. The Court did not resolve this, but they hold, That the Submission by the Father for himself is good, and the Arbitrators may make Arbitration between the Plaintiff and him only; and the Plea doth not answer to this, but pleads Collateral Matter in Bar, 3 *Lev.* 17. *Bloxwith*'s Case. Submission by Father good.

The Father and his Daughter on the one Part, and *K.* on the other Part, submit themselves to Arbitrators of all Quarrels, the Daughter being within Age; the Father is bound to *K.* that he and his Daughter shall perform the Award on their Parts, and *K.* is bound to the Daughter to perform the Award on his Part. They award, That *K.* shall pay to the Daughter so much, and that the Father and Daughter shall release. *K.* doth not pay the Money at the Day; and the Daughter brought Debt on the Bond, (for *K.* is bound to the Daughter only.) It was moved (in this Case), That if the Submission be void, the Arbitrament is void; and if the

Arbitrment is void, the Bond doth not bind *K.* because an Obligation to perform a void Award, is void: And so far the Court agreed.

It was argued, That the Submission of the Infant is void: But *per Cur'*, it is good, because it is for her Benefit; otherwise Infant shall be in worse Case than one at full Age. It is true, if the Infant is bound to the Performance of an Award, the Obligation is void; but the Submission is good. Otherwise, if the Infant may shew this to his Disadvantage; but here it appears to be her Advantage.

Per some, the Submission is not void, but voidable by Infant, and his Election to avoid it is referred to him, during his Infancy; but if an Infant do an Act at his full Age, it shall bind him.

Quære, If this Award be not ill, because it is to be paid to the Daughter? *Latch, p.* 207. *Stone* and *Knight.* 10 *H.* 6. 14. 1 *Rolls Abr.* 730.

Arbitrament concerning an Infant, set aside in Equity.

Matters in Difference, referred by Consent and Order of the Court, to Mr. *B.* and Two others, or any Two of them. Two made the Award, and Exceptions were made to the Award on one Side; and the other Side moved, it might be decreed *per* Lord Chancellor. If the Parties without the Court refer the Differences, they chuse their own Judges; and this Court relieveth not against the Award, unless it be in case of Corruption, exceeding Authority,

rity, or the like; but when a Reference by Consent and Order of Court, if it appear unequitable, the Court will not decree it; and accordingly in this Case set aside the Award and Bond of Submission. The Reason was, because it concerned an Infant, to whom 450 *l.* was awarded; and that Bond should be given by the Guardian, That the Infant should, at his full Age, convey the Lands in Question, which is not reasonable; for he may die, or if he live to Age, refuse to convey: So it is not mutual.

The Lord Chancellor also said, He would never decree an Award which should bind an Infant. 1 *Cases in Chancery* 279. *Cavendish*'s Case.

CHAP. XI.

Of Acts in Law.

Where an Infant shall be bound by Collateral Warranty or not, with a good Diversity: Where a Discent shall toll the Entry of an Infant that hath Right. The Law doth not priviledge Infancy to the Prejudice of another's ancient Right. Priviledge of Infancy holds not against the King. The Difference of Bastard eigne & Mulier puisne *from other common Cases. Where Joint-tenant shall take in Advantage of the Infancy of his Companion. Diversity as to the Entry of a Stranger to the Use of an Infant. Of Remitters of Infants in two or three Diversities. The Nature of Remitter. Diversity between a Feoffment at Common Law, and a Feoffment to Uses. Of Remitter by Entry for Condition broken. Infant bound by Non-performance of Conditions. Who shall take Advantage of the Infancy of his Ancestor, or not. Money tendered for Infant, where good, or not.*

NOW by what Acts in Law an Infant shall be bound or not, comes properly to be treated of, having shewn you by what Acts or Contracts of his own he is obliged. As to this, our first Inquiry shall be, Where an Infant shall be bound by Collateral Warranty, discended upon him during his Nonage, or not.

As

As to this, a good Diversity is taken, 1 *Inst.* 380. *a. b.* where the Entry of the Infant is lawful when the Warranty discendeth; and where it is not lawful, 1 *Inst.* 380. Where Infant shall be bound by Collateral Warranty or not.

Where it is lawful, he may enter upon the Alienee with Warranty, and defeat it, because no Laches shall be adjudged in the Heir within Age. But if he bring his Action against him, he shall be barred by this Warranty, so long as the Estate whereunto the Warranty is annexed continues, and be not defeated by the Entry of the Heir: But if he be within Age at the Time of the Alienation with Warranty, and becomes of full Age before the Discent of the Warranty, the Warranty shall bar him for ever. But if the Entry of the Infant is not lawful, when the Warranty discendeth, the Warranty doth bind the Infant as well as a Man of full Age; and the Reason is, because the Estate whereunto the Warranty is annexed continueth, and cannot be avoided but by Action, in which Action the Warranty is a Bar. With a good Diversity.

A Man seised of Land had two Sons, and deviseth it to his youngest Son in Tail, and dies, the eldest having Issue a Son, the youngest aliens in Fee with Warranty, and goes beyond Sea, and dies without Issue, the Son of the eldest being within Age; if this Collateral Warranty shall bind the Son within Age in Reversion without Assets, was the Question. *Per Curiam*, It is clear, this is a Collateral Warranty, and was a Bar without Assets, notwithstanding his Nonage, because his Entry was tolled. But if the Infant be disseised, and a Collateral Anceſtor releaſe with Warranty to the Diſſeiſor, and dies, and the Infant brings Aſſize againſt the Diſſeiſor; this Collateral Warranty ſhall bind him, becauſe tho' he might have entred and defeated the Warranty, yet in as much as he had brought his Action, he had given Power to the Diſſeiſor to plead it againſt him, *Moor, p.* 96. *Evans*'s Caſe, 25 *H.* 6. 63.

Who ſhall take Advantage of the Infancy of his Anceſtor, or not.

Reſolved in 9 *Rep. Whittingham*'s Caſe, That Privies in Blood inheritable, as general Heir, ſpecial Heir, or as general and ſpecial Heir, ſhall take Advantage of the Infancy of his Anceſtor, and may enter upon a Feoffment made by the Anceſtor within Age: But Privies in Law, as Lord by Eſcheat, ſhall never take Advantage of Infancy, becauſe he is a Stranger to him, and when Infant dies without Heir, the Feoffment is unavoidable.

If Infant convey Lands to the Queen by Deed inrolled before *Stat.* 18 *Eliz.* which eſtabliſheth Grants made to the Queen; or if he levy a Fine of his Lands to the Queen, and afterwards the ſaid Statute is made for the Confirmation of Grants made to the King; yet becauſe the Perſon of the Infant, during his Minority, was diſabled by Law to make any Conveyance at all of his Inheritance, ſuch Parts are not good; but he may reverſe ſuch Fine by bringing a Writ of Error, 11 *Rep. Magdalen College* Caſe,

Where

Where a Discent shall take away the Entry of an Infant that Right hath, or not.

Regularly, No Laches shall be accounted in Infants by Non-entry, or Non-claim, to avoid Discents.

For he hath a Right which the Law preserves for him; but *aliter* where he hath not a Right to enter, for there he shall be bound: As, if a Man is seised of Lands in Fee, his Wife *privement enseint* with a Son, and a Stranger abateth, and dies seised, and after the Son is born, he shall be bound by this Discent, because at the Time of the Discent he had no Right to enter.

Law doth not priviledge Infancy to the Prejudice of another's ancient Right.

And tho' the Law doth priviledge Infancy, yet it doth it not to prejudice another's ancient Right. As, *B.* Tenant in Tail, enfeoffs *A.* in Fee, *A.* hath Issue within Age, and dies, *B.* abateth, and dies seised, the Issue of *A.* being still within Age; this Discent shall bind the Infant, for the Issue in Tail upon his Abatement is remitted, and the Law doth more respect an ancient Right in this Case, than the Priviledge of an Infant, who had but a defeasible Title, 1 *Inst.* 246.

Priviledge holds not against the King.

But if the King dies seised of Land, and the Land discends to his Successor, this shall bind the Infant; for the Priviledge of Infancy in this Case holds not against the King. Now where the Infant hath Right of Entry, if a Discent be cast, the Infant being within Age, he may enter at any Time,

Time, either within Age, or after his full Age, 1 *Inst*. 248. *a*.

The Difference of *Bastard eigne* and *Mulier puisne* from other common Cases.

But the Case of *Bastard eigne* and *Mulier puisne* differ from the common Cases of Discent and Bar: For Discents do only toll the Entry of him that Right hath, but leaveth him to his Action. But now if a Man seised of Lands in Fee hath Issue two Sons, *Bastard eigne* and *Mulier puisne*, and the Father dies, the Bastard enters claiming as Heir to his Father, and occupieth the Land all his Life, without any Entry made upon him by the *Mulier*, and the Bastard hath Issue, and dies seised, and the Lands discends to his Issue who entreth, in this Case the *Mulier* is barred for ever both of his Entry and of his Action; and if the *Mulier* be within Age at the Time of the dying seised, he shall be so barred too; for the Issue of the Bastard is become in Judgment of Law as lawful Heir. For it's the ancient Law, *Justum non est aliquem post Mortem facere Bastardum, qui toto Tempore Vitæ suæ pro legitimo habebatur*. As for this Reason, *sit penes Authorem*. The best of it is, these Cases come but rarely, or else I conceive Infants, *Muliers* legitimate, ought to be reliev'd by an Act of Parliament. But enough of this, and this *in Terrorem fornicandi*, 8 *Rep*. *Lechford*'s Case.

In case of two Joint-tenants being seised, and one is under Age, and he of full Age dies.

Two Joint-tenants, one within Age, the other of full Age, are disseised, and a Discent is cast, and he of full Age dies, the Entry of the other shall be congeable into the whole, 1 *Inst*. 36.

If

Where Joint-tenant shall take no Advantage of his Infant Companion.

If two Joint-tenants in Fee, the one within Age, and the other of full Age, be disseised, and the Disseisor dies seised, and his Issue enter, one of the Joint-tenants being then within Age, and after that he cometh to his full Age, and the Heir of the Disseisor lets the Tenements to the Joint-tenants for the Term of their two Lives, this is a Remitter as to one Moiety to him that was within Age, because his Entry was congeable; but the other Joint-tenant hath only an Estate for Term of his Life, because his Entry was taken away: For the Advantage is given to the Infant in this Case, more in respect of his Person than of his Right, whereof his Companion shall take no Advantage.

Diversity as to the Entry of a Stranger to the Use of an Infant.

As to the Entry of an Estranger to the Use of an Infant, the Difference is fine. If an Infant make a Feoffment in Fee, an Estranger of his own Head cannot enter to the Use of the Infant; for the Estate is voidable, and the Infant at full Age may make it good. But where an Infant is disseised, an Entry by a Stranger of his own Head is good, and presently vesteth the Estate in the Infant, 1 *Inst*. 245. *a*.

But where a Discent shall toll the Entry of an Infant, and where not, *Vide* more fully in 1 *Inst*. in the Chapter of *Discents*.

Remitters of Infants.

As to the Remitter of Infants (which is an Act of Law) the Learning in our Books is very curious, and the Delicacy of Reason is display'd in its full Lustre.

I

I shall give you a Taste of it.

Regula. It's a Rule, That if Tenant in Tail disseiseth his Discontinuee, his Issue shall be remitted, notwithstanding the Infancy, or Coverture of the Discontinuee, and this stands upon the same Reason as the other of Discent; the Law respecteth an ancient Right more than the Priviledge of Infancy, 1 *Inst*. 384.

The Nature of a Remitter. Now Remitter is wrought by Operation of Law upon an Estate past or vested. The Consequence is, That it must be guided by the Estate, and waits thereupon: And therefore Discontinuee, after the Death of Tenant in Tail, makes a Feoffment by Deed to the Issue in Tail, being within Age, who hath Right, and to a Stranger in Fee; and makes Livery to the Infant in the Name of both; the Issue in this Case is not remitted to the whole, but to the Moiety; for first he taketh the Fee-simple, and after the Remitter is wrought by Operation in Law, and therefore can remit him but to a Moiety, 1 *Inst*. 350. *a*.

Diversity between a Feoffment at Common Law, and a Feoffment to Uses. Another Diversity is between a Feoffment at Common Law, and a Feoffment to Uses: For if Tenant in Tail enfeoffs his Issue within Age, he is remitted, and the Law respects the Time of the Feoffment, and not the Time of the Death of the Tenant in Tail, when such Heir was of full Age. But if Tenant in Tail make a Feoffment in Fee (his Heir within Age) to the Use of his Issue, being within Age, and his Heirs, and dies, and the Right of the Estate Tail discends

ſcends to his Iſſue, being within Age, yet he is not remitted; becauſe the Statute executes the Poſſeſſion in ſuch Plight, Manner and Form, as the Uſe was limited, 1 *Inſt.* 348. *b.*

If Tenant in Tail make a Feoffment in Fee upon Condition, and dies, the Iſſue in Tail being within Age, doth enter for the Condition broken, he ſhall be firſt in as Tenant in Fee-ſimple as Heir to his Father, and conſequently and inſtantly he ſhall be remitted; but if the Heir be of full Age, he ſhall not be remitted, becauſe he might have had his Formedon againſt the Feoffee, and the Entry for the Condition broken is his own Act. And for the ſame Reaſon, if Tenant in Tail enfeoffs his Heir apparent, being of full Age at the Time of the Feoffment, and Tenant in Tail dies, this is no Remitter to the Heir, becauſe it was his Folly, being of full Age, he would take ſuch Feoffment, *&c.* and he ſhall, during his Life, be ſubject to all Charges and Incumbrances made by the Anceſtors; but ſuch Folly ſhall not be judged in the Heir being within Age, in reſpect of his tender Years. Remitter by Entry for Condition broken.

Another Difference between Infancy and full Age, in Point of Remitter, is in this Caſe. If Tenant in Tail enfeoffs a Woman in Fee, and dieth, and his Iſſue within Age marrieth the Diſcontinuee, this is a Remitter to him, and the Wife hath nothing, and the Freehold and Inheritance of the Wife vaniſhed clear away. *Aliter,* if ſuch Heir were at full Age at the Time of the Marriage; for

for then the Heir hath nothing but in the Right of the Wife, *&c. Lit.* §. 665.

One ſhall not be remitted by an Act which commenceth by his own Wrong. Tenant in Tail diſcontinues, and dies, his Son procures others to diſſeiſe the Diſcontinuee, and to enfeoff him, then being within Age, he ſhall not be remitted, becauſe the Diſſeiſin is a Wrong which commenceth by the Infant himſelf, 2 *And.* 39.

An Infant ſhall be remitted, tho' he take an Eſtate back by Deed intended, or by Fine, 1 *Inſt.* 353.

Where one ſhall not avoid his own Leaſe by Remitter to Infancy.

And note one Thing more. If Tenant in Tail enfeoffs his Son within Age, who at full Age lets the Land, and after he is remitted by the Death of his Father, yet he ſhall not avoid his own Leaſe, 2 *Rolls Abr.* 422.

Infant bound by Non-performance of Condition.

But Laches ſhall be accounted to an Infant for Non-performance of a Condition, annexed to the Eſtate of the Land, either made to the Anceſtor or to himſelf; and it ſhall bar him of his Right to the Land for ever. So of a Condition in Law, as one annexed to an Office. *Vide ſupra, Plow.* 136. *b.*

Notice of Payment upon a Condition ought to be given to an Infant.

Statute of *Merton, c.* 5.

An Eſtate is deviſed to an Infant, provided ſhe marry with the Conſent of, *&c.* and ſhe marries (being under Age) without Conſent, the Condition is broken, and ſhe forfeits the Eſtate, 2 *Keb.* 758.

If

If a Man makes a Feoffment in Fee to another, reſerving Rent, and if he pay not the Rent within a Month, that then he ſhall double the Rent, and the Feoffee dieth, his Heir within Age, the Infant payeth not the Rent, he ſhall not by this Laches forfeit any Thing. *Aliter* of a Feme Covert. And the Reaſon of the Diverſity is, for that the Infant is provided for by the Statute of *Merton, c.* 1. *Non current Uſuræ contra aliquem infra Ætatem exiſtent'.* But this Statute doth not extend to a Condition of Re-entry, which an Infant ought to perform, for the Forfeiture thereof cannot be called *Uſura,* 1 *Inſt.* 246. *b.*

Eject. Firmæ, on general Iſſue it was found, that *M.* was ſeiſed, and makes a Feoffment to *S.* upon Condition, That if *M.* or his Heirs, pay ſuch a Sum at ſuch a Day, that then, *&c.* Re-entry. *M.* died, having a Son and Heir within Age. The Mother of the Infant provides the Money at the Day, and cauſeth it to be tendered in the Name of the Infant, and there was not any Privity or Conſent by the Infant, nor was the Mother found Guardian in Socage. *Per Cur.* The Tender is inſufficient; but if the Infant was proved to be within 14 Years of Age, and the Mother found Guardian in Socage, the Tender ſhall be adjudged ſufficient, 1 *Mo.* 222. *Watkins* verſus *Aſhwell.*

Money tendered for Infant, where good, or not.

CHAP.

CHAP. XII.

Of Declarations and Pleadings.

Persons shall be enabled by Intendment till the contrary be shewed. Diversity where the Purview of a Statute is restrictive, and where it is general, and after comes a Restraint. Diversity between pleading a Feoffment by Common Law and by Custom. What Averments are needful in Declarations against Infants for Necessaries. If the Bill for Necessaries, how and what Issue shall be taken. Who are Judges of necessary Apparel. Acknowledgment of Satisfaction of Parcel, and saith not what, stops Judgment for any Part. Replication ill in the Conclusion, yet aided after Verdict by the late Statute. Condition to bring in A. *and* B. *at their full Ages, how to be expounded. Consideration of being bound with Security, and saith not in what Sum. Infant, after* Non Assumpsit *pleaded, moved in Arrest of Judgment that he was within Age. If Infant plead* Non est factum, *he shall not have Advantage of his Infancy. What may be given in Evidence on* Non Assumpsit. *Where* Non est factum *must be pleaded, and where the Special Matter, and how to conclude. Where, and what Actions, the Parole shall demur for* Nonage. *Assize. Ancestral Possession. Ancestral Droiturel. Formedon. Appeal. Partition. Torts. Dower.* Quare impedit. *Estrepement.*

4 Debt

Debt on Bond. Error. Trespass. Debt against the Heir in Assize on being ousted by Execution on a Statute Merchant, or Recognizance. Where Parole shall not demur for the Non-age *of the Husband. Where it shall for the* Nonage *of the Wife. Detinue against Executor. Diversity as to the Parole demurring in case of Purchase or Discent. Counterplea of Age. Where the Parole shall demur against all for the* Nonage *of one. Where the Court* ex Officio *shall grant the Age, although the Party do not pray it.*

HAving in the precedent Chapter shew'd by what Acts of his own, and by what Acts in Law, an Infant shall be bound or not, and what Actions, and for what Things, lie against him; it will now be proper to illustrate the same by several Cases and Resolutions concerning the Manner of Declaring and Pleading.

It is a known Rule, That Persons shall be enabled by Intendment, *i. e.* Persons shall be supposed of Ability, except the contrary appear; as, if Obligation be made by a Man or Woman in Action brought upon the Bond, he shall not be compelled to say, That the Man was of full Age, or that the Woman was sole, for that shall be intended till the contrary be shewed. But if one will plead a Feoffment, or Grant of *Cestuy que use*, there he ought to say, he was of full Age, *sane Memorie, &c.* on the Statute of 1 *R.* 3. tho' on the Statute of 4 *H.* 7. of Fine and Nonclaim, he need not do so. And the Reason

Person shall be enabled by Intendment

O is

Diversity where the Purview is restrictive, and where it is at first general, and after comes a Restraint.

is this, The Purview of the Act of 1 R. 3. is, That all Feoffments, Grants, *&c.* being made by any Person being of full Age, of sane Memory, *&c.* to any Person, shall be good and effectual, and the Act doth not warrant any Feoffment or Grant, but of those Persons who are void of such Defects: And therefore, he who will take Advantage by such Conveyances, ought to shew that he who made them was void of such Defects: But otherwise it is where the Purview is general, and the Restraint to some comes after by Exception, as it is in the Statute of 4 *H.* 7. of Fines; or by another Branch, as it is by the Statute of Wills, where the Devisee shall plead the Devise generally, tho' there is a Breach after that Purview, That Wills made by Infants, Feme Coverts, *&c.* shall not be effectual, *Plow.* 176. *Stowell* and *Zouch.*

In Ejectment to be tried at the Bar, to delay and put off Trial, Infancy was pleaded; but it was found by sufficient Proof, and by Examination of the Church Book, that he was of the Age of 63 Years, and Attachment was granted against him, 2 *Bulstrode* 67. *Lord* versus *Thornton.*

Diversity between pleading a Feoffment by Common Law, and by Custom.

If a Man pleads a Feoffment at Common Law, it shall be good; and if the Feoffor was within Age, it shall be shewed of the other Side; but if a Man pleads a Feoffment by Custom, and the other saith the Feoffor was within Age; and the Plaintiff replies, That an Infant within Age may make a Feoffment, the same is not good, but

but a Departure; for he ought to have shewed that at the Beginning of his Declaration. So,

37 *H.* 5. 6. in a *Præcipe quod reddat*, the Tenant pleads, That the Land was devised to him, *&c.* The Plaintiff replies, That the Devisor was an Infant. The Defendant saith, That by the Custom an Infant at such an Age may devise.

But in a *Dum fuit infra Ætatem*, if the Tenant do plead a Release of the Demandant, it is no Plea without saying that he was of full Age; for the Plea shall be taken most strong against himself, that is, that it was made when he was within Age, *Pl. Com.* 104. *a.*

Seeing personal Actions brought against Infants are for Necessaries, or Things relating thereunto, I shall be a little more large about the Declarations, and *Gist* of the Action and Pleadings thereupon.

It must appear by the Pleadings, That the Apparel (for which the Infant made the Contract) was for the Infant himself; and if it be averred that they were for himself, for his own wearing, yet it must be averred that they were necessary and convenient for him to wear, according to his Estate and Degree, as it was adjudged in *Ive* and *Chester*'s Case. *Vide* the Case *supra* in the Chapter of *Contracts*; for the Plaintiff made no such Averment in his Declaration, and therefore it was adjudged for the Defendant. *Ive* and *Chester*. What Averments are needful in Declaration against Infants for Necessaries.

But *per Curiam*, in *Russel* and *Ley*'s Case, 1 *Keb.* 382. The Particulars of the Materials are needless to be set forth: But though it be not laid expresly to be for him or his wearing; yet if there be that which is *Tantamount*, and it appears by the Declaration to be so, it's good enough, as in *Russel* and *Ley*'s Case, 1 *Keb.* 182.

Debt was brought on a Bill given for Security of Money due for Necessaries: The Defendant pleads Nonage. The Plaintiff replies, it was *pro necessario apparatu & vestitu*, not saying it was for him, or that it was suitable to his Degree. The Defendant demurs; but it being said he sold it to him, it shall be intended for him. And if the Bill be unreasonable, then Issue may be taken, that it was not due for Necessaries; and then the Plaintiff must shew the Bill to be suitable to the Price of the Things, and the whole Bill is void, if the Price be unreasonable. And here by the Demurrer, the Defendant hath confess'd it to be due. 2. It was laid to be for Necessaries, *eidem deliberat'*, and does not say it was *pro necessariis* of the Infant, as was *Ives*'s Case, 2 *Cro.* 560. Yet the Court agreed it to be well enough without it, as *Pop.* 151. And *per Cur'*, if the Bill be of excessive Rate, the Defendant may Traverse, *absq; hoc*, That it was for necessary Apparel, and the Plaintiff must reply Specially; also the Jury ought to find in such Case *non est factum*, 21 *Ed.* 4. *Quær.* 1 *Keb.* 382, 416, 423. *Russel* and *Ley*.

If the Bill be unreasonable, then Issue shall be taken.

Debt was brought upon divers Contracts, all for Apparel; some for Fustian Suits, some for Velvet and Sattin laced; Suits laced with Gold Lace, amounting to 44 *l.* whereof he was satisfied 4 *l.* The Defendant pleads Infancy. The Plaintiff replies, That he was one of the Gentlemen of the Chamber to the Earl of *Essex*, and so it was for his necessary Apparel: And it was thereupon demurred. And *per Cur.* we are to judge what is necessary Apparel, and such Suits of Sattin, *&c.* are not necessary for an Infant, though he be a Gentleman. It was prayed for the Plaintiff, that he might have Judgment for those that were necessary Apparel. But *per Cur'*, in regard he had acknowledged Satisfaction for 4 *l.* Parcel, and they did not know wherefore it was paid, therefore he could not have Judgment for any Part; *aliter*, he should have had Judgment for the Contracts, which were allowed of, *Cr. Eliz.* 583. *Makarel* and *Bachelor.*

Who are Judges of necessary Apparel.

Note, In Ejectment Infancy was pleaded, and upon Examination he was found to be 63 Years of Age, and an Attachment was granted, 2 *Bulstr.* 67.

In *Assumpsit* for Wares sold. The Defendant pleads, That at the Time, *&c.* he was within Age. The Plaintiff replies, The Wares sold were necessary and suitable to his Estate and Degree. *Et hoc petit quod inquiratur per patriam. Et præd' Def. similiter.* It was moved, That here was not any Issue joined, because there is not any Negative. *Per Cur'*, He ought to have averred by *paratus est*, &c. and then the Defendant might have

Conclusion ill in the Replication, yet aided after Verdict by the new Statute.

have denied it. But these are Two Affirmatives, and it is Matter *dehors* the Declaration; but yet in this Case the Conclusion *al pais* is good after a Verdict, for the Matter which is the Gist of the Action is void after Verdict for the Plaintiff, the Right of the Cause being tried, *Sid.* 341. *Burton* and *Chapam.*

Condition to bring in *A.* and *B.* at their Age, how to be expounded.

Bond with Condition, That the Obligor should bring in the Son and Daughter of *J. S.* at their full Age, to give such Release as a Third Person shall require. The Defendant pleads, That the Son is alive under Age at *D.* The Plaintiff may demur, for it must be taken of their respective Ages, 1 *Vent.* 58. *Rosvill's* Case.

Action on the Case was brought against an Infant, because he put Cloth to the Plaintiff, being a Taylor, to make a Suit of it, and promised to give him so much for the making of it, and providing all Things necessary (as Trimmings) as he deserved. The Defendant saith, true it is, such a Promise he made, but that then he was within the Government of *A.* and he made this Promise for him, *absq; hoc* that he made any such Promise. *Per Cur'*, The Action lies, though a Bond in such a Case is not good, and the Plea is Repugnant. In this Case there needs not any Averment, that the Apparel was convenient for the Infant for his Quality, because he doth not provide the Materials, only the Making and the Necessaries to it; as Linings, *Latch,* p. 156. *Delamere* and *Clare.*

Debt

Debt was brought on Bond of 20 *l*. The Condition whereof was, Whereas the Plaintiff had paid 10 *l*. for the Meat, Drink and Apparel of the Defendant, if the Defendant should repay the 10 *l*. the Bond to be void. The Defendant pleads Nonage. The Plaintiff replies, The Bond was made *pro Securitate* of the 10 *l*. for the Meat, Drink and Apparel of the Defendant. The Defendant demurs, and Judgment was given for the Defendant, though this Case is differently reported by *Cro. Eliz.* 920. which is of a Bond taken for double the Sum for the Meat, Drink and Apparel of the Defendant, and there adjudged void, *Moor* 679. *Ayliff* and *Archdale, Cro. Eliz.* 920.

Bond taken *pro Securitate* of 10 *l*. for Meat and Drink of an Infant.

Plaintiff, Infant, brought an *Assumpsit* against *J.* and declared, That the Plaintiff bought of the Defendant an Horse for 22 Pieces of Gold paid in Hand, and for 11 *l*. more to be paid at the Death or Marriage of the said Plaintiff, for which he should become bound with sufficient Surety by their Writing Obligatory. The Defendant, in Consideration thereof, promises to deliver the Horse to him when he should be required: Now the Court held the Consideration good; but Verdict was for the Plaintiff, but Judgment was against him for a Fault in the Declaration, because he did not aver that the Bond was ready sealed, and to deliver the same to the Defendant; neither did set down the Sum in which they should be bound for the same. For the Law requires he should be bound in a competent Sum,

Consideration Infant should be bound with Security for 11 *l*. for an Horse, Defendant promised to deliver, *&c.* good Consideration, but Defect in the Declaration.

which is under the Judgment of the Court, and it muſt be pleaded therefore expreſly, that the Court may judge of it, *Hob.* 67; 77. *Auſtin* and *Jervis*. *Roll. Abr.* 19. *Meſme* Caſe.

Infant after *Non aſſumpſit* pleaded, moved in Arreſt of Judgment that he was within Age.

The Defendant pleads *Non aſſumpſit* in Action on the Caſe, and then afterwards he moved in Arreſt of Judgment, That he was an Infant at the Time of the Promiſe, *Et Quer' nil capiat per Billam. Vide Opin' de Keelings*, 1 *Brownl.* 11. *Auſtin* and *Jervis*'s Caſe.

It is agreed in *Fleming* and *Pitman*'s Caſe, *Winch* 63. If Infant plead *Non eſt factum*, he ſhall not have Advantage of his Infancy, *Winch*, *p.* 64.

Where *Non eſt factum* may be pleaded, and where one muſt ſhew the Special Matter.

It's a Rule laid down in our Books: In every Caſe where the Obligation is void, he ſhall conclude *Non eſt factum*; as in the Caſe of a *Feme Covert*, ſhe ſhall plead *Non eſt factum*, for it is void as to her.

So where a Deed is raiſed, *&c.* But it is otherwiſe where the Deed is only voidable; for there in Pleading he ſhall ſhew the Special Matter, and conclude Judgment *ſi actio*.

As if an Infant plead, That at the Time of making the Bond he was within Age, he ſhall not conclude, *Iſſint non eſt factum*, but Judgment *ſi actio*, 1 *H.* 7. 18. 5 *Rep.* 119.

So is 1 *Ventr.* 102. Infancy muſt be pleaded, and the Party cannot be aided on *Non eſt factum*, 1 *Ventr.* 102. *May*, 2 *Keb.* 851. *Paſſiter* and *Bore*, *Mar.* 3 *Keb.* 798. *Tapper*'s Caſe. *Feme*

Feme Covert within Age may be given in Evidence on *Non assumpsit* pleaded, *per Hales*, and not denied. What may be given in Evidence on *Non assumpsit*.

But to plead Nonage at the Time of the Conversion in Trover, *Quære*.

Where the Parole shall demur for the Nonage.

Real Actions being changed into Ejectments, and few brought in our Times, except in some Special Cases, there need not much be said about the Plea tarrying till the full Age of the Infant; yet because it bears a considerable Title in our ancient Books, I shall observe some adjudged Cases, with the Reasons of the Resolution, having an Eye to the Real Actions most usual, and no other.

The Reason given in *Dyer* 137. why Infant shall have his Age, is, because he cannot discern his own Right; and the Court (*ex officio*) ought to speak for an Infant. Age is to be allowed the Infant when he is to defend his Right.

It is regularly true, That in all Real Actions the Infant shall have his Age. Regula.

And although he will not pray it, yet if this appear to the Court, they will grant it; but in Tortious Actions made by him he shall not have his Age, for ***malitia supplet ætatem***, 2 *Roll. Rep.* 17.

Except

Except in ſome certain Caſes hereafter mentioned.

In Real Actions of his own Poſſeſſion.

In all Real Actions which Infant brings of his own Poſſeſſion, although he had the Lands by Diſcent, and although the Tenant plead the Deed or Warranty of his Anceſtor, the Parole ſhall not demur for his Nonage: For by Preſumption of Law, the granting that the Parole ſhall demur is for the Benefit and in Favour of the Infant; becauſe, for want of good Intelligence of his Eſtate, and of the Verity of the Matter, he ſhall not be prejudiced of his Right.

As the Parole ſhall not demur in a Writ of *Entry ſur diſſeiſin* made to the Infant himſelf, nor in a Writ of *Right* of a Deforcement to the Infant himſelf: So in a Writ of *Eſcheat, Ceſſavit*, Writ of *Right ſur Diſclaimer* brought by Infant, or in a Writ of *Meſne*.

Where the Tenant may plead, that the Parole ſhall demur.

But in Actions *Aunceſtrel Droiturel*, when nothing diſcend but a naked Right from the Anceſtor in Fee-ſimple, who once was in Poſſeſſion, to an Infant; there the Tenant, without Plea pleaded, may pray that the Parole ſhall demur; as in a Writ of *Right*, as Heir to the Anceſtor.

So if Infant bring a *Formedon* in Reverter, as Heir to the Donor.

But in *Formedon* in a Remainder, tho' he demand a Fee-ſimple, yet his Anceſtor never was in Seiſin, nor took the *Eſplees*; there the Tenant without Plea ſhall not pray, that the Parole ſhall demur.

In

In all Actions *Auncestrel possessory*; as in *Cosinage*, *Ayel*, *Besayel*, *&c.* where the Ancestor dies seized, there the Tenant, without Plea pleaded, may not pray, that the Parole shall demur for the Nonage of the Demandant.

In *Formedon in Discender*, where the Demandant does not recover a meer Right, but a limited Estate *per formam doni*, the Parole shall not demur: But in *Assize* and *Assize* of *Mortdancester*, the Parol upon any Plea pleaded shall not demur. *Formedon.*

Formedon in Remainder was brought against Infant in *C. B.* The Infant by his Guardian pleads he was in by Discent, and prays that the Parole may demur; and upon this Issue is taken, and found for the Tenant in the *Formedon*, and Judgment final was there given, (*viz.*) That the Demandant shall be barred. And for this a Writ of *Error* brought in *B. R.* and Judgment was affirmed. The Reason is, because this Issue is upon a Matter in Fact, which is supposed to be in the Conisance of the Party; and if he will give so much Trouble and Charge to the other Party, it's Reason he should be barred. *Aliter* upon Demurrer, because the Party is not supposed to be Conisant of the Law. And it is a Rule in all Dilatories, or other Matters pleaded in Abatement, If Issue be taken, its peremptory, and the Prayer is, *Quod breve cassetur*, *Sid.* 252. 1 *Keb.* 869. *Ampcot*'s Case. *Regula.*

In

In all Real Actions at Common Law (and in some few it's taken away by Statutes) if the Tenant was within Age, and in any Discent, he shall have his Age; As in *Scire fac'* upon a Fine; in Error, if he be Tenant; in *Formedon in Discender*, in *Ayel*, unless it be founded in his own Tort.

Vide pluis de hoc in 6 *Rep. Markal's* Case.

The first Statute about Age is *Westm.* 1. *c.* 47. which ousts the Heir of the Disseisor from having his Age.

The second is the Statute of *Gloucester*, *c.* 2. which ousts the Heir of his Age in a Writ of *Ayel* and *Besayel*.

The third is *W.* 2. *c.* 44. in a *Cui in vita*, 3 *Bulst.* 137, 138.

Regula. And it's a sure Rule, The Parole shall not demur for the Prejudice of the Infant; but for his Benefit, 2 *Inst.* 291.

Appeal. The Parole shall not demur in an Appeal, 2 *Inst.* 32.

Partition. The Infant shall not have his Age in a Writ of *Partition*, brought upon the Statute, because nothing is in Demand but Partition, *Hob.* 179.

Diversity. And the Diversity is taken between those Things that concern the Hereditary Right, (for which the Parole shall demur) and those Actions which are brought and grounded *de son Tort demesne*; as Wast, Disseisin, &c. for there *Malitiosa supplet ætatem*, *Cro. Jac.* 467.

In

In a Writ of *Dower* the Parole shall not demur for the Favour of Dower, and perhaps the Wife may die before his Age, *Trin.* 4 *Jac. B. R. Epp's* Case. Dower.

In *Quare Impedit* the Parole shall not demur for the Nonage of the Patron, Defendant; for the Lapse may incur before his full Age. *Qu. Impedit*

In a Writ of *Estrepement* against Infant, he shall not have his Age, because this Action is in Nature of a Trespass, and this is made by himself, 3 *H.* 6. 16. *Estrepement.*

And for the same Reason in Assize the Tenant shall not have his Age. *Assize.*

If a Man by Bond bind himself and his Heirs to pay 100 *l.* at such a Day; and if he pay it not at the Day, that then he and his Heirs shall pay 10 *l.* for every Quarter that is behind. Obligor dies, and leaves Assets in Fee-simple, his Heir within Age, he shall have his Age by the Common Law, and after his full Age he shall be freed of the 10 *l. per* the Quarter, by the Statute of *Merton, c.* 5. Debt on Bond. Stat. *Mert. c.* 5.

Infant Imparls till another Term, where he appears by his Guardian, yet he shall have the Benefit of his Age, 21 *Ed.* 4. 78. After Imparlance.

In a Writ of *Error* against the Heir of the Recoveror, by Real Action the Parole shall demur for his Nonage, although he had nothing in the Land; but the other is Tenant, because he is presumed not to have Conisance of his own Right, or to know what is best for himself, 9 *H.* 6. 46. Error.

In

In Error to reverse a Fine, the Defendant, if he be Tertenant in Tail by Discent, shall have his Age. The Defendant to a Writ of *Error* pleads a Discent of Lands to him within Age, and prayed his Age; and the Age was granted, because he that prayed it was Tertenant: But if he had not been Tertenant, he should not have his Age in Error, *Mo.* 847.

If *Baron* and *Feme* levy a Fine of the Land of the Husband, and after the Husband dies, and the Conisee dies, his Heir within Age, against whom the Wife brings a Writ of *Error*, being Tertenant; but the Wife pleads she claims only Dower in the Land, yet the Plea shall demur, because the Wife may make other Title in the Land when it is reversed. And the Dower is not demanded in this Action, as in a *Quod ei deforceat*; tho' there was some Doubt upon the Demurrer, *H.* 13 *Jac. B. R.* *Herbert* and *Bincot*.

Dower.

A Fine levied by *Baron* and *Feme*; the Baron dies, the *Feme* brings Error against the Heir of the Conisee, being an Infant; after being well argued by Council and Judges, *Resolved*, Age should be allowed to the Defendant, and that the Plea should stay till the Defendant's full Age, 3 *Bulstr.* 134. *Vide pluis ibid.* about the Parole demurring.

Trespass, and justifies for Rent.

In Trespass *Vi & armis* against an Infant, who justifies for Rent and the like, as Heir to his Father; if the other shew forth the Deed of the Ancestor in Discharge, yet the Plea

Plea shall not demur; but he ought to answer to the Deed presently.

In a Writ of *Debt* against the Heir he shall have his Age, because he may at his full Age discharge himself, by saying, That he had nothing by Discent, *H.* 7 *Jac. Vivian* and *Trelawny*. (Debt against the Heir.)

If a Man sue Execution upon a Statute-Merchant against an Heir within Age, and ousts him by it, an Assize lies for the Heir; for he shall have his Age. (*Assize* being ousted by Execution on Statute Merchant.)

So if a Man sue Execution upon a Recognizance against an Heir within Age, he shall have his Age although he be partly charged as Tertenant, 3 *Rep.* Sir *William Herbert*'s Case. (So of a Recognizance.)

The Infant who had the Tenancy by discent, shall have his Age in a *Per quæ servitia* brought against him, 9 *Rep.* 85. *Coney*'s Case.

In Action brought by *Baron* and *Feme*, for the Inheritance of the Wife, the Parole shall not demur for the Nonage of the Husband, because it is in Right of his Wife, *Dyer* 137. But, (Where Parole shall not demur for the Nonage of the Husband, and where it shall for the Nonage of the Wife.)

In a *Præcipe quod reddat* against *Baron* and *Feme* of the Land of the Wife had by Discent, the Parole shall demur for the Nonage of the Wife, although the Husband be of full Age.

In Action of *Debt* brought against *Baron* and *Feme* upon the Bond of the Ancestor of the *Feme*, the Parole shall demur for the Nonage of the Wife.

In

Detinue against Executor. In Detinue against Executor, upon Bailment to the Testator, the Parole shall not demur for the Nonage of the Executor, 11 *H.* 6. 40.

Regula. If the Infant be in by Purchase, he shall not have his Age.

As if Lease for Life be, the Remainder to the right Heir of *J S.* who dies, his Heir within Age; he shall not have his Age.

Purchase. So if a Gift is made to the Father for Life, the Remainder in Tail to the Son, the Remainder to the Right Heirs of the Father; and after the Father dies, and the Fee discends to the Son within Age, yet he shall not have his Age, because he hath the Estate Tail by Purchase, 7 *H.* 4. 5.

If Lessee for Life surrender to an Infant, who had the Reversion by Discent, he shall not have his Age.

Heir of the Disseisee shall have his Age. If the Infant be in by Abatement, and not by Discent, he shall not have his Age; but if the Heir of the Disseisee enter, he shall have his Age, 9 *H.* 4. 5.

Discent. If Tenant in Tail enfeoffs his Issue and dies, the Issue shall have his Age; for he is remitted, and so in by Discent.

If an Infant be enabled by the Custom to sell his Land at a Time certain, as (suppose) at the Age of Fifteen; after this Time, and before his full Age of One and twenty Years, he shall have his full Age, for the Custom doth not extend to this collateral Thing, 11 *H.* 4. 36.

If a Man saith in an Action in which Age lies, That his Ancestor was seized in Fee, and died seized, and this discended to him within Age, and pray his Age; it is a good Plea that his Ancestor died not seized, 29 *Ed.* 3. 6. What shall be a good Counter-plea.

One seized in Fee-simple, makes a Feoffment in Fee to one and Heirs; afterwards he levies a Fine to him and his Heirs; the Conisee dies, and this discends to his Heir within Age. The Heir of the Conisor brings a Writ of *Error* against the Heir of the Conisee, to reverse the Fine, who prays Allowance of his Age. The other Counterpleads, and saith against this, *You ought not to have your Age, because you have a Feoffment made by my Father, to your Father and his Heirs.* This Plea shall not oust him of his Age.

Where the Parole shall demur against all, for the Nonage of one.

If Two are vouched, if the Plea demur for the Nonage of the one, it shall demur for the other also.

So if one Coparcener had Aid of the other within Age, if the Plea demur for the Nonage of the one, it shall demur for both, 9 *H.* 6. 47. 1 *Inst.* 164. *a.*

In *Dum fuit infra Ætatem* by Two Coparceners of the Seisin of their for the Nonage of one of the Demandants, all the Plea shall demur, *Dyer* 137.

If Four enter into Recognizance, and after one dies, his Heir within Age; in a *Scire fac'* againſt the Heir and the others, the Parole ſhall demur againſt all, 29 *Aſſ.* 37.

The Parole ſhall demur for the Nonage of one Coheir upon the Obligation of their Anceſtor, *Mo. p.* 74.

Where the Court ex officio *ſhall grant the Age, although the Party do not pray it.*

Note, If the Parole ought to demur for the Nonage of the Infant; although that the Tenant would anſwer, yet the Court ought to award that the Parole ſhall demur, 6 *Rep.* 5. *a. Marſhal's* Caſe.

Where Parole ſhall demur for the Nonage of the Infant, or not, *Vide Addenda infra.*

CHAP.

CHAP. XIII.

Of Infant Executors and Administrators.

Of the Power of Infant Executor. A Release of an Executor for Principal Money and Interest, Quære, *if a* Devastavit. *The Release of Infant Executor shall not bar him, and why. In what Cases it will bar. Of the Infant's Agreement to a Devise. Infant Executor may Sue by Attorney; but not Defend without a Guardian, and why. In Debt against Infant Executor, he cannot appear by Attorney, but* per *Guardian. Executors, some under Seventeen, and others above; all may join in one Suit, and they may Sue by Attorney. Of Administration* durante minori Ætate: *It is General or Special. This Sort of Administration is not within the Statute of* 21 Hen. 8. *Where and when, and for what Reason, Administration* durante minori Ætate *ceaseth. The Office and Power of an Administrator* durante minori Ætate; *and what Acts done by him shall be good and binding, or not. Not to proceed in any Action after his Authority is determined. How such Administrator may grant Leases: Or such Administratrix gives Bond to Creditors, and then takes Husband, the Husband may retain the Value. Of Actions and Suits brought by and against an Administrator during Minority, with Declarations and Pleadings. Administrator,*

strator; how he shall be named during the Minority of an Executor of an Executor; both must be named in Action brought. If Administrator durante minori Ætate *be Plaintiff, the Nonage of the Executor must be averred:* Aliter *where he is Defendant, and why. Averment that the Executor is under the Age of* 21 *Years, vitiates the Declaration. Trover by Administrator during Minority.* Scire facias *by Executors at full Age, on Recovery by Administrator during Minority. Promise to pay by Administrator during Minority, on Forbearance of Suit, if the Executor were above* 17 *at the Time of the Promise, it's no good Consideration. Prohibition on Agreement pleaded in Account to the Ecclesiastical Court. In Debt, such Administrator pleads Judgment against him by a Stranger, and the Infant was then above* 17 *Years; yet the Bar is good, and the Judgment not void. Pleads, That such a Day the Minor came to* 17, *and after that he refused. How the Law is after the Executor comes to* 17 *Years, in reference to the Administrator* durante minori Ætate. *How such Administrator shall be charged, and the Pleadings thereon. One is in Execution at the Suit of the Administrator* durante minori Ætate, *and then the Executor comes of full Age, how he shall be relieved.* Scire facias *by Executor at full Age, upon Recovery by Administrator during Minority. Administration* durante minori Ætate *is repealed and granted to another, who calls him to Account; yet the Executor may call him to account again. Leases are*

are Assets to pay Debts, notwithstanding the Assent of the Executor, to the Devise of them.

And first, of the Power of Infant Executor, or Administrator.

INfant Executor takes the Principal Money forfeited upon a Bond, and gives a Release; it was argued, Whether the Release was good, because Interest properly is not due at Common Law, and there is no Conscience he should have the Forfeiture. But it was agreed, that this Release shall not bar him, for the entire Sum is due to the Executor: But if he takes all the Money, and makes a Release, it is good; and if the Defendant will have Remedy, he must go into a Court of Equity; but he cannot plead this Release in Bar at Common Law. But it was agreed by Two of the Judges, That such Release by Executor at full Age, upon Receipt of the Principal Money and Interest, shall be only Assets for the Interest and Principal so received, and shall not be a *Devastavit* for the Residue, because he did that in good Conscience which he ought to do, *Cro. Car.* 490. *Kniveton* and *Lathar.*

Release by Infant Executor, for Principal Money and Interest. *Qu.* of a *Devastavit.*

But *Rolls* is more positive in the Report of the Case, 1 *Abr.* 730. If *A.* be bound to *B.* in 100 *l.* for the Payment of 52 *l.* at the End of Half a Year, and after *B.* dies, making Three Executors; and after the Obligation is forfeit, one of the Executors comes to 18 Years of Age, and then accepts the 52 *l.* in full Satisfaction of the Obligation, and makes a Release of the said Obligation; yet this doth not release the Obligation, for that the Release is made by an Infant, and by the Forfeiture of the 100 *l.* it was a Debt of the Inteftate, and the 52 *l.* may not be in Satisfaction of the 100 *l.* and in Equity there may be good Cause to take the Forfeiture; and in an Action of *Debt* against Executor, he may plead a Judgment upon an Obligation forfeit in Bar, *Ultra quæ* he had not Assets, which shews that the Sum forfeited is the Debt, and Infant Executor may not release the Debt of the Testator without Satisfaction.

The Reason why the Release of Infant Executor shall not bar him.

Now the Reasons why the Release of an Infant Executor shall not bar him, are Two:

1. Because if it should bar him, it should be a *Devastavit*, and charge him of his own proper Goods.

2. It would be a *Tort*, which the Infant may not do by his Release; but all Things else which he doth, according to the Office and Duty of an Executor, shall bind him; and therefore he may give a Discharge for so much as he receives.

In what Cases it will bar him.

And the Book of 16 *H.* 6. *Release* 45. is to be understood, when the Infant receives full Satisfaction; So that for his Release there must be a true Consideration.

Per

Per Cur. All Things which an Infant Executor doth according to the Office and Duty of an Executor, ſhall bind him, 5 *Rep. Ruſſel's* Caſe, 27. *b.* Upon Payment or Satisfaction to the Infant Executor, he may acquit and diſcharge the Debtor for ſo much as he receives, *Ibid.* 1 *Inſt.* 172. *a.* And therefore, 16 *H.* 6. *Releaſe* 45. Releaſe by Infant Executor, as Executor, is good, and he ſhall not avoid it. *Per Cur.* Shall be intended where the Infant, as Executor, receives full Satisfaction; for he doth not act as Executor, if he receives little or nothing.

But if one indebted to the Teſtator by ſingle Bill, if Infant Executor receive the Money, and make an Acquittance, the Acquittance is good, *quia eſt de Neceſſitate,* otherwiſe the Obligee is not bound to pay the ſame, 1 *And.* 177.

It was ſaid to be adjudged in the Caſe of one *Manning,* That where Infant Executor ſold the Goods of his Teſtator for a leſſer Price than they were worth, and afterwards brought Action of *Detinue* againſt the Vendee *in Retardatione Executionis Teſtamenti,* that the Sale was good, and ſhould bind the Executor, notwithſtanding his Nonage, 4 *Leon. p.* 210. *Sed quære,* 3 *Leon. p.* 143.

The Agreement of an Infant Executor, That the Deviſee ſhall take the Thing deviſed to him by Will, is not good, 5 *Rep.* 29. *b.* The Infant's Agreement to a Deviſe.

If Infant Adminiſtrator, being above 17 Years of Age, by Aſſent of his Friends, ſells a Leaſe for Years, which he had of Land as

Administrator to another, to the Intent to pay the Debts of the Inteſtate, and to diſcharge Debts which were for the Infant himſelf, Apparel or Diet, this ſhall bind the Infant.

Infant Executor may ſue by Attorney, but not defend without a Guardian, and why.

It hath been much queſtioned, Whether Infant Executor ſhall ſue by Attorney? But it was reſolved in *Foxwiſt* and *Tremain's* Caſe, That Infant Executor, after 17 Years of Age, may ſue by Attorney, but not defend without a Guardian, *Sid.* 449. *Foxwiſt* and *Tremain*.

(So it was adjudged in *Cro. Jac.* 441. *Cotton* and *Weſtcot.*)

For in ſuch Caſe the Executor, Plaintiff, cannot draw any Loſs upon himſelf. But *Twiſden contra*, That he cannot ſue by Attorney, becauſe, Firſt, he cannot make a Letter of Attorney. This ſeems to be a good Law Reaſon: And by him it hath been adjudged, that he ought to ſue by Guardian, 1 *Ventr.* 54.

His ſecond Reaſon was, He may be injured by the Attorney's Plea, and cannot remedy himſelf, as he may do againſt his Guardian.

As, if in Debt the Defendant pleads a Releaſe, and the Attorney confeſſeth it, and if the Adminiſtrator be above 17, yet he ought to ſue *per Gardianum*; for tho' by the Civil Law he is able to undertake the Adminiſtration, yet the Manner of his Suing is to be determined by our Law, and that cannot be by Attorney till the Age of 21, *Mich.* 1649. *Colt* and *Skeward*.

When

When Infant is made Defendant, he must appear by Guardian, not by Attorney, for he hath not Capacity to chuse one; the Appearance by Guardian is the Act of the Court. When he is Plaintiff, he may sue by *Prochein amy*, 3 *Mod.* 236.

If he is Administrator, he may bring Action of Debt *per Attornat'*, because he sueth in the Right of another, 3 *Mod.* 248.

And if one Executor be 17 Years of Age, and the other Executor within 17, both may join in one Suit: Or if one be of full Age, and the other under 17, they may join in one Suit, because both are Executors *quoad esse*, tho' not *quoad Executionem*, 2 *Saund.* 212. Executors, some under 17, and others above, may all join in one Suit.

But this Case is more fully reported in *Saunders*; which is,

Four Infant Executors bring an Action of the Case upon an *Assumpsit*; the Defendant pleads in Abatement, that two of the Plaintiffs are within the Age of 17 Years, (*viz.*) of 13 Years, and no more. The Plaintiff demurs.

It was Resolved,

(1.) That the Action was well brought in the Name of all; which the Resolution in *Hutton* and *Mascew*'s Case seems to favour: Which was,

Scire facias was brought by one Executor upon a Judgment obtained by the Testator. The Defendant pleads in Abatement, That there was another Executor in full Life, not named in the Writ. The Plaintiff replies,

This

This other Executor was within the Age of 17 Years: And upon Demurrer, it was ruled in the *Exchequer-Chamber*, That the Action was well brought by one Executor only, without naming the other, who was within the Age of 17 Years, *Mich.* 15 *Car.* 2. *B. R. Hutton* and *Mascew*, 1 *Keb.* 750.

This Case of *Hutton* and *Mascew* is reported in *Raym. p.* 198. and agreed, That where one makes his Executors, some of full Age, and one within Age, that the Action might be brought by all the Executors jointly, because they make but one Person as it were, and all represent the Testator jointly. Or it may be brought as in *Hutton* and *Mascew*'s Case, the Executors of full Age may sue without the Infant, and adjudged, *quod Def. respond. ouster*, *Raym. p.* 198.

And they may sue by Attorney.

(2.) It was Resolved, They may sue by Attorney, and the Executors of full Age may make Attorney for those within Age: And *Stat.* 24 *Jac. c.* 13. aids the Defect, if Infant, sole Executor, sue by Attorney; and in the principal Case, the Plea being in Abatement, a *Respondeas ouster* was awarded, So that these two Points are now settled.

The Nature of an Administrator durante minori Ætate.

If one under the Age of 17 Years be made an Executor, the Ordinary shall grant Administration

niſtration to another during his Minority; but if the Infant Executor be 17 Years of Age, or above, ſuch Adminiſtration committed by the Ordinary is void, 5 *Rep. Pigot*'s Caſe.

But ſuch Adminiſtration is granted, either

It is General or Special.

{ Generally, or Specially.

And that granted Specially runs thus:

—— **Ad Opus, Commodum & Utilitatem Executoris durante minori Ætate, & non aliter, nec alio Modo.**

The Form of a Special Adminiſtration, *durante minori Ætate.*

And the Obſervation of this Diverſity will be of Uſe, as you may ſee by ſome Caſes following.

As to the Nature of an Adminiſtration *durante minori Ætate*, it's a Truſt, and ſomething more, as you may ſee *infra*, *Tit. His Office and Power.*

This Administration, during the Minority of an Executor, is not within the Statute of 21 *H.* 8. to be granted of Neceſſity to the Widow of the Teſtator, becauſe there is an Executor.

This Adminiſtration *durante minori Ætate*, not within the Statute of 21 *H.* 8.

And ſo this Adminiſtation differs from another Adminiſtration, which the Ordinary is bound to grant upon Pain of 10 *l.* to the *Feme*, *Hob.* 250. *Briers* and *Goddard*, 1 *Roll. Abr.* 18, 21.

When

When and for what Reason Administration durante minori Ætate *ceaseth.*

This Administration shall continue but to Infants Age of 17 Years; and if there are three Executors, and one is of full Age, no Administration *durante minori Ætate* can be granted; and if four Executors are made under Age, and one comes to 17 Years, the Administration *durante minori Ætate* is determined. So if Executrix, under 17, takes an Husband of 17, it ceaseth; and so if he be of full Age, for the Husband may administer as Executor.

And the Court *ex officio* ought to take Notice, if the Age appear in Pleading, 1 *Leon.* 74. 5 *Rep.* 29. *Prince*'s Case, *Cro. Car.* 210. *Wells*'s Case.

The Office and Power of an Administrator, dur' minori Ætate, *and what Acts done by him shall be good and binding, or not.*

Generally an Administrator *dur' minori Ætate* cannot do any Act to the Prejudice of an Infant, but may sell Goods, pay Debts, and do all Things as an Executor may. But he cannot sell any of the Goods of the Deceased, unless it be for Payment of Debts, or *bona peritura*: Also he cannot assent to a Legacy, unless there be Assets to pay Debts; but this is to be understood where it is granted Specially, 5 *Rep.* 29. *Prince*'s Case.

Now

Now whether Administrator *dur' minori Ætate* may grant Leases, and in what Cases he may, and in what not, the third Resolution in Sir *Moyl Finche's* Case will inform us. When the Administration is not committed Specially, but Generally without any Restraint or Limitation, there the Administrator during *minori Ætate* may grant Leases. As a Man having a Lease for 50 Years expectant upon a Lease for Life, dies, his Executor being of the Age of 3 Years, and after Administration is committed to one during the Minority of the Executor, who make a Lease for 10 Years, this Lease is good. But when Administration is committed Specially, he cannot grant such *Interesse termini*, 6 *Rep.* 67. *b.* Sir *Moyl Finche's* Case. How such Administrator may grant Leases.

Administratrix *durante minori Ætate* of the Daughter Executrix made divers Obligations to the Creditors of the Testator, and after took Husband. *Per Cur'*, So much of the Testators as amounted to the Value of the Debts paid and undertaken by the Wife, the Husband may retain them as his own. Administratrix gives Bonds to Creditors, and then takes Husband, the Husband may retain the Value.

Quær. if the Wife die, for then the Husband is no longer chargeable by her Bond, *Hob.* 250. *Briers* and *Goddard*.

A. enfeoffs *B* on Condition that if he pay 10 *l.* to the Feoffee his Executors, and assigns within three Years next ensuing, that then, *&c.* Feoffee hath three Sons whom he makes Executors, and dieth before Payment; the Ordinary commits Administration to *J. S.* during the Minority of the Executors. By *Dyer*, It is the surest Way for *A.* to pay the Money Of Payment of Mortgage Money to him.

Money to the Executors, and he shall be accountable to them, and if the Money be paid to one of the Executors it is sufficient; 4 *Leon. p.* 100.

Of Actions and Suits brought by and against an Administrator during Minority, and Declarations.

It was the Opinion of some, That Administrator *durante minori Ætate*, in our Law cannot sue or be sued, because he is rather a Bailiff to the Infant than an Administrator; but this is a Fancy, *Godb.* 30. 104. *Owen* 35.

The Writ is brought by the Plaintiff as an absolute and compleat Administrator, and by the Court it appears that he is but a qualified and limited Administrator; this seems to be a material Variance, 1 *Lut.* 343.

Administrator during the Minority of an Executor, how he shall be named.

Administrator during the Minority of an Executor, shall be named Administrator of the Goods of *T. C.* during the Minority of *M.* Executor of the said *T. C.* late Executor of *E. C.* and shall not be named Administrator of the Goods of *E. C.* not administred by *T. C.* But had the Infant been Defendant, he should have been named but Executor of the Executor, for the rest follows, but the committing Administration is of both, *Hob.* 246. *Morton's* Case.

Administrator during the Minority of an Infant Executor, both must be named in Actions brought.

B. made his Wife, and *J.* his Son being one Year old, Executors, and the Wife only proved the Will; yet she cannot bring an Action

Action without naming the other Executor, and if he be not named, the Bill shall abate; and altho' the Mother had Administration during the Minority of the Infant, yet the Infant ought to be named, for they are both Executors, and his being named affirms him to be Executor, 1 *Brownl.* 101. *Smith's* Case, *Yelv.* 130. *Mesme* Case cited, 2 *Sanders* 213.

W. brought Debt as Administrator *omnium Bonorum*, &c. of *A. E.* during the Minority of *J.* Executor of the said *A. E.* Executor of *R. E.* By this Administration he cannot meddle with the Goods of the first Testator, and so the Action lies not, *Limner and Every.*

If Administrator *dur' minori Ætate* be Plaintiff, the Nonage of the Executor must be averred; *Aliter* where he is Defendant, and why.

But if Administrator *durante minoritate*, and doth not aver that the Infant is within the Age of 21, if the Defendant doth plead in Bar, the Count is made good by this, *Lut.* 632.

If Administrator *durante minori Ætate* be Plaintiff, the Nonage of the Executor must be averred, *i. e.* that he is within 17 Years of Age, for he is to take Cognizance how long his Authority shall continue, and he ought to shew it to enable himself to the Action. (*Quær.* if not aided after a Verdict.) *Secus* if he be Defendant, for in an Action against Administrator *durante minori Ætate* of an Executor, he needs not aver the Executor was still within the Age of 17 Years.

1. Because the Plaintiff is a Stranger to the Power given to the Defendant, and he cannot be Conisant of what Age the Infant is.

2. Be-

2. Because the Defendant (in *Croft*'s Case) had joined Issue, by which he admitted that his Power continues. And so long as the other continues his meddling he shall be sued. And the Plaintiffs are not to take Conisance of the Age of the other, as where Jointenancy is pleaded on the Part of the Plaintiff, the Defendant need not shew how; but if he plead it on his own Part, he ought to shew in particular how; and here if his Authority were determined, it should be shewn on the Defendants Part, 1 *Rolls Rep.* 400. *Hob.* 251. *Carver* and *Hasebrig. Yelv.* 128. *Crofts* and *Walbanck.* 5 *Rep. Pigots*, 2 *Rolls Rep.* 466. *b. Cr. Jac.* 590. *Walthall* and *Ald.*

Regular in Pleading.

An Action was brought against the Defendant as Administrator during the Minority of *J. S.* and the Plaintiff shews in his Count, that the said *J. S.* at the time of the Writ brought, was and yet is under the Age of 21 Years, and Verdict *pro Quer.* But Judgment was arrested, for the Declaration was insufficient, because the Administration ceaseth at seventeen; so that he may be eighteen, nineteen or twenty Years of Age, and yet the Administration ceaseth, and so doth the Action against such Administrator according to the Resolution in *Pigot*'s Case, 2 *Brownl.* 247, 248. *Brownhead* and *Spencer*.

Averment, that the Executor is under the Age of 21, vitiates the Declaration.

Administration granted during the Minority of Infant, till he come to 21.

Administration granted to one during the absence of another, good in Law.

If an Administrator *durante minori Ætate* of the Estate of an Infant Executor hath

Not to proceed in any Action after his Authority is determined.

Judgment, and after the Executor comes of full Age, he ſhall have *Scire fac'* to execute the Judgment. Adminiſtrator ſhall not proceed in any Action after his Authority is determined, *Lut.* 342. *Major* verſus *Peck.*

Trover by Adminiſtrator *dur'. minori ætate.*

Adminiſtrator *durante minori ætate* may have Action of Trover of the Goods of the Teſtator, for he had more than the bare Cuſtody of them, for he had the Property it ſelf, 1 *Roll. Abr.* 911. *Seth* and *Seth.*

Declaration is during the Minority of 3, and on the *Profert, &c.* it appears to be of 4, and Verdict *pro Quer.* *Quære.*

An Action of the Caſe was brought by one as Adminiſtrator during the Minority of three, where it was of four; and the Plaintiff declares as Adminiſtrator during the Minority of three, and upon *Profert in Curia Literas Adminiſtrationis* it appears, that it was committed during the Minority of four, and Iſſue was taken upon Collateral Matter and found for the Plaintiff; and it did not appear, whether he was within the Age of ſeventeen, or above. And whether this were good after a Verdict, the Court was divided, in *Bennet* and *Maude*'s Caſe.

Scire fac' by Executor at full Age on Recovery by Adminiſtrator during Minority.

Adminiſtration is granted to one Executor during the Minority of another, and he in his own Name brings a *Scire fac'* againſt the Defendant, on Recovery in *Scire fac'* had by the Teſtator as Executor of *A.* who recovered againſt him; this is good, and ſo adjudged for the Plaintiff on Demurrer of the Defendant to the *Scire fac'*. And it's agreed, in 2 *Leon. p.* 278. *pl.* 36. *Knight*'s Caſe, That if an Adminiſtrator during Minority recover, the Executors at full Age may have a *Scire fac'* thereupon, *Tr.* 16 *Car.* 2. *B. R.*

Hutton and *Mascue.* 2 *Leon.* *p.* 278. *Knight's* Case.

Promise to pay by Administrator *dur' minori ætate*, on Forbearance of Suit, if the Executor were about 17 at the Time of the Promise, it's no good Consideration.

Now the Cognizance of this Administration ceasing at 17, appears in *Dumport's* Case. Action on *Assumpsit* was brought against the Administrator *durante minori ætate* upon a Promise to pay upon Forbearance of Suit, *&c.* The Defendant pleads, That the Executor was above 17 Years of Age at the Time of the Promise made, for that it being then ceased, it is no good Consideration, and so adjudged a good Bar, 1 *Rolls Abr.* 910. *Cro. Car.* 14 *Car.* 2. *Dumport* and *Pinser.*

Of Pleading by Administrator durante minori Ætate, *in Actions brought against him, what is good or not.*

It is taken for a Rule in 1 *Roll. Abr.* 910. If Administration be granted to *A.* *durante minori ætate* of *B.* if it appear to the Court in Pleading, that *B.* was of the Age of 16 Years, the Court *ex Officio* ought to take notice of the Ecclesiastical Law, that the Administration is determined and void, 1 *Rolls Abr.* 910.

Executor of the Infant calls the Administrator, *dur' minori ætate*, to account in the Ecclesiastical Court. Prohibition granted on Agreement pleaded.

C. is Administrator *durante minori ætate.* The Infant dies, and makes the Wife of *B.* Executrix, the Executrix calls C. to account in the *Ecclesiastical Court.* C. pleads Agreement with the Husband of *A.* and that he gave 80 *l.* in Satisfaction of all Accounts, and a Prohibition was granted, *Hetly p.* 18. *Creedland's* Case.

In

In Action of Debt against the Administrator, if the Defendant pleads a Bar, a Judgment may be had against him by an Estranger upon an Obligation, and in the Record he is named Administrator *durante minori Ætate* of *J. S.* who was then within the Age of 18 or 20 Years: This is a good Bar of the Action; for though the full Age of such Infant Executor is 17, if an Action was brought against the Administrator after, and this Age of the Infant appears to be passed, yet if Judgment be given against the Administrator it is not void, *Tr.* 14 *Car.* 1. *B. R. Good* and *Pinsent.* In Debt, Administrator *dur' minori ætate* pleads Judgment against him by a Stranger, and the Infant was then above 17 Years of Age, the Bar is good, and the Judgment not void.

The Defendant Administrator *durante minori ætate* pleads *plene Administravit*; it was found he had paid 1400 *l.* in Discharge of Debts and Legacies, and had accounted with the Infant Executor when he came of full Age, and that upon 91 *l.* paid to the Infant he released all Actions. *Quære*, if it is a good Administration, *Vide Creedland*'s Case *supra. Mod. Rep.* 174. *Brooking* and *Jennings.* Account with the Infant, and Release found, on *plene Administravit* pleaded

Scire fac' was brought upon a Judgment against an Administratrix *durante minori ætate*; she pleads, that such a Day the *Minor* came to 17 Years of Age, and after that she refused, and Administration was granted to another. The Plaintiff replies, *Quod devastavit*, *Hetly* 35. *Margery Rivet*'s Case. Pleads, that such a Day the *Minor* came to 17, and after he refused, *&c.*

In Debt as Executor, the Defendant pleads, That the Testator made C. and another Infant Executors, and that after his Death, and before the Action, the Administration was committed to *H. C.* during the Demands Judgment *de brevi*, where ill.

 Minority

Minority of the Executors, and that he administred, and demanded Judgment of the Writ. And the Bar was held to be ill, in demanding Judgment of the Writ, 3 *Keb.* 202. *Kellar* and *Weſtcom.*

In *Anderſon*'s Time, in 1 *Anderſon p.* 34. when the Infant comes to Age and proves the Will; the Queſtion was, What Remedy he ſhall have againſt the Adminiſtrator for the Goods. *Per Cur.* He cannot have an Action of Account, but *Detinue* for the Goods, or ſue for them in *Court Chriſtian.* 1 *Anderſon* 34.

Prerogative. But Prerogative may ſomewhat alter the Caſe of Pleading, as it was in *Scaccario, Miller* and *Gore*'s Caſe, cited in *Godb.* 104. The Infant pleaded in a *Scire fac'* upon Aſſignment of a Bond to the Queen, that *S.* and *E.* were Adminiſtrators during his Minority. And *per Cur.* it is no Plea, but he ought to anſwer as Executor.

How the Law is after the Executor comes to 17 Years of Age, in reference to the Adminiſtrator during his Minority, and how ſuch Adminiſtrator ſhall be charged, and the Pleadings thereon.

It hath been a great Queſtion in our Books, If the Executor or Adminiſtrator, *durante minori ætate,* continue the Poſſeſſion of the Goods after the full Age of the Executor, or waſt them, how he ſhall be charged? And there are three ſeveral Opinions:

1. Some held, That he may be ſued as Executor

cutor *de son Tort*; but this was denied by others, because he comes to the Goods lawfully.

2. Others hold, That he may be sued as Executor *durante minori ætate*, (as a Sheriff may be sued after the Delivery over of the Prisoners, for Money received on a *Fieri facias* executed, or for not delivering over his Prisoners that he hath in Execution to the next Sheriff,) because an Estranger cannot know the Age of the rightful Executor; and the only notorious Act for Discovery of this is, the ceasing of the Administrator, *durante minori ætate*, to intermeddle. Of this Opinion was *Hobart* 265. and *Windham* Justice agreed to it, That it was the fittest Way to charge him as Administrator *durante minori ætate* continuing, in *Lawson* and *Croft*'s Case.

3. But most held, That he may be charged upon the especial Matter disclosed.

The Case was: Debt was brought against the Defendant *durante minori ætate* of the Executor. He pleads, That such a Day the Infant came to the Age of 17 Years, and that after he did not take Administration. The Plea, by *Allen*, is not good, for if he did administer the Day the Plaintiff came of Age, he shall be charged: But how he shall be charged was the Question, and how the Creditor should be relieved; for the Goods never came to the new Executor's Hands, tho' perhaps he may have an Action against the former Executor for so much as he did wast; and against the Vendees he can have no Remedy, or elſe the Adminiſtrator may remain Adminiſtrator ſtill for that Purpoſe, the Executor being none in effect for thoſe Goods: But the beſt Opinion is, That he ſhall be charged eſpecially. But all agreed, that he muſt plead fully Adminiſtred. And by *Twiſden*, this Plea which here he pleaded ſhould have been pleaded in Abatement, and not after Imparlance, *Sid.* 157. 1 *Keb.* 157, 158. *Lawſon* and *Croft*.

Plene Administravit pleaded.

Adminiſtration was committed to one during the Minority of the Executor, who waſted the Goods of the Teſtator, and after the Executor attained the Age of 17 Years, and an Action of Debt was brought againſt the Executor. And the Opinion of the Court was prayed, whether he may plead *unques Executor*, or excuſe himſelf by pleading the ſpecial Matter; but the Court agreed, That it is moſt ſafe to plead the ſpecial Matter, 1 *Brownl.* 80.

The Jury found the Adminiſtrator *durante minori ætate*, after the Executors were of full Age, had in his Hands 4000 *l.* Aſſets, to which Adminiſtrator, the Executors at their full Age did releaſe all Demands. *Per Cur.* This Releaſe is Aſſets in the Hands of the Executors, 4 *Leon. p.* 402. *Knightley*'s Caſe.

One is in Execution at the Suit of Adminiſtrator during Minority, and then the Executor come of full Age, how he ſhall be relieved.

A. Adminiſtrator *durante minori ætate*, brought Debt againſt the Debtor and recovered, and had him in Execution, and now the Infant Executor comes of Age: It hath been a Queſtion, How the Party ſhall be diſcharged, in *Godb.* 104. *pl.* 122. for the

Authority

Authority of the Administrator is now determined, and he cannot acknowledge Satisfaction, nor make an Acquittance, and the Executor is not Party to the Record, and he cannot sue Execution; yet the Recovery and Judgment stand in Force. It may be relieved by *Audita Querela*, and in 2 *Brownl.* 83. it was the Opinion of the Court, that the Executor may sue a special *Scire fac'* upon the Record, and so sue Execution in his own Name, 27 *H.* 7. 8. *a.* And so it was resolved in *Wright*'s Case, 1 *Rolls Abr.* 888, 889. If Administrator *durante minori ætate* of an Executor recover in Debt, and after the Executor comes to full Age, he shall have a *Scire fac'* upon this Recovery, for that he is privy to the Judgment, *M.* 9 *Jac. B. R.* 1 *Rolls Abr.* 888. *Wright*'s Case.

Scire fac' by Executor upon Recovery by Administrator during Minority.

Administration *durante minori ætate* is repealed, and another is made Administrator during Minority, and the second Administrator draws the first Administrator to Account, and gives him a Release; yet the Infant at his full Age may compel the first Administrator to account again, 1 *Rolls Abr.* 910.

Account or Detinue.

Administration is committed *durante minori ætate*, Infant comes of full Age and proves the Will: It's said, the Infant shall not have an Action of Account for the Goods but *Detinue*, or he may sue in the Court of the Ordinary, *Bendl.* 101. 1 *Anderson* 34.

Thomas Chamberlaine possess'd of Leases of 3000 *l.* Yearly, and owing several great Debts, made his Will, and made his Wife Executrix, who paid the Debts as far as the Chattels Personal and Stock would reach, and no further, and there being Debts unpaid above the Value of the Leases, she assents to a Bequest of the said Leases by the Will, *viz.* to *Elizabeth* his Wife for her Life, and afterwards in Remainder to another; after which Assent she dies, and leaves Mr. *Crofts* her Executor, who articled with the Plaintiff to sell the Leases for 900 *l.* *Qu.* was, Whether Debts being unpaid at the Time of the said Assent, and nothing liable to make good the said Debts saving the said Leases, the Leases might be Assets in the Hands of Mr. *Crofts*, so that he might sell them to answer the said Debts, notwithstanding the said Assent; or whether the said Bequest of the Leases were vested in the Remainder by the Assent, and could not be divested of the Sale of the said *Crofts* the Executor? And it was Decreed, That the said Leases should be Assets to pay the Debts, notwithstanding the Assent. So if an Infant Executor assent, it's no good Assent if there be not other Assets for Debts, which the Common Law provides for the Security of Creditors, much more shall this Court provide for them. 1 *Cases in Chancery* 256. *Chamberlaine*'s Case.

Leases for Assets to pay Debts, notwithstanding the Assent of the Executor to the Devise of them.

CHAP.

CHAP. XIV.
Of Devises.

The Determination, at what Age one may make his Testament of Goods, belongs to the Ecclesiastical Law. By our Law, Infant at 18 Years of Age may make his Will of Goods and Chattels. New Publication at full Age of a Will made under Age, good. Devise of Lands by an Infant to Charitable Uses, good. Devises to Children unpreferred, how to be construed. Possibility. Where a second Husband shall have the Estate or Profits devised to a Feme, till the Son come to Age. Where there needs no Admittance to a Copyhold Estate. Legacy to a Woman at 21 Years, or Day of Marriage, and she died before either, the Executor shall have it; aliter *if the Money were bequeathed to one at the Age of 21 Years. How the Civil Law is in such Cases. Diversity at Common Law, where the Executor of an Infant dying before the Time of Payment of a Legacy shall have it or not. Portions to be paid on Condition of Marriage within 16, or without Consent,* &c. *to be void. Pleading to the Condition of a Bond for the Payment of Portions. Administrator of a Legatee, who died before Contingency happened, had the Money. Maintenance and Education not discounted out of a Child's Portion in Equity.*

THE next Thing that falls under Consideration is, The Construction of Law upon Devises, and Legacies to Children and Infants,

Infants, which is one of the most material Parts of this Treatise. But first, I shall shew what Wills, Devises and Legacies, made or given by Infant, shall be good or not.

The Determination, at what Age one may make his Testament of Goods, belongs to the Ecclesiastical Law.

In the Case of the Chancellor of *Litchfield*, Prohibition was prayed to the Consistory Court of *Litchfield*, because a Testament of of Goods made by one but of 16 Years old, being there exhibited, was admitted, and Proceedings and Sentence given for the Testament; but it was denied; for the Cause was proper for the Spiritual Jurisdiction, and the Determination, at what Age one may make his Testament of his Goods belongs to them. And the Inferior Court, having given Sentence against their Law, the Party may appeal, Sir *Thomas Jones p.* 210. 1 *Inst.* 89. *b.*

And in *Smallwood* and *Brickhouse*'s Case, the Suggestion was, That *B.* being under the Age of 16 Years had made a Will, and the Prerogative Court proceeded to the Proof of it, whereas by the Common Law a Person is not capable till 17 Years. But Prohibition was denied before the Proof of Wills, and the Validity of them doth belong to the Ecclesiastical Court, 2 *Mod.* 315.

Infant at 18 Years may make a Will of Goods and Chattels. New publication at full Age, and of a Will made under Age.

But it's settled in our Law, That an Infant of the Age of 18 Years may make a Will, and constitute Executors for his Goods and Chattels, but he cannot thereby dispose of Lands until the Age of 21 Years. Now put the Case, that an Infant makes his Will of Lands under the Age of 21 Years, and dies at full Age without a new Publication, this Will

Will is void; but if he make a new Publication of it at full Age, it is good; but then such Publication must be guided by the Statutes of Fraudes and Perjuries, and be so qualified as is required by that Statute, or else it will not be good in Law. So if a new Publication of it be made the same Day he comes of full Age, and which Day is the Day of his Death (as it was in *Herbert*'s Case) it is good; and so a Will made the Day he comes of Age, is good, 1 *Inst.* 89. *b. Sid.* 102. *Herbert* and *Turbal*.

An Infant makes a Will, and signs and seals it in the Presence of three Witnesses, who sign it in his Presence as the Statute directs, afterwards he comes of full Age, and being sick, sends for his Will, and in the Presence of three Witnesses declares this to be his Will, and adjudged a void Will, for it was void in its Creation, and could not be made good by any future Publication.

A Devise of Lands, tho' it be void in it self, yet shall bind an Infant to Charitable Uses, as was in *Collison*'s Case. The Case was:

Devise of Lands to Charitable Uses by an Infant.

Collison devised an House in *Kent* to *L.* his Wife for Life, and after her Death made *J. B.* and others Feoffees (as he called them) of the said House, to keep the same in Reparation, and to bestow the rest of the Profits in the Reparations of the Highways. *Collison* and his Wife are dead, and the Land descended to an Infant.

This

This Caſe was in *Chancery*, between the Pariſhioners and *R.* the Infant, and it was referred to *Hobart* and *Tanfield*; and they reſolved clearly, That it was within the Relief of the Statute of 43 *Eliz.* for tho' the Deviſe were utterly void, yet it was within the Words [*Limited and appointed to Charitable Uſes.*]

Aliter, If he were an Infant Lunatick or the like that gave it, or where one appointed that which was not his own, *Hob.* 136. *Colliſon*'s Caſe.

By the Statute of 12 *Car.* 2. *c.* 24. the Father under 21 Years may deviſe the Cuſtody and Poſſeſſion of his Child. *Vide ſupra*, Tit. *Guardian.*

Now as to Deviſes of Lands and Legacies, and Profit to Children, and at what Time the ſame ſhall take Effect, and what Conſtructions the Law makes thereupon, the Reſolutions following will give ample Direction for your better underſtanding of Caſes of that or the like Nature.

Of a Deviſe to an Infant in *Ventre ſa mere*, *Vide ſupra* at large, *Cap.* 1.

What is a Deviſe of two ſeveral Rents, and not a joint Rent.

A Man deviſeth a Rent-charge of 20 *l. per Annum* to his Wife and his Son for their Lives, and for the Life of the longer Liver of them; and that after his Son ſhall attain his Age of 13 Years, he ſhall have 20 *l. per Annum* of his Rent *pro meliori manutenentia ſua*, during the Life of his Wife; this is an entire Deviſe of the 50 *l. per Annum* to the Wife, until the Son ſhall attain that Age, and after

after they are two ſeveral Rents, and not a joint Rent, 2 *Sand.* 283, 284.

A Man makes his Will thus:

I bequeath to my Wife the Leaſe of my Houſe during her Life; and after her Death, I will it ſhall go amongſt my Children unpreferr'd. Deviſe to Children unpreferr'd.

It was ſaid by ſome, That here is neither Poſſibility or Remainder in any Perſon certain; and therefore they concluded, that the Term was wholly in the Wiſe. But *per Cur.* in this Caſe the Poſſibility ſhall riſe well enough by the Death of the Wife, to the Daughter unpreferr'd. Poſſibility.

And ſo it was reſolved in *Amner* and *Lodington*'s Caſe; That a Man poſſeſſed of a Term deviſeth it to *B.* his Wife for Life, and after her Death to his Children unpreferred, and after *B.* dies, *C.* being then the ſole Daughter of *A.* ſhall have it; for an Executory Deviſe, which had a Dependance on the firſt Deviſe, may be made to a Perſon uncertain. For it was uncertain, whether the Daughter ſhould have this as long as *B.* lived, or whether ſhe might have been advanced in the Life of *B.* 1 *Roll. Abr.* 612. *Amner* and *Lodington*'s Caſe.

Now where a ſecond Husband ſhall have the Eſtate or Profits deviſed to a *Feme* Legatee, or not, we are to obſerve theſe Differences: Where a ſecond Husband ſhall have the Eſtate or Profits to a *Feme* Legatee, till the Son came to Age.

Deviſe to a *Feme*, and that ſhe ſhall take the Profits until the Son comes of Age to maintain and bring him up; her ſecond Husband

Husband surviving her shall not take the Profits; for that nothing is devised to the Wife, but a Confidence, which by her Death is determined.

Diversity. *Aliter*, Had he devised the Profits of the Land to the Wife till the Age of the Infant, to educate him, *&c.* the same had amounted to the Devise of the Land it self, and so a Chattel in the Wife, and consequently the surviving Husband shall have it, 2 *Leon.* 221.

So is 1 *Brownl.* 79. One seised in Fee, made his Will thus:

Item, I Will that my Wife and Executrix shall have the Education of my Daughter, with the Portion of Money and Profits of my Land to her own Use until my Daughters Age of 18 Years; Provided she pay the Out-Rent, and keep her Daughter at School.

The Devisor died; the Wife married one *P.* and performed the Condition, and afterward died; and Judgment was given, That it was a Term, and the Husband shall have it.

Regula. For if an Infant be devised, it vests in the Wife as a Chattel; as was *Dedicot's* Case.

Certain Customary-Lands were surrendred into the Hands of the Lord, to the Intent that the Lord should grant the same *de novo* to *Dedicot* for Life, and afterwards to *Jane* his Wife, during the Nonage of the Son and Heir of *Dedicot*. *Dedicot* died before any New Grant; afterwards the Lord granted

granted the Land to the Wife during the Nonage of the said Heir, the Remainder to the Heir in Tail, the Heir at that Time being of five Years of Age; so as the said Wife, by Force of the said Surrender and Admittance, was to have the Land for 16 Years; the Wife took another Husband and died, the Husband shall have the Land during the Nonage of the Infant, and that without any Admittance: For the Wife had the said Estate to her own Use, then the Husband surviving her, he shall have it; and he comes not in as of any new Estate, but as of the Estate of his Wife as Assignee, 1 *Brown*. 79. *Balder* and *Blackborn*.

Where there needs no Admittance to a Copyhold-Estate.

Where one bequeathed a Sum of Money to a Woman at her Age of 21 Years, or Day of Marriage, to be paid her with Interest, and she died before either, the Money shall go to the Executor; and so it was decreed by my Lord Chancellor *Finch*. But he said, If Money were bequeathed to one at the Age of 21 Years, if he dies before that Age, the Money is lost. On the other Side, if the Party die before, it shall go to the Executor, 2 *Ventr*. 342. *Cloberry*'s Case.

Legacy to a Woman at 21 Years or Day of Marriage, and she died before either, the Executor shall have it.

Aliter, if the Money were bequeathed to one at the Age of 21 Years.

It was said in my Lady *Lodge*'s Case, by Dr. *Awbrey*, Dr. of Civil Law, that in their Law, *If a Legacy be given to an Infant, to be paid when he shall come to the Age of 21 Years, if such a Legatory die before such Age, yet the Executor or Administrator of such Legatory shall sue for the said Legacy presently, and shall not expect until the Time in which if the Infant had continued in

* How the Civil Law is in such cases.

in Life he had attained his full Age. But *aliter* in our Law. Lady *Lodge*'s Case, 1 *Leon.* 274.

And the Difference stands thus:

Diversity, where the Executor of the Infant dying before the Time limited for Payment of a Legacy, shall have it or not.

If one gives to *J. S.* 20 *l.* when he comes to 21 Years of Age, or when he shall be married; and he dies before, and makes Executor, his Executor shall not have the Legacy.

But if it be thus:

I give to *J. S.* 20 *l.* and I will that it be paid him at the Age of 21 Years; his Executors shall recover the Legacy.

Or if it be:

I give to *J. S.* 20 *l.* toward his Marriage, and he dies before, his Executors shall have the Legacy, and may recover it in Court, *Godb.* 182, 183. *Brownl.* 32. 2 *Bulstr.* 126.

Portions to be paid to the Children, as they are named in order.

A Man deviseth One hundred Pounds to his youngest Daughter, One hundred Pounds to his middle Daughter, and One hundred Pounds to his eldest Daughter, and that all these Sums shall be levied out of the Profits of his Lands. *Per Cur.* The youngest Daughter shall be first paid, and then the middle, and then the eldest, *Conyer*'s Case, cited 3 *Leon. p.* 55.

The Condition of a Bond was for Payment of Childrens Portions when they married, or came to their Age of 21 Years. In Action of Debt for Non-performance, the Defendant pleads, That he had paid the Sum *cum & quam cito*, they came unto their full Age, generally, without shewing how. Demurer, because he hath not shewed in his Plea when they came to their full Age, and when he had paid the same, the Payment being to be upon Request. Pleading to the Condition of a Bond for the Payment of Portions.

Per Cur. The Plea is not good, for that Reason; and *per Doderidge*, if there had been a Day certain set down in the Condition, then to plead Payment, *secundum formam & Effectum Chartæ*, had been good. 2 *Bulst.* 266, 267. *Haulsey* and *Carpenter*.

R. had two Daughters, and bequeathed by Will to each 20000 *l.* apiece, provided that if either of them married before the Age of 16 Years, or that the Marriage were without the Consent of such Persons, that then they should lose 10000 *l.* of their Portion, and that 10000 *l.* should go to his other Children. Lord *Salisbury* married one of the Daughters under the Age of 16 Years; but with the Consent of all the Parties. It was the Opinion of the Lord Keeper, that both Parts must be observed; and she must be of 16 Years of Age, as well as have Consent, Lord *Salisbury*'s Case, 2 *Ventr.* 368. Portions to be paid on Condition.

A Thousand Pounds is devised to *J. S.* at One and twenty Years of Age, and if *J. S.* died under Age, then *J. N.* and *J. B.* to have the 1000 *l.* or else the Survivor of them. *J. B.* and *J. N.* die both in the Life of *J. S.* and before the Age of 21 Years, and then *J. S.* dies under the Age of 21 Years; the Administrator of *J. N.* (who survived Administrator of a Legatee, who died before the Contingency hapen'd, yet the Money decreed to him.

J. B.) sued and obtained a Decree for the Thousand Pounds, tho' he died before the Contingency hapen'd, 2 *Ventr.* 347.

Mainte-nance and Education not dis-counted out of a Child's Portion. *Aliter* of Apprentice Money.

One deviseth 250 *l.* to his Son, and makes his Wife Executrix, and she marries another Husband; by Bill in *Chancery* brought by the Son for the Legacy, the Defendants would have discounted Maintenance and Education: Which was not permitted by the Court, so as to diminish the Principal Sum; for it was said by the Court, That the Mother ought to maintain the Child; but a Sum of Money paid for binding him out Apprentice, was allowed to be discounted, 2 *Ventr.* 353.

Fee upon a Contin-gency.

A. had two Sons *B.* and *C.* by several Venters, and seised in Fee of *Black-acre* and *White-acre*, deviseth *Black-acre* to *B.* in Fee, and *White-acre* to *C.* in Fee, under this *Proviso* following: That if it shall so please God either of my said Sons to die before such time as they shall be married, or before they shall attain to their Age of 21 Years, and without Issue of their Bodies to be begotten; then I give all the said Lands, which I have by this my Will given to such of my said Sons which shall so decease before Marriage, or before their Age of 21 Years, and without Issue of their Bodies begotten, unto such of those my said two Sons as shall the other survive; any former Gift thereof notwithstanding in this Will to the contary. And after *B.* takes Wife, and hath Issue a Daughter and

and dies, and after *C.* comes to full Age and dies without Issue before Marriage; in this Case it is not any Estate Tail in *B.* and *C.* but a Fee upon the said Contingent of Marriage, or dying before the Age of 21 Years without Issue, to come to the Survivor for Life only, *Hill.* 1650. *Hanbery* and *Cockerell.*

A Devise, That the eldest Son shall take the Profits till the younger Son be of Age, and the Remainder to the younger Son; the eldest hath a Fee Conditional, 3 *Leon.* *p.* 216. Fee in eldest, till the youngest come to Age.

Or, as it is reported in the first Part of *Leonard:* One having Issue two Sons, devised that his eldest Son, with his Executors, should take the Profits of the Lands, until his youngest Son should come to the Age of 22 Years, and that then the youngest Son should have the Lands to him and the Heirs of his Body. *Per Cur.* Clearly the eldest Son shall have Fee in the Interim till the youngest Son come to Age, 1 *Leon.* *p.* 101. *Gates* and *Hallywel.*

Land was devised to the Son and Heir, and if he die before his Age of One and twenty Years, and without Issue of his Body then living, then the Remainder over. He survives One and twenty, and then sells the Land and dies. *Per Cur.* He hath a Fee presently, and so the Sale is good; for the Estate Tail is limited to Commence upon a subsequent Contingency, *Dyer* 330. *Clatch's* A Fee, because the Estate Tail is limited to commence upon a subsequent Contingency.

Case, *Cro. Jac.* 675. *Chadwel* and *Cowley*; *Sid.* 148. *Collenson* and *Wright*.

Portionary Legacies, in what Court suable.

One who dwelt in *Somersetshire* made his Will, and by his said Will did bequeath to each of his Children, being Infants, a Legacy of 20 *l.* apiece. The Procurators of the Infants did libel in the Court of *Arches* against the Executors of the Testator for the said Legacies, being out of the Diocess; and a Prohibition was awarded. And *per Cur.* The Exception in the Statute of 32 *H.* 8. *c.* 9. doth extend only to Probate of Wills; and that an Averment might be, That the Parties were sued out of their proper Diocess, if the same doth not appear in the Libel, *Godb.* 214. *Pl.* 306.

A. seised of Lands in Fee, and having Issue two Sons, *R.* and *G.* deviseth, That if his Son *R.* die before Issue, so that the Lands discend to my Son *G.* then I will, that my Overseers shall have the Government of my Lands, and of my Son *G.* *R.* took a Wife, and died, she being young with Child with a Daughter. Devisor dies; the Daughter was born. *Per Cur.* The Daughter is excluded from the Inheritance, and *G.* shall have the Land. *Sed quære*, 4 *Leon.* *p.* 32.

A. having Nine Children, and possess'd of a Lease for Years, deviseth it in this Manner:

I devise my two Rectories (whereof the Lease was) to be divided between my Children, and that all the Profits thereof shall remain between my Children; and if my Son Richard *die,* *then*

then the two Daughters of Richard *shall have his Part; and if any of the rest of my Children die, then his Part shall come to my Children.*

And after Four of the Nine Children die, by which an equal Part of these Parts comes to *Richard*, and after *Richard* dies. *Per Cur.* The two Daughters of *Richard* shall only have the 9th Part, which first was devised to *Richard*, and nothing of the four Parts, which by the future Devise comes to *Richard* by the other Four Children; for the Devise to them is only limited to the first Part of *Richard*, and the future Devise upon the Death of the other Children comes after this Limitation, *Mich.* 10 *Jac. B. R. Rimer* and *Belcher.*

Vide infra plus sub Tit. Cases in Chancery.

CHAP. XV.

Of Apprentices.

The Nature of the Relation between Master and Apprentice. He is not within the Statute of 5 Eliz. *as to Departure: Nor within the Statute of* 21 H. 8. *Servants imbezelling Goods of* 40 s. *Value, Felony; not so of Apprentice. That Statute explained. How and to what Covenants Apprentices are liable at Common Law or Custom, and Declarations and Pleadings thereupon. Declaration on Covenants in general against Apprentice, who pleads* deins Age. *Replication by the Custom of* London. Quære, *If it be a Departure? Collateral Covenants shall not bind Infants.* Et sic —— *where a sufficient Averment. Covenant to instruct, if discharged by Death. Account lies not against an Apprentice, except for collateral Receipts. Covenant lies not on the* Stat. 5 El. c. 4. *Covenants incident to the Estate. The Statute of* 5 Eliz. *pleaded, That the Father had not* 40 l. per Annum. *Retainer. If the Intent of a Statute be fulfilled, sufficient. Of Actions on the Statute of Labourers. Declaration ill, for that a Retainer is not averred. Of Obligations, with special Conditions, relating to Apprentices. Proof of wasting and imbezelling Goods, how to be made. No Action of Covenant for imbezelling Goods within the Statute of* 5 Eliz. *Notice, where requisite. Though the Indenture and*

and Retainer according to the Statute be void, yet the Bond to deliver a just Account is good. Release to the Apprentice before Forfeiture, saves the Bond given by a third Person for his accounting. Bond not to use a Trade, void; but an Assumpsit *is good. Whether the Master may send his Apprentice beyond Sea. Of the Custom of* London *as to Apprentices. The Statute of* 8 Anne, *of the Tax on taking of Clerks and Apprentices. Inrolment. The Custom, how tried. Assignee of an Apprentice turned over may have Covenant by Custom. How Apprentice free of one Trade, may exercise another by the Custom of* London. *Explication of the Statute of* 5 Eliz. c. 4. *relating to Apprentices. Indictment for exercising a Trade not being an Apprentice, how to be laid. In Debt for using a Trade not being Apprentice, how to declare. Diversity where a Statute creates an Offence with Qualifications, and where it gives a Penalty to the King. Difference between Action of Debt and Indictment on the Statute of* 5 Eliz. *as to laying the Action. Of discharging an Apprentice, and the Explanation of the Statute of* 5 Eliz. *as to that Clause. If the Difference between Master and Servant may come before the Sessions originally, or by Way of Appeal only. If Justices of Peace may compel one to take an Apprentice. Of Masters correcting Apprentices. Who may be compelled to be bound Apprentices. Of.* Stat. 2 Anne, c. 6. *of Apprentices being bound to Mariners. Remedies for abusing, enticing,* &c. *Servants. General Damages given, where ill. If Ser-*

vant dies of a Battery, no Action lies for the Master.

THE Relation betwixt a Master and an Apprentice is of general Consideration, and differs from all other Minors, not only in that the Law favours more the Acts of the Master towards his Apprentice, by reason of such Relation, but also in respect of Obligation, especially by the Custom of *London*, to which Infants shall be bound, which they shall not in any other Case.

Servants imbezelling Goods of 40 *s.* Value, Felony: Not so of Apprentices.

By *Stat.* 21 *H.* 8. *c.* 7. 'All and singular 'such Servants to whom any Caskets, Jewels, 'Money, Goods or Chattels, by his or their 'Masters or Mistresses, shall be delivered to 'keep, if any such Servant or Servants with-'draw them or any of them from their said 'Masters or Mistresses, and go away with 'the said Caskets, *&c.* or any Part thereof, 'to the Intent to steal the same, and defraud 'their Masters and Mistresses thereof, con-'trary to the Trust repos'd in them, or else 'being in the Service of his said Mistress, 'without Assent or Commandment of his 'said Master or Mistress imbezel the same 'Caskets, Jewels, Money, Goods and Chat-'tels, or any Part thereof, or otherwise con-'vert the same to his own Use with like 'Purpose to steal it, that if the said Caskets, 'Jewels, Money, *&c.* that any such Servant 'shall go away with, or which he shall im-'bezel with Purpose to steal, be of the Va-'lue of 40 *s.* or above, That then the same

'false

'false and fraudulent Act or Demeanor from 'henceforth shall be deemed and adjudged 'Felony, and he or they so offending shall 'be punished, as other Felons be punished 'for Felonies committed, by the Course of 'the Common Law; Provided this Act shall 'not extend or be prejudicial to any Ap'prentice, or any other Person within the 'Age of Eighteen Years, going away with 'his or their Masters Goods, *&c.* otherwise 'converting the same to his or their own 'Uses during the Time of their Apprentice'ships, or being within the Age of Eighteen 'Years.

One is put Apprentice to a Master for Seven Years, and the Master covenants to instruct him in the Trade, and to find him with Meat and Drink during the Seven Years, and after dies, having left an Executor, the Apprentice remains Apprentice to the Executor. Though the Executor cannot instruct him in the Trade, yet he is bound to find him Meat and Drink during the Term of Seven Years, *Sid.* 216. *Wordsworth* and *Guy*. He remains Apprentice to the Executor, tho' he cannot instruct him.

If the Apprentice misbehave himself, the Master may correct him, or the Justices may punish him, *Cro. Car.* 127. *Gilbert's* Case.

* It is lawful for the Master to maintain his Apprentice with Money, in an Action brought against him, *Moor* 814. * Master gives his Apprentice Money to defend Actions, it's no Maintenance.

Apprentice is not within the Penalty of the Statute of 5 *Eliz.* for Departure: And by *Hobart*, It was never the Intent of that Statute to make an Infant who is Apprentice Apprentice not within *Stat.* 5 *El.* as to Departure.

tice to be within the Danger of it: For an Infant at the Age of Fourteen may be bound to be an Apprentice; and the Punishment which is given by the same Statute, is, That such Person shall be whip'd as a Rogue; which plainly proves the Statute intends those of full Age.

Nor within *Stat.* 21 *H.* 8. of departing with Goods.

If Apprentice departs with his Master's Goods delivered to him, he is not within the Statute of 21 *H.* 8. as another Servant is.

How, and to what Covenants, Apprentices are liable, and by the Custom of London; *and of Declarations and Customs thereon.*

Infant cannot bind himself Apprentice by the Common Law; but by the Custom of *London* he may bind himself Apprentice by Indenture, and it shall be good, 2 *Bulstr.* 192. in *Burton*'s Case.

Declarations on Covenants in general against an Apprentice, and replies by Custom of *London*, is a Departure by the better Opinion.

Covenant was brought against an Apprentice on Indenture. The Defendant pleads, he was within Age. The Plaintiff in his Replication maintained his Action by the Custom of *London*, that he may bind himself at the Age of Fourteen.

The Question in 4 *Leon. p.* 77. and in *Cro. El.* 652. *Walker* and *Nicholson*'s Case, was, Whether this was a Departure in Pleading? And it was much doubted there, and 19 *R.* 2. cited there, how that an Infant brought an Action against his Guardian in Socage, who pleaded, that the Plaintiff was within Age. The Plaintiff did maintain his Declaration,

ration, That by the Custom of such a Place an Infant of Eighteen Years of Age might bring an Account against his Guardian in Socage, and it was held it was no Departure, *Cro.* 652. 4 *Leon.* 77. *Walker* and *Nicholson.*

In the principal Case it was much argued in *Mould, alias Bold,* and *Wallis*'s Case, 14 & 15 *Car.* 2. *B. R.* because he brought his Action, as at Common Law, generally, and maintained it by a Custom.

Some argued, That it was a Departure, and cited 1 *Inst.* 304. and *Kel.* 76. *Abbot of Buckface*'s Case; which was,

Action was brought against *H.* as Bailiff generally. Defendant pleads, He was Receiver. The Plaintiff replies, That the Tenants of the Manor have used to elect a Tenant, which shall be Bailiff to collect the Lord's Rents; and this was adjudged a Departure, 1 *Inst.* 304. *Kel.* 76.

Yelv. 13. *pl.* 22. *Wood* and *Hawkshead*'s Case, it was argued there, If a Man entitle himself by the Feoffment of one *A.* and the Defendant shews how *A.* was an Infant at the Time of the Feoffment, if the Plaintiff in his Replication will induce a Custom to make the Feoffment good, that this is a Departure, the Custom being a Matter of Title, and is variant from the Declaration.

They on the other Side cited 21 *H.* 7. 17. *Feoffment.* The Defendant pleads Nonage.
The

The Plaintiff replies by a Special Custom, That this is not good; *contra* to 37 *H.* 6. 5.

But it was agreed by all, That where one alledgeth a General Custom in a Count, and replies by a Special Custom, that that is not good.

Departure in Pleading. By *Windham* Justice: This is no Departure in the principal Case, being no Matter varying from the Count; that being but Supposal, and always General, this Special Matter is a good Support; and that this is no Departure from the Title, but an Answer to a Disability pleaded in Bar, *Yelv.* 13. *Wood* and *Hawshead.*

Foster held it to be no Departure, the *Gist* of the Action being laid in *London,* and the Title is the same still, only the Person enabled, *Winch* 63.

But by *Twisden*: All the Precedents are to Count on the Custom, as being the Ground of the Action; and he was of Opinion, That it is a Departure, as whensoever the Count is General, and cannot be made good by any particular Manner, *Winch* 63.

What is a Departure in Pleading. Count on a Statute that gives a Penalty. The Defendant pleads, It was repealed. The Plaintiff replies, and sets forth, It was confirmed by another Act, this is good. *Contra,* If I count on a Temporary Statute, and the Defendant shews it to be expired, the Plaintiff in his Replication shews it to be confirmed by a new Statute, is a Departure, as is resolved in Dr. *Butler*'s Case against the *College* of *Physicians, Lit. Rep.* By all the Judges:

Judges: So Feoffment generally pleaded may be made good by Leaſe or Releaſe. But in Treſpaſs, if *H.* juſtify by a Leaſe from an Abbot for 60 Years, he cannot rejoin, it is good for 20 Years, *Plowd.* 105. by the Act of *Diſſolutions* of 31 *H.* 8.

And further he ſaid, as in *Gilbert* and *Fletcher*'s Caſe, *Hill.* 5 *Car.* 1. The Action is founded on the Covenant, and not on the Cuſtom, and Infant is not bound by Collateral Covenant.

But the Court gave Leave to the Plaintiff to diſcontinue his Action, and to declare on the Cuſtom of *London*, that an Infant may bind himſelf.

I have been the larger in the Recital of this Caſe, becauſe it may give ſome Light to other Caſes of the like Nature, and which are not yet well ſettled in our Books; I mean, as to Departure in Pleading.

Now as to what Covenants an Indenture ſhall bind, or not bind, the Infant.

Collateral Covenants ſhall not bind Infant. As in Action of Covenant brought againſt the Infant on Covenant to ſerve his Maſter faithfully as an Apprentice in the Myſtery of a Draper, and he lays in the Action, That he defrauded him of his Goods. *Per Cur.* The Statute of 5 *Eliz.* is not ſo ſtrong againſt Infants as to make Collateral Covenants good. Infant is not bound by thoſe Words at Common Law, and no Collateral Covenant ſhall be maintainable upon that Statute. Action on the Caſe

Collateral Covenants ſhall not bind Infant.

Case lies upon the Covenant in Law, but not on the Covenant in Fact; and for that he ought to have Collateral Security, and the Retainer is for the Benefit of the Infant to learn his Trade; but the Covenant is to his Disadvantage.

Tho' *Winch* thought the Covenant to be good, being incident to the Retainer. *Per Cur.* There is no Remedy but by Action on the Case, *Winch p. 63. Fleming* and *Pitman. Vid. Helt. p. 63.*

Quære, How that lies against an Infant for Disceit. *Vide supra.*

Covenant was brought upon Indentures of Apprenticeship, containing the usual Covenants in such Indentures, and he ran away with his Master's Moneys in *London*.

And two Exceptions were taken to the Declaration:

Covenant implied.

1. In the Indenture the Words are, That the Infant shall be *Loyal and Faithful*, and *secreta sua velare, &c.* without any Words of Covenant express.

But it was resolved, that the words imply a Covenant.

That Infant shall be bound by Covenant, where pleadable.

2. It was excepted, That Infants shall be bound by Covenant, is pleadable no where but in *London*. (The Custom is, That Infant shall not wage his Law upon Covenant for Tabling.) *Sed non allocatur*, It is pleadable at any Place: This Covenant is allowable at Law, and the Words are, That the *Covenants* shall become of such Effect and Efficacy, as if he had been at full Age at the time of his

4

his Sealing the Indenture; and then he shall be bound in every Place within the Realm.

The Court seemed to be of Opinion, that it was a good Custom, and the Action was well brought, *Moor* 135. *Stanton's* Case.

Infant Apprentice departs from his Master, the Master may not have Action of Covenant against him upon his Indenture of Apprenticeship, *per Cur.* in 8 *Car.* 1. *B. R.* for *per Cur.* Covenant in Indenture of Apprentiship binds not the Infant at Common Law before Statute 5 *Eliz.* c. 4. if it be not upon a Custom, *Fitzh. N. B.* 168. and it does not lie on the Statute of 5 *Eliz.* c. 4. for the said Statute saith, the Indenture shall bind him, and if he depart and will not serve the Master, the Master may complain to the Justices, and by this make him to serve. But if the Master might have Action of Covenant against the Apprentice for not serving, then he shall recover all the Damages, and then he ought not to have the Thing it self.

Covenant, lies not upon Statute 5 *Eliz.* c. 4

If Infant, Man or Woman, of 12 Years, or other Person, who is not compellable to serve, yet if he make a Covenant to serve in Husbandry, he shall be bound by his Covenant, and shall be punished if he then depart, *Dalt. Just.* 83. *Edit.* 6. Yet by Common Law the retaining an Infant under 12 Years of Age was void, he not being of Ability of Body, or of Years to consent; for Infant at Common Law is not of Age

to

to bind himself by Covenant before *Annos nubiles*, which are 12 in a Woman and 14 in a Man, 7 *Rep.* 43. 9 *Rep.* 73. nor before such Age are they accounted *Potens* in Body, which were the Words used in the Statute 23 *Ed.* 3. although the said Words are omitted out of the Statute 5 *Eliz.* But now by Statute 5 *Eliz.* c. 4. any Person above the Age of 10 Years, by his Consent and Agreement, may by his Indenture be bound as Apprentice to Husbandry, *Dalt. Ibid.*

Custom by By-Law, That the Bonds and Covenants shall be void, its ill.

In an Action of Covenant on Apprenticeship, the Defendant pleads a By-Law in *London* by the Common-Council there, That if any Free-man take to Apprentice the Son of an Alien, the Bond and Covenant shall be void.

And *per Cur.* this is no Plea; for the Common-Council cannot make the Bonds and Covenants void, but they may inflict a Fine or Punishment upon such a Master for taking such an Apprentice, *Moor* 411. *Doggerel* and *Peck.*

Covenant incident to the Estate.

Justice *Jones* in his solemn Argument of *Bland*'s Case, *M.* 8 *Car.* 1. *B. R.* said, That Covenant incident to an Estate, as for Reparations, bind Infant, if he accept the Estate, tho' he doth not seal.

Action of Covenant was brought by an Apprentice, and assigns for Breach, That the Testator of the Defendant had covenanted to instruct the Plaintiff in the Art of a Sadler for Seven Years, and to find him Meat and Drink during the Term; and that the

the Defendant after the Death of the Testator did put the Plaintiff out of his House, and so kept him from Meat and Drink.

It was agreed, —— *Et sic* —— is a sufficient Averment of the Breach, and that it is not but Matter of Form. And as for the Law, the Opinion of the Court was, That the Apprentice remains an Apprentice to the Executor; for altho' he cannot Instruct him, yet he may find him Meat and Drink, *&c.*

Et sic —— Where a sufficient Averment.

Per Hide, This general Covenant to Instruct, is not gone by his Death, altho' there be no particular Custom, as in *London*, especially since the Statute of 5 *Eliz.*

Covenant to Instruct, if discharged by Death.

To which the Court inclined: Tho' some were of Opinion, had it been only to Instruct, it had been discharged by Death; and if it were, yet the Breach is sufficiently assigned if either Part be true, as here, in turning him out. Judgment *pro Quer.* *Sid.* 216. 1 *Keb.* 761, 820. *Wadsworth* and *Eye.*

Infant of 12 Years of Age, shall be bound by his Covenant to serve in Husbandry, *Fitz. N. B.* 168. *d.*

Action on the Statute of Labourers against *A. E.* Servant, and *R.* who detains him, and *A.* was of the Age of 5 Years, and therefore by *Finch* the Action doth not lie against him, for his Covenant is void *ratione* of his tender Age, and therefore it lies not against *R.* who accepts him, 41 *Ed.* 3. 17.

As on the Statute of Labourers.

Action was brought upon the Statute of Labourers against a Damsel of the Age of 10 Years, upon Retainer and Departure.

Defendant faith she is not 10 Years of Age, and because *constat Cure* by Inspection, that she is not of Age to make a Covenant, the Writ shall abate by Award.

Action on the Statute of Labourers, 23 *Ed.* 3. *c.* 1. *Quod quilibet potens in corpore*, ought to serve; and *per Hancks*, Infant of 21 Years of Age ought to serve.

Trespass on the Statute of Labourers, for taking his Servant out of his Possession. Defendant saith, That the Servant is an Infant under 10 Years of Age, and because the Plaintiff could not deny it, he took nothing by his Writ, 38 *Ed.* 3. 5. *b.*

If Infant at 7 or 8 Years of Age covenant to serve me, he may depart at his Pleasure, 21 *H.* 6. 9.

Vide plus, Stat. 5 Eliz. *c.* 4.

Tr. 20 *Jac.* in *B. C.* it was held by Lord *Hobart* and Justice *Hutton*, in *Jennings* and *Pitman*'s Case, (which was enter'd *P.* 19 *Jac. Rot.* 3014.) That Covenant made by Infant in Indenture of Apprenticeship, that he will not wast the Goods of his Master, will not bind him, for the Statute 5. *Eliz.* does not bind him to any Covenants which are not implied in the Indenture of Serving; and the sole Thing that binds him in the said Statute is, That he shall be bound to serve when he is bound by Indenture, being within Age, as well as if he were of full Age, and if the Covenant be only a Covenant to serve, no Covenant lies for imbezelling of Goods; and if the Covenant be to serve him faithfully and dili-

No Action of Covenant for imbezelling Goods within 5 *Eliz.*

diligently, that shall not bind him upon this Covenant; and *per* Just. *Hutton*, this is like to a Custom that shall be taken strictly; but by Justice *Winch*, this is a Thing incident and *quasi* consequent, if he shall be bound to serve, by consequence it shall be to serve faithfully and truly, *Hutton Rep.* 6. 62.

It is generally said, that Action of *Account* lies not against an Apprentice, *Winch* 11 *Rep.* 89. And it is regularly true with this Difference; although an Apprentice cannot be charged in this Action, for ordinary Receipts upon his Master's Trade, yet upon collateral Receipts, which do not concern the ordinary Trade of his Master, he shall be charged as well as another. And therefore in the Case of *Rivers* and *Pudsey*, in Action of *Account*, the Defendant pleaded, That at the Time, *&c.* and now he is the Plaintiff's Apprentice; and it was held to be no Plea, 3 *Leon.* 63. *Rivers* and *Pudsey*, 11 *Rep.* 89.

Account lies not against an Apprentice except for Collateral Receipts.

H. Brought Action of Debt against *P.* and declared upon Indenture; and that the Defendant covenanted to serve him honestly and faithfully, as an Apprentice, in the Mystery of a Draper for Seven Years; and that he had defrauded him of his Goods, *&c.* The Defendant pleaded the Statute of 5 *Eliz.* That none shall be an Apprentice to any of the most worthy Trades (amongst which Drapery is one) except his Father have Freehold to the Value of 40 *s. per Annum*, to be certified to the Place in which he

5 *Eliz.* pleaded, That the Father had not 40 *s. per Annum.*

he is to be Apprentice, by three of the Justices of the Peace of the same County, and this Certificate to be enrolled in the Town-Book: And he pleaded, That no such Certificate was made, and pleaded the Branch of that Statute, which made every Retainer, contrary to the Form of the Statute, void. The Plaintiff replied, He had 40 *s. per Annum*: Defendant rejoined, he had not 40 *s. per Annum*: And the Plaintiff demurs, because the Defendant said in his Rejoinder, that he had not 40 *s. per Annum*, and in his Plea he pleaded no such Certificate.

Retainer. *Per Cur.* The Retainer is good, tho' there is not any such Certificate or Inrolment, if *revera* the Father had 40 *s. per annum*; for the Intent of the Statute is fulfilled.

If the Intent of a Statute be fulfilled, it is sufficient. As upon the Statute of 21 *H.* 8. Of *Pluralities*, it was adjudged in one *Robin*'s Case, That a Dispensation is good, tho' it be not inrolled; and yet there are as strong Words of Inrolment as may be.

Departure. But the Court agreed clearly, that this is a Departure. But the Doubt was, if the pleading of the Certificate were good.

Hutton conceived, there ought to be a Certificate. Certificate to precede the Indenture: But others thought the Bar is Good, (*viz.*) the pleading the Want of the Certificate, and the pleading that he had 40 *s. per Annum* in the Replication is ill; and tho' the Rejoinder of the Defendant is ill, and a Departure; yet it appears, that the Plaintiff had not any Cause of Action, for that the said Statute shall not extend to make collateral

Cove-

Covenants good, *Winch* 63. & 64. *Fleming* and *Pitman*. *Vide supra* this Case in *Hutton's* Reports, by the Name of *Jennings* and *Pitman*

Declaration ill, for that a Retainer is not averr'd.

In Consideration of 40 *l.* given by the Plaintiff to the Defendant, the Defendant did assume and promise to take the Son of the Plaintiff for his Apprentice for Nine Years, and to teach, &c. and to find him with Meat and Drink; and doth not say, that the Defendant had taken the Plaintiff's Son to be his Apprentice, and so no Cause of Action, 3 *Bulstr.* 221. He alledgeth no Retainer, 1 *Rol. Rep. mesme* Case, and *Cro Jac.* 406. *mesme* Case; the Declaration was adjudged not good; for he never avers that he put him Apprentice, or that the other accepted him, 3 *Bulstr.* 221. *Talker* and *Wright*; *Cro. Jac.* 40. *b. mesme* Case.

Obligations relating to Apprentices.

Having done with Covenants on Indentures of Apprenticeship, I shall now consider of Obligations, with Special Conditions, relating to Apprentices, and the Construction of Law thereupon, with the Pleadings.

And first, as to Conditions concerning faithful Service; and the Cases of *Crookhay* and *Woodward*, *Cardinal* and *Hesket*, *Gold* and *Death*, are settled Cases.

Proof of imbezelling Goods, how to be made.

Condition of a Bond was, That if *J. S.* (the Apprentice) did wast his Masters Goods; and this should be proved by Confession under his Hand in Writing, or otherwise; and if within three Months after Satisfaction

tisfaction was not made to him, then the Bond to be in Force. And the Question was, How this Proof shall be? And the Difference was, Where the Proof is General, there it must be by Jury in the Action brought: Otherwise where the Proof is with reference to Time, and before Persons certain, or by Confession; and tho' he did confess it, yet it must be averred, that he did imbezel, *Cro. El.* 723. *Cardinal* and *Hesket*, *Cro. Jac.* 381. *Hob.* 92. 3 *Bulstr.* 55. *Gold* and *Death*, 1 *Leon.* 344. *Tedcastel* and *Hallywel*, *Cro. Jac.* 488. *Lee* and *Hedge*.

The Condition was, That his Son should render to C. his Master a just Account *de omnibus Monetis, Bonis, &c.* without imbezelling any way; and that if he did imbezel any, upon due Proof made of it, he would pay the same to him within three Months after Demand.

Per Cur. Before Payment, ought to precede Account and Arrears, and in this Action Proof ought to be made, and he must give Notice to the Defendant, 1 *Bulstr.* 40. *Cockain* and *Goodlage*, *Hob.* 217. *mesme* Case, *Crookbay* and *Woodward*.

But this Case is more fully and sensibly reported in *Hob.* 217. by the Name of *Crookbay* and *Woodward*.

The Case was on Covenant, and declared, That the Defendant, by his Deed shewed in Court, did covenant to satisfie him all such Sums of Money as *J.* his Son, the Plaintiffs Apprentice, should imbezel from him within three Months after Request, and then lays the

the Imbezelling and Requeſt, &c. The Defendant prays *Oyer* of the Deed, which was entred *in hæc verba*; and there the Covenant was to ſatisfie within three Months after Requeſt, and due Proof made of ſuch Imbezelling. The Iſſue was, Whether he imbezeled? and it was found *pro Querente*. And Judgment was arreſted, becauſe it appears by the Entry of the Deed, that the Plaintiff ought not to have brought this Action until the three Months were incurred, as well after Proof as after Requeſt; whereas the Plaintiff had averred no Proof in the Declaration. Proof. Requeſt.

And *per Cur'*, the Word *Proof* generally laid, ſhall be underſtood Proof Judicial, by *Jury*, *Confeſſion* or *Demurrer* in Court; but if the Form of Proof were by the Writing appointed otherwiſe, that ſhall prevail; as by Witneſſes before two Aldermen, by Certificate, &c. which Proof ſhall be ſet down in the Plea with all the Circumſtances; and then it ſhall be in the Diſcretion of the Court, Whether that Proof were competent according to the Meaning of the Writing? But in this Caſe, becauſe the Word [*Proof*] is left at large, and may be made in Court judicially in Action brought againſt the Apprentice, before the Action brought on this Covenant made by another, it may be well taken in this Caſe of a Proof by Trial in Court, and ſo it is every way againſt the Plaintiff, *Hob.* 217. *Crookhay* and *Woodward*, 2 *Roll. Rep.* 40. *Lee* and *Skey*, *Cro. Jac.* 488.

Breach laid in three Parts.

In *Cutler* and *Brewster*'s Case, the Condition was of Three Parts:

1. If he well served the Plaintiff?
2. If he duly Accounted?
3. If he should make Satisfaction in three Months after Notice?

Breach was, That upon Account he was found 60 *l.* Polish-Money in Arrears, which he converted to his own Use, and so not well served him, and good; for it was a Breach of the first Part, for every Part is several by it self, *Cro. El.* 83. *Cutler* and *Brewster*.

The Condition of a Bond was, That if Apprentice turned over should wast the Goods of his Master, the Defendant should pay what the Master was damnified, and pleads *Nul damage.* The Plaintiff sets forth a Breach in wasting the Goods, but sets forth no Notice given to the Defendant; and for that Cause the Defendant demurred.

Notice, where requisite.

But *Per Cur.* no Notice is necessary, because both Parties are of equal Capacity to take Notice. Also when any one undertakes for a Third Person, he must answer for him at his Peril, and the Imbezelment is not in the Conisance of the Plaintiff.

Where the Particulars of the Goods need to be shewed or not.

And *Twisden* thought, the Particulars of the Goods wasted ought to be set forth, and not to say of such a Value, or at least the Kind: But afterwards he agreed with the other Judges, That no Particulars need to be shewed; as in Debt against Executors they plead fully administred, the Plaintiff may sug-

ſuggeſt, they have waſted *diverſa bona*, without ſhewing what; and Judgment *pro Quer'*, *H.* 14, & 15 *Car.* 2. 1 *Keb.* 467, 471. *French* and *Perry.*

Tho' the Contract or Indenture for Retaining an Apprentice according to the Statute is void, yet if ſuch Apprentice give Bond to deliver up a true and juſt Account of Merchants Wares, the Bond is good; it being for a Collateral Matter, the Bond is good and out of the Statute, 3 *Bulſtr.* 179. *Bennet* and *Field.*

The Indenture and Retainer contrary to the Statute, is void; but a Bond to deliver up a juſt Account, is good.

Condition of a Bond entred into by a Stranger, That if ſuch an one did become the Apprentice of the Obligee, and tranſport his Merchandizes beyond Sea, and make Return of them, and make Account to the Obligee, and pay the Money upon Account within a certain Time, that then, &c. and afterwards the Obligee releaſed by Deeds to the Apprentice, but not to the Obligor, and in Debt upon the Bond the Obligor pleads this Releaſe.

Re[illegible]e to the Apprentice before Forfeiture, ſaves a Bond given to a third Perſon for his Accounting.

Per the Lord *Dyer* & *tot. Cur.* By the Releaſe to the Apprentice the Obligation is ſaved, if the Releaſe were made before any Forfeiture, or before the Apprentice had broken any Point, according to the Conditions or Covenants: But if it was made after any of them were broken, then ſuch a Releaſe to the Apprentice did not diſpenſe with the Obligation which was made by the Stranger; becauſe an Obligation once forfeited, cannot be ſaved by any Act or Releaſe made or done to a Stanger, 3 *Leon.* *p.* 45.

Regula.

As

Bonds not to use a Trade void, but an *Assumpsit* good.

As to Bonds for not using a Trade, there are several Cases in our Books, and upon the whole, the Law to that is settled, That a Bond that a Tradesman shall not use a Trade is void, though it be in such a Town or particular Place, and for a Time: But an *Assumpsit* in such a Case is good, 2 *H.* 5. 5. *March* 191. *Pl.* 238. *Barrow* and *Wood*, 77. *Pl.* 121. *Cro. El.* 872. *Colgate* and *Batchelor*, *Noy* 98. 2 *Bulst.* 136. *Rogers* and *Parry*, 2 *Leon.* 210. *Cro. Jac.* 596. *Broad* and *Jolliff*, 2 *Keb.* 377. *Ferby* and *Arrowsmith*.

Whether the Master may send his Apprentice beyond Sea.

Condition of the Bond was, To teach and employ his Apprentice in his House and Service of the Art of Chirurgery for Eight Years: The Master sends him a Voyage to the *Indies*. The Defendant pleaded, he did it for the better Instruction of his Servant. The Plaintiff demurs; and Judgment *pro Quer.*

Per Cur', The Defendant could not send his Apprentice out of *England*, except he went with him, (but to any other Part of *England* he may) unless the Nature of the Trade require it; as a Master Adventurer, 1 *Bulstr.* 67. *Coventry* and *Weedale*, 1 *Roll. Abr.* 427. *Mesme Case* 445. 1 *Brownl.* 97.

The Condition of a Bond was, To pay to his Apprentice, his Executors or Assigns, Ten Pounds, at the Time of the End or Determination of his Apprenticeship. The Apprentice serves Six Years, and then dies.

Per Cur. The Obligation is discharged, and the Money shall not be paid, 1 *Brownl.* 97. *Cheyney* and *Fell*.

By

By the Statute 8 *Anne*, certain Rates and Duties upon Candles, and Clerks and Apprentices; it is enacted, 'That there shall 'be raised and paid the Sum of 6 *d.* for 'every 20 *s.* of every Sum of 50 *l.* or under; 'and the Sum of 1 *s.* for every 20 *s.* above '50 *l.* which shall be after the First Day of '*May*, 1710. and during the Term of Five 'Years thence next ensuing, paid or contracted for, with every Clerk, Apprentice or Servant, put to, or with, any Master or Mistress, to learn any Profession, 'Trade or Employment; which Sums shall 'be paid by the said Masters or Mistresses 'respectively; the full Sum and Sums of 'Money received or given, and paid or 'agreed for, with such Apprentice and 'Servant, shall be truly inserted, and written in Words at Length, in some Indenture or other Writing, which shall contain the Covenants, Articles and Agreements, relating to the Service of such 'Clerk, Apprentice or Servant, upon Pain, 'That every Master or Mistress, to whom any 'such Sum or Sums of Money shall be paid or 'contracted for, which shall not be truly 'specified in some such Indenture or other 'Writing, (which is to bear Date the Day 'of Signing and Sealing the same) shall 'for every such Offence forfeit double the 'Sum so paid, given or contracted for: 'The Forfeitures to be one Moiety to the 'Queen, the other Moiety to the Informer.

Of

Of the Custom of London, *as to Apprentices.*

Inrolment.

The Custom of *London*, as to inrolling of Apprentices, is certified by the Mouth of the Recorder.

And at Fourteen Years of Age the Apprentice may bind himself by the Custom of *London*, as an Apprentice, and it shall bind him, though he be not inrolled.

The Apprentice, at any Time before one Year (if his Master do not inrol the Indentures) may exhibit a Petition in *French* to the Lord Mayor and Aldermen, and have a *Scire facias* against his Master, to shew why the Indenture was not inrolled; and if he doth not shew a sufficient Cause, (as that he could not bring the Apprentice Personally, as he must, or some such Cause) then he may sue out his Indenture and be discharged of his Master, *Palm.* 361, or 31.

But this Case is more fully reported in 2 *Roll. Rep.* 305.

How the Covenants shall bind the Apprentice, tho' not inrolled.

In a Writ of *Error* between the Master and the Apprentice, they were at Issue upon the Custom of *London*, and the *Certiorari* awarded to the Mayor; and the Recorder certified, That where any Man, within the Age of One and twenty Years, and not under the Age of Fourteen, binds himself by Indenture, in which are many Covenants; these shall bind the Infant, although the Deed was not inrolled before the Chamberlain within the Year; but with this Difference, That the Apprentice may come

come in before the Mayor and Aldermen, and there ſhew the Matter by Petition in *French*, that the Deed is not inrolled within the Year; and upon this a *Scire facias* ſhall iſſue forth to the Maſter, to know why the Deed was not inrolled. And if upon his Default the Deed was not inrolled, the Defendant (the Apprentice) may ſue out his Indentures, and ſhall be diſcharged; but if it was not inrolled through the Default of the Apprentice, as if he would not come to be preſent before the Chamberlain, but abſent himſelf, then he ſhall not be diſcharged; for the Deed may not be inrolled, unleſs the Infant be preſent in Court, 2 *Roll. Rep.* 305.

21 *Jac. B. R. Cole* and *Holme*'s Caſe, ſuch Action was brought againſt an Apprentice, (*videlicet*) That he departed from his Maſter's Service, *&c.* Defendant pleads Nonage; the Plaintiff replied the Cuſtom of *London*, and that the Indenture was inrolled, as it ought to be; and this was certified by the Recorder to be the Cuſtom; and Judgment was given againſt the Defendant, 21 *Jac. B. R. Cole* and *Holmes*.

In Action of *Debt* on Bond, whereof the Condition is to perform Covenants in Indenture of Apprenticeſhip in *London*. The Defendant pleads the Cuſtom of *London*, That the Indenture ſhall be void, if it be not inrolled within the Year; and this Cuſtom is traverſed. This ſhall be tried by the Mayor and Commonalty by the Mouth of the Recorder, *Co. Entr. tit. Debt* 144. Cuſtom, how certified, and Trial.

The

Assignee of Apprentice turned over may have Covenant by Custom.

The Custom of *London* is, To turn over an Apprentice from one to another; and he to whom such Apprentice is turned over, may have an Action of *Covenant* upon Special Issues on the several Breaches assigned; and the Plaintiff in such Case had a Verdict.

Though it was moved in Arrest of Judgment,

1. That *abstraxit se à servitio* so many Nights, and during that Time did not serve him; which *per Cur.* being found against him, is good enough.

Et sic non tenuit conventionem pleaded by Assignee.

2. It is said, He did not serve according to his Covenant; whereas no Covenant was made with the Plaintiff, yet it is good enough; and the Conclusion, *Et sic non tenuit conventionem* made with the Plaintiff, is as good as can be, and Judgment *pro Quer.* 1 *Keb.* 250. *Bowcher* and *Coster.*

Tale Remedium implies Remedy by Action of *Covenant.*

Action of *Covenant* was brought upon the Custom of *London*, That an Infant above 14, and under 21, may bind himself Apprentice; and that the Master shall have *tale Remedium*, as if he were One and twenty. It's good, and he need not alledge that the Custom is, That he shall have Action of *Covenant* against him, for *tale Remedium* implies as much, *Mod. Rep.* 271. *Horn* and *Chandler.*

In

In Covenant it was laid, That every Freeman may take an Apprentice, and that Infants may bind themselves to serve.

How the Custom to be pleaded.

It was objected, That this Custom was alledged in *fieri*, not in *facto*; for Usage is not added to it as a Custom of a Manor, that every Tenant *potuit & potuisset sursum reddere* is ill. So *licet & licuit* for the Lord to assess a Pein.

But the Court *contra*, as *Old Entries* 141. a Custom, that every Citizen and Freeman might devise in *Mortmain*, allowed good. *Vid.* 1 *Cro.* 347. *Raymond's Rep. Windhurst* and *Gibbs*.

It has been a Question, Whether and in what Cases an Apprentice, by the Custom of *London*, being bound and free of one Trade, may exercise another; and it is setled in *Fletcher* and *Bagshaw's* Case, 2 *Roll. Abr.* 579.

How Apprentice free of one Trade may exercise another by the Custom of *London*.

The Case was,

Action of Debt *tam pro Dom. Rege, quam pro seipso*, upon the Statute of 5 *Eliz.* for using the Trade of Making and Heading of Points, not being bound to the Trade as an Apprentice, against the Statute.

The Defendant pleads, that there is a Custom in *London*, That every Freeman of *London*, being free of any Art or Mystery, or Occupation, may use any other Art, Mystery or Occupation, within the City whereof he is not free, nor had been Apprentice by the Space of Seven Years. Upon which Issue was joined, whether there be such a Custom in *London*.

Now

Now this ought to be tried by the Mouth of the Recorder, although it concern the King as well as a Subject; and also, altho' this is not like to the Custom of *Mortmain*, and such ancient Customs concerning Lands, and the Devisees of them, which have been used to be tried by the Mouth of the Recorder.

And in *Appletoft* and *Stoughton*'s Case, *Pasc.* 11 *Car.* 1. *B. R.* This was certified by the Mouth of the Recorder *Mason*, upon a Writ directed to him, and he certified that there was not any such Custom in *London*; for he said, by the Custom, He who is free of a Manual Trade cannot use any other Manual Trade whereof he is not free, nor had been Apprentice to it for Seven Years; but otherwise it is of other Trades that are not Manual.

And his Certificate was received by the Court *de bene esse*; but the Court doubted, whether this ought to be tried by him.

And therefore this Matter was moved in Arrest of Judgment, *Trin.* 10 *Car. B. R. Rot.* 56. But after divers Arguments it was adjudged, *M.* 14 *Car.* 1. that this was well certified by the Mouth of the Recorder, and Judgment given accordingly for the Plaintiff.

And in *Trin.* 10 *Car. B. R. in Informat'* by *Fletcher* against *Bagshaw*, *tam pro Dom. Rege quam pro seipso*, upon the said Statute of 5 *Eliz.* Issue being joined, the Recorder *Littleton* certified by his Mouth, that there was not any such Custom, 2 *Rol. Abr.* 579. *Fletcher* and *Bagshaw*.

 This

This Case being a Resolution upon 5 *Eliz.* I shall go on in the Construction and Explanation of that Statute, as far as concerns Apprentices, which will be the Subject of the next Section.

Explication of the *Stat.* 5 *Eliz.* relating to Apprentices.

Of using a Trade without being Apprentice.

And First, of using a Trade, not being an Apprentice.

At Common Law, before this Statute of 5. *Eliz.* it was lawful for any Man to use what Trade he could without being Apprentice, 1 *Saund.* 312.

But by the Statute of 5 *Eliz. c.* 4. It is enacted, 'That it shall not be lawful to 'any Person or Persons, other than such as 'now do lawfully use or exercise any Art, 'Mystery, or Manual Occupation, to set 'up, occupy, use or exercise any Craft, 'Mystery or Occupation, now used or occupied within the Realm of *England* or '*Wales*, except he shall have been brought 'up therein Seven Years at the least, as an 'Apprentice, in the Manner and Form aforesaid; nor to set any Person in Work 'on such Mystery, Art or Occupation, being not a Workman at this Day, except 'he shall have been Apprentice, as aforesaid, or else have served as Apprentice, as 'is aforesaid, shall or will become a Journeyman, or hired by the Year, upon Pain 'that every Person willingly offending, or 'doing the contrary, shall forfeit and lose 'for every Default 40 *l.* for every Month.

Infant for exercising the Trade of a *Chandler*, not having been Apprentice to the same for Seven Years; but he was Apprentice to a *Taylor* for Seven Years.

Per Cur. If one hath been Apprentice for Seven Years at any Trade mentioned within the Statute, he may exercise any Trade named in the said Statute, although he hath not been Apprentice to it, 4 *Leon.*

But now the Charters of the City of *London* may not be any Dispensation with this Statute, That no Person shall use a Trade to which he hath not been Apprentice, although they are confirmed by Act of Parliament: And therefore in *Kilderby*'s Case, who was indicted at the Sessions in *Suffolk*, for using the Trade of a *Woollen-Draper* in *H.* in the said County, for Three Months next before the taking of the Indictment, he never having served as an Apprentice to it, against the Statute of 5 *Eliz. c.* 4.

Which Indictment being removed into the *King's-Bench* by *Certiorari*, the Defendant pleads a Special Plea, That he is a Freeman of *London*, and pleads the Charter of 11 *Jan.* 15 *H.* 3. That the Citizens of *London* may *libere & sine impedimento*, negotiate *de rebus & merchandizis suis*, and may reside where they will in *England* for that Purpose; and pleads the Confirmation of the said Grant by Act of Parliament, and that he did reside at *H. præd. cum quibusdam Mercimoniis Pannariis emen' & venden', &c.* which is the same using the Trade of a *Draper*, supposed in the Indictment; and traverseth, that he used the

the Trade of a Draper for Three Months, mentioned in the Indictment. *Aliter vel alio modo.*

And Judgment was given for the King; for the Intent of the Charter is only to give Citizens and Freemen of *London* Leave to sell their Merchandizes, and reside where they will, notwithstanding some Boroughs and Cities claim a Liberty to exclude Foreigners, *Dyer* 279. 8 *Rep.* 128.

And the Traverse is ill, *aliter vel alio modo*; for he was not charged by the Indictment with using it, *aliter vel alio modo.* Also the Traverse goes to the entire Time only, where it ought to go to every Part of the Time *distributive*; for if he had used the Trade by one Month, though he had not used it for Three Months, yet he ought to be convicted for One Month, and acquitted of the other, if the Traverse had been rightly taken, 1 *Sand.* 311. *Le Roy* and *Kilderby*, *Sid. p.* 427. *Mesme* Case.

Traverse, Indictment for not using a Trade not being Apprentice, how to be laid.

Indictment was, That he used the Trade of an *Upholsterer* 11 Months, *& amplius*; the *mplius* there is void, *Sid.* 368.

But in Debt on the Statute of 5 *Eliz.* for using a Trade, not having been Apprentice to it; the Plaintiff ought to declare, That the Defendant did not use it at the Time of the Statute, as well as in an Indictment. And Diversity was taken between a Statute which creates an Offence; which was not so before with Qualifications as here, and gives Action to the Prosecutor: For in this Case no Action lies, without shewing that the De-

In Debt, for using a Trade, not being Apprentice, how to declare. Diversity where a Statute creates an Offence with Qualifications, and where it gives a Penalty to the King.

Defendant is within the Qualifications, and to make it perfectly appear that the Defendant is such an one who had broken this Law, without which he is not liable to this Action: But where a Statute gives a Penalty to the King, he may sue for it without shewing all the Sayings, for there it shall come on the other Part; and it's sufficient for the King to say, *contra formam Statuti, Siderfin* 303. *Wade*'s Case.

Difference between Action of Debt and Indictment on the Statute of 5 *El.* as to laying the Action.

And there is another Diversity well to be observed, between an Action of *Debt* on this Statute, and an Indictment, as to the bringing the Action: Debt for using a Trade, not being Apprentice to it, lies elsewhere than in the proper County; but Information or Indictment ought to be brought in the proper County. And therefore Action of *Debt* brought for it in the King's-Bench is good, notwithstanding the Statute of 21 *Jac.* 1. which saith, That *all Actions, Bills, Pleints,* &c. *for Penal Laws there expressed, whereof this of* 5 Eliz. *is one, shall be commenced and prosecuted in the County where the Offence was committed, before the Justices of Assize,* Nisi prius, Oyer *and* Terminer, *and Justices of Peace, in the respective Counties and Liberties only, and elsewhere*; for it was not the Intent of this Statute to oust the Courts above at *Westminster-Hall* of this Action of Debt, and no Original out of *Chancery* in Debt was ever made returnable before the Justices of Assize, *&c. Sid.* 400. *Barnes* and *Haylers,* 1 *Cro.* 112. 146. *Green* and *Gadye*'s Case.

Note,

Note, A Man may not be punished in a Leet for using a Trade.

Of the Discharging an Apprentice.

Of the Discharging an Apprentice, and Explication of the Statute of 5 *Eliz.* c. 4. as to that Clause.

It is enacted by the said Statute of 5 Eliz. c. 4. 'That if any Master shall misuse, or evil-'intreat his Apprentice, or that the said 'Apprentice shall have just Cause to com-'plain, or the Apprentice do not his Duty 'to the Master; then the said Master or 'Apprentice being grieved, and having 'Cause to complain, shall repair to one 'Justice of Peace within the said County, 'or to the Mayor, or other Head Officers 'of the City, Town-Corporate, Market-'Town, or other Place where the said Ma-'ster dwelleth; who shall, by his Wisdom 'and Discretion, take such Order and Di-'rection between the said Master and his 'Apprentice, as the Equity of the same 'shall require: And if for want of good 'Conformity in the said Master, the said 'Justice of Peace or other Officer cannot 'compound and agree the Matter; then 'the said Mayor, or other Head Officer, 'shall take Bond of the said Master to ap-'pear at the next Sessions, *&c.* and upon 'his Appearance, and hearing of the Mat-'ter before the said Justices, *&c.* if it be 'thought meet to discharge the said Ap-'prentice of his Apprenticehood, that then 'the said Justices, or Four of them at the 'least, whereof one of them to be of the

'*Quorum*, or the said Mayor, *&c.* shall
'have Power in Writing under their Hands
'and Seals to pronounce and declare, that
'they have discharged the same Apprentice,
'and the Cause thereof, and that the Wri-
'ting so being made and inrolled by the
'Clerk of the Peace, and the Town-Clerk,
'shall be a sufficient Discharge for the said
'Apprentice against his Master. And if
'Default shall be found to be in the Ap-
'prentice, then the said Justices, *&c.* shall
'cause such due Correction and Punish-
'ment to be ministred unto him, as by their
'Wisdom and Discretion shall be thought
'meet.

The Intent of this Act is, That an Apprentice shall be discharged of an ill Master, as the Master shall be discharged of an ill Apprentice; and that Clause which gives Power to them to minister Punishment to an ill Apprentice, does not restrain, but enlarge the Power of the Magistrates further than it gave to them concerning the Masters; for they may not minister Punishment to the Masters for their Faults, but only discharge their Apprentices; but for the Faults of the Apprentices they may inflict Corporal Punishment, or discharge them at their Discretion: But there was a *Quære* in this Case, and the Case of *Walker* and *Edwards*, If the Defendant, who was sued in an Action of Covenant, ought to have gone to one Justice first, as the Statute directs, that he might take Order in it; and then

Q. If the Difference between the Master and Apprentice may come before the Sessions originally, or by Way of Appeal only.

then if he could not agree it, to make his Application to the Sessions. Another *Quære* was made in *Hawksworth*'s Case, If it ought not to appear, That the Order made at Sessions for discharging an Apprentice should be under the Hands and Seals of the Justices there, 1 *Sand.* 315. *Hawksworth*'s Case, *Mod. Rep.* 287. *Walker* and *Edwards*.

If the Master refuse to keep the Apprentice any longer; this is a good Cause of Discharge, 1 *Sand.* 315.

A Record was removed out of *London* into the *King's-Bench* by *Habeas Corpus*, and it was on Debt on a By-Law, That no Freeman should employ any Person in any Trade which had not been Apprentice to it, or a Freeman of *London*, and that the Defendant had employed one in the Trade of an Upholsterer, which had not been an Apprentice to it, and a *Procedendo* was granted, *Sid.* 269. *Player* and *Petill.* *Procedendo*, or By-Law.

Per Windham, Upholsterers were a Corporation in *Henry* the Seventh's Time. And the Question here is, Whether an Upholsterer be a Trade, and a *Procedendo* ought to go upon 11 *H.* 7. c. 19. 1 *Keb.* 930. *Mesme* Case.

It hath been a Question, Whether the Justices of the Peace may compel one to take an Apprentice; and adjudged by all but *Twisden*, That they may, by the Statute of 5 *Eliz.* c. 4. for they are to be Executioners of the Statute, and that it would be fruitless, unless they had Authority to compel a Man Justices of Peace may compel one to take an Apprentice.

to take an Apprentice. But *Twisden* said, *Then the Son of my Enemy might be put to me, which would be dangerous.* But it was so ruled in *Gislfer's* Case, 14 & 15 *Car.* 2. *B. R. Sid.* 99. *Canterell's* Case.

The Case was,

The Churchwardens and Overseers of a Parish in *Darbyshire* placed a Child, which was the Bastard Child of *M. N.* with the Defendant, according to the Statute of 43 *Eliz. c.* 2. and doth appoint the Defendant to receive the said Child. The Defendant appeals to the Sessions; and there the Justices make an Order, That the Defendant shall take the said Child as an Apprentice, and the Defendant by *Certiorari* removed the Order into the *King's-Bench.* Some Exceptions were taken to the Form of the Order:

1. It appears not to be a Poor Child.

2. Nor in what Trade he shall be an Apprentice. But *per Cur'*, It shall come on the other Side, that she is not a Child within the Statute. And Secondly, Husbandry is intended in that Statute, and so shall be intended in the Order, until the Contrary appear. But as to the Case in Law, the Order was confirmed by Three Judges. *Windham* said, the Judges in *Serjeants-Inn* in *Fleet-street* were divided in the Case. Therefore it was agreed, That the Law might come in Debate, that an Information should be exhibited against the Defendant for not performing thereof.

And

And in *P.* 19 *Car.* 2. *B. R.* The Court was moved to quash an Order for imposing an Apprentice; but the Court refused to quash it, or to give any Opinion, whether they might impose so or not, but directed the Party grieved by the Order to have an Action on the Case if he will. But *Quær.* against whom it must be brought, *Sid.* 411.

As to Masters correcting of Apprentices.

If the Apprentice misbehave himself, the Master may correct him, or the Justices may punish him. Of Masters correcting Apprentices.

Trespass was brought for Battery. The Defendant justified, because the Plaintiff was his Apprentice, and because he neglected his Service, *moderate castigavit.* The Plaintiff replies, *Non moderate castigavit*; the Jury found *Non moderate castigavit*, and 20 *l.* Damages. It was moved in Arrest of Judgment, that *moderate castigavit* is not any Answer to the Declaration, which doth not import any Beating, and it's a *negativum infinitum*, to reply to it *Non moderate castigavit*, where it ought to be *De injuria sua propria.* *Per Cur.* This were ill upon Demurrer, yet it's good after a Verdict by the Statute of *Jeofails*, *Car.* 2. because here is an Affirmative and a Negative, *Sid.* 444. *Awbry* and *James*. *Non moderate castigavit*, no good Issue, yet helped by *Jeofail.*

Trespass of Assault, Battery and Wounding. The Defendant traverseth the Wounding, and on this Issue is joined, *Et quoad verberationem*; he pleads, *Quod diu ante præd' tempus quo & eodem tempore quo supponitur transgressio*

gressio præd' fieri; the Plaintiff was his Servant, and for Neglect of his Service, *mollit' manus imposuit*; *quæ est eadem verberatio*; and pleads further; That such a Day and Year the Plaintiff released to him all Actions; and saith not by Deed; yet *per Cur.* the Plea was held to be ill, as being double, 1. *Keb.* 661. *Sid.* 175. *Bleeke* and *Grove.*

Remedy for Abusing or Inticing a Servant.

One brings an Action on the Case against another for procuring and inticing his Apprentice from him, (which is before the Time expired,) and declares, *per quod idem (le Pl.) totum proficuum commodum & easiamentum ratione servitii servientis præd' per totum residuum Termini prædicti ventur' recipere potuisset totaliter perdidit & amisit*, to the Plaintiff's Damage of 100 *l.* The Jury find for the Plaintiff, and assess Damages generally, and Judgment was arrested, for he ought to recover no more Damages than from the Departure, till the Time of the Exhibition of the Bill, and not for the future, for he may return again to his Master, and the general Damages being as well for the Time to come as the Time past, it is ill, 2 *Sanders* 169. *Hambleton* and *Vere*, *Raymond* 200. *Mesme* Case.

General Damages given, where ill. And it shall not be intended, that Damages were only given for the Loss for the Time past, because he hath declared for the Time to come, and the Jury have found generally according to his Declaration.

If

If one beat the Servant of *J. S.* so that he die of that Beating, the Master shall not have an Action against the other for the Battery and Loss of Service; because the Servant dying of the Extremity of the Beating, it is now become an Offence against the Crown, and turned into Felony; and this hath drowned the particular Offence. *Quære,* If after Conviction it doth not lie, as in Case of Robbery, *Vide* in *Stiles* well argued, 1 *Brownl.* 205. *Huggin*'s Case, 2 *Rolls* 557. *Mesme* Case, *Stiles* 347. *Dawke*'s Case, *Mod. Rep.*

If the Servant die of the Battery, no Action lies for the Master.

H. was indicted for Practice in withdrawing and inticing an Apprentice. After Not guilty pleaded and Verdict, he demurred to the Indictment on the Precedent in *Coke*'s *Entries* 303. which the Court disallowed; and *Twisden* conceived that was some *Scire fac'* against the Party; and Judgment was for the King, 1 *Keb.* 726. *Cok. Ent.* 303.

Indictment for inticing away an Apprentice.

Who may be compelled to be bound Apprentices.

Any one Justice of the Peace (upon Complaint made to him) may compel any Person meet (in his Discretion) to be bound an Apprentice with any one that shall require him to Husbandry, or any other Art; and upon their Refusal, may commit him to Ward, there to remain till they will be bound.

Such Children, whose Parents are not able to maintain them, though they be under 12 Years of Age, may be bound Apprentices by the Overseers of the Poor, with the Assent of any Two Justices of Peace, by the Satute of 43 *Eliz. c.* 2.

Of Apprentices bound to Mariners.

Per the Statute of 2 *Ann. cap.* 6. Two Justices in their Counties, *&c.* or Mayor, Aldermen, or other Chief Officers of any City, or Town-Corporate, and Church-wardens and Overseers of the Poor, with the Consent of such Justices of Peace, *&c.* may bind out Boys above 10 Years of Age, who, or whose Parents, are chargeable to the Parish, to be Apprentices to the Sea-Service to any Subject, Master, or Owner of any Ship or Vessel belonging to any Port in *England, Wales* or *Berwick,* until the Age of 21. The Age of the Boy to be bound shall be mentioned in his Indenture.

The said Church-wardens and Overseers shall pay 50 *s.* to the Boy's Master for Cloathing and Bedding, which shall be allowed them on their Accounts.

Any to whom any poor Parish Boy is Apprentice, by the Statute of 43 *Eliz.* may, with the Consent of Two Justices of Peace, Mayor or Chief Officer, *&c.* where such poor Boy was bound, to turn over such Boy to any Master or Owner of such Ship or Vessel, for the remaining Time of his Apprenticeship; which shall be certified. The Counterpart of the Indenture is to be executed at the Port, in the Presence of the Collector and Officer conducting the Boy, and to be returned to the Church-wardens and Overseers.

Two Justices, all Mayors, Chief Officers, *&c.* in or near the Port to which Ships shall arrive, may hear and determine Complaints of hard Usage of all Apprentices to Sea-Service, 2 *Annæ*, *c.* 6.

Of the Master's making the Apprentice free.

In *London*, if any Master shall refuse to make his Apprentice free, when the Term in his Indenture is expired, upon Complaint thereof made to the Chamberlain, he will cause such a Master to be summoned before him, and if he cannot shew good Cause to the contrary, will make the Apprentice free.

In other Corporations, he may have a *Mandamus* to be directed to the Mayor, *&c.* to make him free, if the Master refuse to do it. And this was *Townsend*'s Case, and the Mayor of *Oxford*, *Raymonds* 69. *Townsend*'s Case.

So it was in *Norwich*. And in *Hill.* 15 *&* 16 *Car.* 2. The Mayor and Commonalty of *Oxford* retorned to the *Mandamus*, That if any Person binds himself to be an Apprentice, it is by the Course of their Corporation to be inrolled; and *Townsend* bound himself Apprentice to C. by which he covenanted he would not contract Matrimony during his Apprenticeship, and that the Indenture was inrolled, and that he within the first Two Years of his Apprenticeship did

did marry, and after this he ſerved rather as a Journyman than an Apprentice.

Per Cur. Exceptions to this Retorn:

1. Tho' he covenants he will not marry, yet if he marry, this is only a Breach of his Covenant, but not any Cauſe to bar him of his Freedom.

2. The Retorn, That he ſerved him rather as a Journyman than an Apprentice, is uncertain and not poſitive, and Reſtitution was awarded, *Raymond* 92. *Meſme* Caſe.

CHAP.

CHAP. XVII.

Orphans.

Of the Court of Orphans in London; *and the Customs in relation to Orphans. The Chamberlain of* London *a sole Corporation to this Purpose. Though Security to account,* &c. *hath been given at Common Law, and in the Prerogative Court, yet the Court of Orphans will compel him to give new Security. Hotchpot, the Nature of it. Prohibition lies, if any sue in the Ecclesiastical Court. Orphans not to marry, or be put out Apprentice, without Leave of this Court. Marriage without Consent is finable, and Imprisonment till Payment. Bar is good to common Intent. The Custom extends to Lands out of* London. Quære, *If a Freeman discontinue the City and his Trade, how much he may dispose by Will? The Custom of* London *as to the Distribution of the personal Estate. Freeman cannot devise the Disposition and Custody of the Body of an Infant. Orphans Money not devisable when payable by the Custom.*

ORphanage being one of the most considerable Customs of *London*, in reference to Infants of Freemen there, deserves next to be considered.

By

By an Act of Parliament, *Rot. Par.* 1 *R.* 2. N° 130. It is enacted, 'That the Mayor 'and Chamberlain of *London* for the Time 'being shall have the keeping of all the 'Lands and Goods of such Orphans as hap-'pen within the City, saving to the King 'and other Lords the Rights of such as 'hold of them out of the same Liberty.

The Court of Orphans.

The Court of Orphans is held before the Lord Mayor and Aldermen of the City of *London*, who are Guardians to Children of all Freemen of *London*, that are or shall be under the Age of 21 Years at the Time of their Fathers Decease. The Common Serjeant of the City is the only Person intrusted by the Court of Aldermen to take all Inventories and Accounts of Freemen's Estates.

The youngest Attorney in the Ld. Mayor's Court is always Clerk of the Orphans, and is appointed to take all Securities for Orphans Portions, which Securities are constantly taken in the Name of the Chamberlain of *London* for the Time being: And to this Purpose the Chamberlain is a sole Corporation to him and his Successors for Orphans. And in *Fullwood*'s Case, 4 *Rep.* A Recognizance or Bond made to him and his Successors concerning Orphans, shall by the Custom of *London* go to his Successor: And this is not like the Case of a Bishop, Parson, Vicar, Master of an Hospital, *&c.* or such sole Corporation; for there no Chattel either in Action or Possession shall go in Succession.

The Chamberlain of *London* a sole Corporation to this Purpose.

But

But the Executors or Administrators shall have them.

1. Because they cannot take Recognizance or Bond in their Politick Capacity.

2. Neither have they such Custom, 4 *Rep. Fullwood*'s Case.

But for Judgment in Law as to the Custom of Orphans, you have a clear Case resolved in *Hob.* 474. *Latch*'s Case.

It was resolved, There hath been a Court of Orphans Time out of Mind in *London*, and there hath been a Custom, If any Freeman or Freewoman die, leaving Orphans within Age unmarried, that they have had the Custody of their Bodies and Goods; and that the Executors and Administrators have used, and ought, to exhibit true Inventories before them; and if any Debt appears due, to become bound to the Chamberlain to the Use of the Orphans in a reasonable Sum, to make true Account upon Oath of them after they have been received; and if they refuse, to commit them till they will become bound. This was adjudged to be a reasonable Custom upon the Retorn of a *Habeas Corpus*. The Case was, One *Jane* (Widow, Freewoman, and Fishmonger of *London*) died, leaving divers Orphans, and one *Latch* was Administrator, and had exhibited an Inventory of 1000 *l.* Debts unreceived, and was required to give Bond of 2000 *l.* which Sum he refused, *per quod, &c.* It was adjudged good and reasonable; and if the Ecclesiastical Court will compel them to make Account there against this Custom,

Custom of *London* as to Orphans.

U a Pro-

Tho' Security to account hath been given at Common Law, or in the Prerogative Court, yet the Court of Orphans will compel him to give new Security.

a Prohibition lies. And it was alledged for the Prisoner in that Case, That he was already bound in the Prerogative Court to make Account, and so he should be twice bound.

And to this Purpose was the Case of *Andrews*, P. 17 *Jac. B. R.* which was, A Woman, before she contracted Marriage with *J. S.* agrees with him, that she shall have Power to devise a Sum of 200 *l.* to any Person, and after the Marriage she by her Will gives this to the Children of her first Husband, and dies; the Husband after acknowledges a Judgment at Common Law for the Security of it; yet by the Custom of the Orphans of *London*, he may be compelled by the Court of Orphans to give new Security for this to the Chamberlain of *London*.

As for the Manner of Process, Summons, Conditions of the Bond for exhibiting an Inventory, the Appraisement, the Security Bond, (if the Money be not paid into the Chamber, &c.) *Vide Lex Londinensis*, or the City Law.

Note, The Custom of *London* is, That if the Father advance any of his Children with any Part of his Goods, that that shall bar them to demand any further Part, unless the Father under his Hand, or by his last Will, did express and declare, that it was but in Part of Advancement, and then that Child so partly advanced shall put his Part in Hotchpot with the Executors and Widow, and have a full third Part of the whole, ac-

Hotchpot.

counting

counting that which was formerly given to him as a Part thereof; and this is that which the *Civilians* call *Collatio Bonorum*.

Some expound the Custom thus; That as if a Man has two Children, and gives to one of them 100 *l.* in Part of his Advancement, and then dies worth 900 *l.* in this Case, the Wife, the Issue not advanced, and the Executors, shall have but three equal Parts of the 900 *l.* (*viz.*) 300 *l.* apiece, and then the 100 *l.* so given shall be in Hotchpot between the Children, which my Lord *Coke* conceives cannot be; for then there shall be no Equality amongst the Issues, as the Custom doth require, 12 *Rep.* 113.

It was in *Beckford's* Case in *Chancery*, 1 *Jac.* 2. declared the Custom of *London* to be, That Children not fully advanced were to bring in what they had recover'd into Hotchpot with the Orphanage, though after the Estate is divided into Thirds, and not into Hotchpot with the whole Estate, and decreed accordingly, *Beckford's* Case.

This Court of Orphans is such a peculiar Court, that if any Orphan sue in the Ecclesiastical Court for any Goods, Money or, Chattels, due to them, or by the Custom of *London*, or for any Legacy, or to have an Account, a Prohibition lies, 5 *Rep.* 73. Prohibition lies, if sued elsewhere.

Orphans not marry, or be put out Apprentice, without Leave of this Court.

Note, The Security must take particular Care that none of the Orphans marry, or be put out Apprentices, without the Leave of the Court of Aldermen first obtained for that Purpose.

Marriage without Consent is finable, and Imprisonment till Payment.

The Court of Aldermen do commit the Custody of Orphans to such Person and Persons as they shall think fit; and if any Person do intermarry with any Orphan without the Consent of the same Court first obtained, such a Person may be fined by them according to the Quality and Portion of the Orphan, and unless such Person do pay the Fine, or give Security to pay it, the Court may commit him to *Newgate*, to remain there till he submit to their Order: And this hath been adjudged good in the Court of *King's-Bench*; and it was one *Wilkinson's* Case against Sir *William Bolton*, *Pasch.* 17 *Car.* 2.

An Action of Trespass was brought for Battery and false Imprisonment. The Defendant justifies by the Custom of *London*, of the Court of Orphans, and that a Freeman died, and left his Daughter under 18 Years of Age (for such is the Age of a Female) and unmarried; and that the Court committed the Custody of her to Sir *William Bolton*, and set forth the Custom, That if any such Ward be taken away, *&c.* they may commit the Party to *Newgate* who does this, to be imprisoned till he produce the Infant, or be deliver'd by due Course of Law, and because the Plaintiff took her away,

away, he was committed, *P.* 17 *Car.* 2. *Wilkinson* and Sir *William Bolton*.

The Plaintiff demurs upon this Plea.

1. Becauſe the Cuſtom to impriſon is unreaſonable, for that no Time is allowed to the Party to make his Defence.

2. And it's general, to impriſon all, and ſo a Peer may be impriſoned. But by the Court, It's a great Offence and Contempt, and the Cuſtom is reaſonable: But there ſeemed to be a Fault in the Plea. For the Bar was, That the Infant was of ſuch an Age, and unmarried at the Time of the Death of the Anceſtor, but does not ſay ſhe was unmarried at the Time of the taking. But it was over-ruled, for that a Bar ſhall be good to common Intent. *Vide* the Caſe reported in *Raymond*, *p.* 116.

Pleading.

Bar good to common Intent.

Note, This Cuſtom to have the Cuſtody of the Perſon, and of all the Eſtate real and perſonal, extends to Lands out of *London*. But it hath been a Queſtion, If a Freeman diſcontinue from the City and his Trade, and dies, leaving his Children and Eſtate in the Country, whether the Court of Orphans ſhall intermeddle with them? And it was the Opinion of *Hide* Chief Juſtice, That they ſhould not intermeddle.

The Cuſtom extends to Lands out of *London*.

Quære, If a Freeman diſcontinue his Trade and the City.

By the Cuſtom of *London*, a Freeman's Widow may require a third Part of his perſonal Eſtate, after his Debts paid, and the Funeral diſcharged, and his Children may require another third Part thereof, and he

What a Freeman may deviſe by Will.

The Custom of *London* as to the personal Estate.

may by his Will give away another third Part of his Estate: But if he have no Children, the Widow may require a Moiety of his personal Estate; but a Freeman in the Time of his Sickness cannot give away any Part of his Estate. But if a Freeman die without a Will, Administration shall be granted to his Wife, and she will claim one third Part, and one Third must be divided amongst the Children, and the other between the Wife and Children, and usually the Widow is allowed two Thirds of the Freeman's Estate.

A Freeman cannot devise the Disposition of the Body and Custody of an Infant.

If a Father is a Freeman of *London*, he cannot devise the Disposition of the Body of the Infant, and if he do, yet the Infant shall remain in the Custody of the Mayor and Aldermen. And as well in the Statute of 4 and 5 of *Philip* and *Mary*, *c.* 8. concerning the taking of Infants Females out of the Possession of the Guardian, as the Statute of 12 *Car.* 2. *c.* 24. which impowers Fathers to dispose of the Custody of their Children, there are Proviso's to save the Custom of *London*, and also of other Vills, *Sid.* 363. *Bastian*'s Case.

Orphans Money in the Hands of the Chamberlain, not devisable by the Husband.

A. B. an Orphan of *London*, married to *W. P.* before he was at the Age of 21 Years, and not having taken out the Money, dies, having bequeathed this Money to his Wife, provided she should not claim Dower. She brought Dower against *P. P.* Brother of *W. P.* her late Husband. He brings a Bill in *Chancery*, to make Discovery of the Estate, and to compel her to release Dower, or renounce the

the Devise. The Question is, Whether the Money in the Court of Orphans were devisable or not?

Per Bridgman, Keeper, *Twisden* and *Wild*, it is a *Chose en Action*, and so not devisable; The Custom of Orphans is, under Age they find them Money (that is) for their Maintenance, and no more; yet when the Orphan comes of full Age, or the Female marries, it is cast up, and the Interest is fully paid. In this Case it was the Laches of the Husband that he did not recover it; for by the Custom it is to be paid at the full Age or Marriage of the Female Orphan: And the Custom is, Upon the Marriage of Orphans, to appoint the Common Serjeant to treat and take Security for the Orphan, 2 *Ventris* 240. *Phesant*'s Case.

When the Orphans Money becomes payable by the Custom.

It is the Custom of *London*, That if any Freeman of *London* devise a Legacy to an Orphan, that the Executor shall be constrained to find Sureties to pay the Legacy according to Law. *Quære*, If this Custom be good, for perhaps he shall not have Assets after Debts paid, 1 *Rolls Rep.* 316.

It was adjudged in *Hanmond* and *Honywood*'s Case in *Chancery*, 32 *Car.* 2. That by the Custom of *London*, a Declaration made by a Freeman by Writing, tho' such Writing were made for his last Will, and revoked, is such a Declaration as will let in the Child to have a customary Part of the personal Estate.

What is a good Declaration of customary Part.

A Citizen of *London* cannot devise his Child's Part over to another, in case the Child die in Minority.

A Citizen and Freeman of *London* deviseth to his Son a groſs Sum, which did exceed the cuſtomary Part, and deviseth, if his Son die before he attain Twenty one, that Sum over to another. The Queſtion was, If the Deviſe over were good? It was decreed, 23 *Car.* 2. in *Chancery*, That the Deviſe over for ſo much as was the cuſtomary Part was void, and that the Orphan dying within Age, his Adminiſtrator was intitled to ſo much as was the cuſtomary Part, and the Surplus of that groſs Sum to go to thoſe to whom it was deviſed over, 1 *Caſes in Chancery* 99.

CHAP.

CHAP. XVIII.

Trial, Judgment, Execution.

Regula. *Infancy, where and in what Cases tried by Inspection, Proofs, or* per Pais. *Infant himself examined on a* Voire dire. *The Manner of Inspection. Evidence of Nonage upon* non Assumpsit. *A Rule of Court about Inspection. Reinspection granted; and why the Court judge of Infancy by Inspection, not a Jury. Nonage, where tried in the County where the Land lies, or where the Action is brought. The Birth of an Issue where it shall be tried. Infant, if bound by Verdict upon Issue tried upon a Plea in Abatement. If Judgment against an Infant* Quod capiatur. *No Execution against an Infant-Heir on Recognizance. Trial in* Ætate probanda.

THE Trial of Infancy, the Manner and Place where to be tried, comes next to be treated of.

It's laid down as a Rule:

In all Cases where the Matter may be tried by the Examination of the Justices, they may, if they be in Doubt, refuse that, and compel the Party to put it upon Trial *per Pais. Per touts Justices,* as in case of Infancy. *Regula.*

Now

Infancy tried by Inſpection per Proofs, or *per Pais*.

Now I ſhall recite ſome Reſolutions, where and in what Caſes Infancy ſhall be tried by Inſpection, by Proof, or *per Pais*.

In what Caſe Nonage ſhall be tried by Inſpection, *Per Pais*, Infant appearing by Attorney.

In Error to reverſe a Fine for Nonage, or in *Audita Querela* to reverſe a Statute or Recognizance for Nonage, the Age ſhall be tried by Inſpection of the Juſtices, and not by *Pais*: But if an Infant appear by Attorney, this is Error; but it ſhall be tried *per Pais*, and not by the Juſtices: For the making of the Warrant of Attorney is the Act of the Party, without the Examination of the Juſtices.

By Inſpection.

If the Tenant in a real Action vouch *A.* as Heir within Age; or if Tenant for Life be impleaded, and pray in Aid of one in Reverſion within Age, and prays that the Parol ſhall demur, *&c.* there if the Demandant reply, that he is of full Age, this ſhall not be tried by *Pais*, but a Writ ſhall be directed to the Sheriff, (*viz.*)

Quod Venire fac' tali die A. ut per aſpectu corporis ſui conſtare poſſit pdictis Juſticiariis noſtris ſi ſit plene etatis necne, &c. non teſtiu teſtimonio, non Juratorum veredicto ſed judicii Inſpectione.

But the Judges (as is uſual) by *adminicula* may inform themſelves by Witneſſes, by Church-Books, *&c.*

Account *per Pais*.

In Account againſt *Baylee* (*Account Fitz.* 121. 12 *Aſſ.* 37.) Infancy ſhall be tried in *Pais*. 9 *Rep.* 31.

If

If an Appeal be brought by Infant, the Infancy shall be tried by Inspection, 11 *H.* 4. 94. Appeal Per *Inspect.*

In a Writ of *Error* to reverse a Judgment, if Nonage be alledged for Error, this shall be tried by Inspection. So upon a common Recovery, or to reverse a Fine, *Anne Hungate's* Case. *Vide supra.* *Dyer* 104. *Contr. Trin.* 11 *Car. B. N. Scawen* and *Arundel.* Error *per Inspect.*

Trial of Inspection in case of Dower is by Proofs in case of Death *per Pais.* In a *Dum fuit infra ætatem*, Infancy may be tried *per Pais*, 1 *Keb.* 929. By Proofs *per Pais.*

If the Question be, Infant or not? If the Party be of full Age, it shall be tried *per Pais*, *Bulstr.* 7 *Jac. Moreton* and *Ords.* Where the Party is of full Age, *per Pais.*

If the Parole be prayed to demur for the Nonage of one Party, and the Nonage is confessed by the other Party, the Parol shall be adjudged to demur without Inspection of the Infant, 29 *Astr.* 37. *Adjudged.* *Parol* demur.

If Infant appear by Attorney in Action brought against him, in which he ought to have appeared by Guardian, and after Judgment is given against him, being within Age, and after in a Writ of *Error* he assigns this for Error; this shall not be tried by Inspection, but by Proofs; for if he be now of full Age, Judgment shall be reversed; and the first Judgment was reversed. By Proofs.

Trin. 39 *El.* B. R. *Sydbery* and *Raunt*, but cited by the name of *Selborough*'s Case, in *Cro. El.* 580. *Stone* and *Matches* Case. The Defendant in Debt confesseth the Action by Attorney, and assigns for Error that he was within

Confession in Debt *per Pais.* within Age at time of the Confession; and they were thereupon at Issue, and tried *per Pais*, *Cro. El.* 580. *Selborough*'s Case.

Appearance by Attorney *per Pais.* Infant brought a Writ of *Error* by Guardian, to reverse a Judgment given against him, in which he appeared by Attorney, and assigns for Error, That he was within Age at the time of the Judgment given against him, he appearing by Attorney; this shall not be tried by Inspection, but *per Pais*, *Trin.* 11 *Car.* 1. B. R. *Scawen* and *Arundel.*

Bartholomew brought a Writ of *Error*, for that *Dighton* recovered against him in an Action of *Imprisonment*, in which he being within Age did sue by Attorney, and the Judgment was reversed, and the Nonage was tried *per Pais*, *Bridgm. Rep.* 75.

Infant himself examined upon a *Voire dire.* The Court may examine Infant upon a *Voire dire*, whether he be within Age, 11 *H.* 4. 15.

In Trial at Bar, the Question was, If one was at full Age at the time of the Will made by him? To prove his Nonage, the Defendant produced an Almanack, in which his Father had writ the Nativity of the Devisor; and it was allowed to be strong Evidence, *Raym.* 84. *Herbert* and *Tuckal.*

Evidence of Nonage, upon *non Assumpsit.* In *Assumpsit*, the Defendant pleads *non Assumpsit*, and upon Trial before *Hale*, in *Middlesex*, he permitted the Defendant to good Evidence of Nonage at the time of the Promise, on which the Plaintiff was nonsui. 2 *Lev. Seaton* and *Gilbert* 144.

As

As to the manner of Inspection, and the *Adminicula* the Judges use, I find, The manner of Inspection.

That in a Writ of *Error* to reverse a Fine levied by Infant *Feme Covert*, the Court was moved for a Day to bring in the Party that levied the Fine to be inspected, which was granted, and at the Day she was brought into Court and viewed; and two Witnesses deposed, that she was within Age at the time of the Fine levied, which was entred upon the Roll: Upon which the Issue was tried, *Styles* 451.

The Rule of Court was

Martis 22 die Junii, Anno Regni Regis *Jacobi* Angliæ, *&c.* Inter, *&c*

Habita isto die per Curiam hic inspectio corporis pred. Quer. videtur dicte Curie hic eundem Quer' infra etatem vigint' & unius annorum modo existere, sed quia dicta Curia hic se advisare vult priusquam ad judicium in hac parte reddend' procedatur Ordinatum est per eand' Curiam hic quod pred. querens possit producere in dicta Curia hic testes quoscunque & alias probatione ad veritatem in promissis probandum.

And in *Sherlock*'s Case, *Stiles* 456. upon Trial by Inspection, *Affidavit* was made by one in the Court who knew the Infant that was there present, and the Time of her Birth, and her being Baptized, and swore the Day precisely. The Church-Book was also produced in Court, and proved by Oath,

Oath, wherein the Time of her Baptizing was entred, and that she was the same Person; and the *Affidavits* were recorded, and the Inspection entred, and she had a Guardian assigned her by her own Election; and a *Scire facias* was awarded against the Heir, *Stiles* 456.

In *Michaelmas* Term, 20 *Jac.* one *W.* being of 20 Years, brought a Writ of *Error* to reverse a Fine, being levied by him during his Nonage, and was inspected by the Court, and the Church-Book where he was Christned was shewed to the Court, and the two Church-wardens were sworn that this was the true Book, and that he was the Party then Baptized, and a Knight, who was then his Godfather, affirmed it upon Oath, *Palmer* 326.

It was prayed that an Infant might be inspected to reverse a Fine, and forasmuch as he had not his Proofs there, he was not inspected; but *dies datus est usque Octab' Michaelis proximas*, at which time the Infant came the Day which was wont to be the Day of Essoin, and prayed *Justice Crooke* (who was there to adjourn the Term) to Inspect him and take his Proofs, which he did *de bene esse*.

And now before the Month of *Michaelmas* the Infant came of full Age; and whether this Inspection was well taken, was the Question.

Per Cur. The Day of Essoin is a Day in Term, and the Court was full, tho' there was but one Judge; and if the Inspection had been

been the Day of Effoin, and before the *quarto die poft* he had come of full Age, this fhall be very good.

But the Doubt was, If upon the Day of Adjournment the Judge had Power to do any thing but to adjourn the Term. *Qu. de hoc.* 2 *Brownl.* 278. Infpection on the Effoin-day, if good.

In Points, 2 *Crook* 230. and 1 *Bulftr.* 31. The Infpection of an Infant was taken by one of the Juftices upon an Effoin Day. The Queftion was, whether it were good, and the Judgment upon the Infpection of him was given the fame Day, and by the Opinion of all the Juftices, the Judgment was well given.

The Court was moved in behalf of an Infant to difcharge a Guardian affigned by the Court, and to make another, and that the former Infpection may be difcharged; and that the Infant may now be infpected again; becaufe there was no Action depending in Court againft the Infant, when the former Infpection was; and it was granted, *Stiles p.* 456. Reinfpection granted, and why.

Error was brought to reverfe a Fine for Infancy; it was moved, that the Party being in Court fhe might be infpected, and the Infpection recorded; and there was produced a Copy of the Regifter-Book, fworn to be true, and feveral Affidavits of her Age.

Per Cur. Let the Infpection be recorded. The Iffue of her Infancy may be tried at any time hereafter, tho' fhe comes of Age, 1 *Ventr.* 69. *Coufin's* Cafe.

A

A Woman during Coverture joined with her Husband in levying a Fine of her own Lands with her Husband within Age, and she was brought into Court to be inspected; whereupon a *Scire facias* issued out to the Tertenants, who came and pleaded, That she was of full Age at the time of the Fine levied; upon which Issue was joined, and a Verdict *pro Quer.* And now she came and prayed Judgment upon the Verdict. The Court said, That we are to judge of Infancy upon Inspection, and not the Jury: And upon Inspection, we judge her to be within Age, and therefore let the Fine be reversed. *Vidian* and *Fletcher*'s Case, *Stiles* 474.

The Court judge of Infancy by Inspection, not a Jury.

It was doubted in *But*'s and *Jenning*'s Case, 1 *Bulstr.* 296. Whether Infant bringing a Writ of *Error* to reverse a Judgment given against him in Action of Debt, because he then was and still is an Infant, whether he is to be inspected by the Court as in case to reverse a Fine? *Per Man* Secondary, This is an usual Course for him to come into Court by his Writ of *Error* to be inspected, and a *Scire facias* is to issue against the others to come in. *Et per Curiam*, We may well inspect him when he comes in by Writ of *Error*, and if he be of full Age, the other Side ought to aver this, and Day was given to the other Side to shew Cause, or else for this Error Judgment to be reversed.

Error is assigned in Fact (in *Action sur Case*) that he was an Infant, and shews no

Place where he was an Infant. To this Error the Plaintiff pleaded that he was of full Age, and it was tried at *H.* in *Suffolk.*

Whitlock Just. Every *Venire fac'* properly is to be from the Place where the Writ is brought, unless it be drawn away by Plea. This is new Matter, and not helped by the Statute of 20 *Jac.* The Matter is Collateral to the first Record, and it is a new Record upon Error.

Per tot. Cur. It's out of the Statute, and a Repleader was granted; for there is no Trial, nor no *Venire.* But if in this Action he had alledged a Place of his Infancy, *scil.* at *Dale*, and the *Venire* had been of *Sale*, there the Trial had been good, *Godb.* 382. 2 *Rolls* 373. *Latch* 194. *Tayler* and *Tollwin.*

Where Nonage shall be tried.

It hath been much argued where Nonage shall be tried, whether in the County or Place where it is alledged, or where the Land lies, and it is Resolved as follows, with the Diversity:

Error was brought, for that Judgment was given by Default against the Defendant, being an Infant; Issue was taken that he was of full Age, and the Question was, where the Issue shall be tried, Whether in *Norfolk*, where the Land lies; or in *Middlesex*, where the Action was brought? And *per Cur.* it shall be tried in the County where the Land lay, *Cro. El.* 818. *Green* and *Rosse.* (Nonage, whether tried in the County where the Land lies, or where the Action is brought.)

X And

And so is *Morgan* and *Vaughan*'s Case:

Error was of a Judgment in the Grand Sessions at *Brecon*; Error assigned was, That the Tenant within Age appeared by Attorney; and alledgeth, that he was within Age at *Abergaveney* in the County of *Middlesex*, and Issue being joined in the County of *Monmouth*. And Issue was joined upon the Nonage, the Trial was by a Jury of the *Venue* of *Abergaveney*, and found for the Plaintiff in Error.

It was moved in Arrest of Judgment, That the Plaintiff in this Writ of *Error* appears by Attorney, and he was within Age at the time of the Writ brought, as appears by the Record: For it is alledged, That 7 *Septemb.* 20 *Car.* 2. he was within Age, *Videlicet*, the Age of Fourteen Years, and no more; and he brought the Writ of *Error* 14 *July*, 26 *Car.* 2. and in the Term following assigns the Error.

(*Videlicet*) where no Estoppel.

Sed non allocatur; for the [*Videlicet*] is not the Material part of the Issue; and the [*Videlicet*] goes not to the right of the Action, and so cannot be an Estoppel.

2. It was said, That Trial for Dower being a Real Action, Error upon it is of the same Nature, and every Issue joined in this ought to be tried where the Land lies: And to *Green* and *Rosse*'s Case, the Original Action was *Ejectione firmæ*; but here it is Dower.

But

But *per Cur.* the Trial is good enough; and the Difference was taken as to the Nature of the Original Action, where the Title depends upon the Nonage alledged, and where the Nonage is pleaded, as it is here by Matter *dehors*. Diversity.

In the first Case, the Tryal shall be where the Land lies, and not so in the other. And Judgment was given for the Plaintiff in Error, Sir *Tho. Jones*'s *Rep.* 170. *Morgan* and *Vaughan*, *Green* and *Rosse*'s Case.

If *A.* recover against *B.* in *Ejectione firmæ* in *Durham*, upon which *B.* brought Error in *B. R.* at *Westminster*, and assigns for Error, That the said *A.* at the time of the Trial of the first Action, was *commorans* and within Age at *Westminster* in *Middlesex*, and that he sued in the said Action by Attorney, and upon the Nonage the Parties are at Issue; this shall be tried at *Westminster*, and not at *Durham*, where the Land lies; because that the *Ejectione firmæ* is not any Real Action; and inasmuch as it is specially alledged, that he was within Age, and *commorans* at *Westminster*, where the Writ of *Error* is now brought, 1 *Brownl.* 150. *Trin.* 11 *Jac. B. R.* *Ords* and *Moreton*. In *Ejectione firmæ*. Nonage tried where it is alledged, not where the Land lies.

And in the Report in *Bulstrode* of this Case, the Difference is taken in Real and Personal Actions, 1 *Bulstr.* 131.

Infant pleads, That at the time of making the Release of all his Right, he was within Age, and born in another County; yet the same shall be tried where the Land is. *Aliter*, in Personal Actions, 1 *Bulstrode* 134.

The Birth of an Issue, where it shall be tried.

If Issue be, Whether *D.* was born before Marriage at *A.* or within Marriage at *B.* in the same County; this shall be tried in both Vills, 11 *H.* 4. 84.

In an *Assize*, if the Birth of him who claims as Heir be alledged in a Foreign County, and the Issue is, whether he be Heir; this shall be tried where the Land is, and not where the Birth is alledged; for the Inheritance is the Principal, and where the Land lies it may be best known who is to inherit, 46 *Ass.* 5. *fo.* 355. *b. Adjudged.*

If the Issue be between the Heir and a Man who claims to be Tenant by the Courtesie, whether he had Issue by the Wife during the Coverture in a Foreign County; this shall be tried where it is alledged, 13 *H.* 4. 44.

Stat. Glouc. c. 2. Explained.

The Statute of *Gloucester, c.* 2. gave the Infant a Trial during his Minority; but it gave it him in such Actions, as he might not be foreclosed in his Right: But tho' he were barred in any of the said Actions (Actions *Auncestrel possessory, Mortdauncestor, Ayel, Besayel, Cosinage)* during his Minority, he may have Recourse to a Writ of an higher Nature, so as he should not be Remediless, nor any final Judgment given against him during his Infancy; and therefore the *Formedon in discender,* which is in Nature of his Writ of *Right* for the Issue in Tail, he can have no Writ of an higher Nature, and therefore is not within the Statute, 2 *Inst.* 291.

Infant,

Infant, who was Party to an Ejectment in a Trial at Bar in the *King's-Bench*, answered to a Bill in *Chancery* by Guardian; that Answer shall not be read in Evidence against the Infant, 1 *W. & M. Leigh* and *Ward*.

Judgment against an Infant was reversed, because it was *Capiatur*.

Error of Judgment in a Formedon in Remainder, where the Tenant pleads Infancy, and that the Remainder discended to him, and prays his Age. Demandant pleads, the Remainder did not discend to him. Issue joined, and found for the Demandant, and Judgment final, and this was assigned for Error. But the Judgment was final; and in *Respond' ouster*, it was agreed, that generally that upon Issue upon a dilatory Plea, Judgment final ought to be. In all Cases, when Issue is upon a dilatory Plea and tried *per Pais*, Judgment is Peremptory; otherwise in all Cases where it's tried *per* Demurrer, unless it be in one only, and that is in case of Demurrer upon Evidence where it's Peremptory, because no *Respond' ouster* can be, because the Parties are at the end of their Pleading, 1 *Lev.* 163. *Amcots* Case. Infant, if bound *per* Verdict on Issue tried, *sur* Plea in Abatement.

The Case was:

Ejectione firmæ was brought against Four, whereof one was an Infant, and appeared by his Guardian; and upon *Not Guilty* pleaded, and found for the Plaintiff, Judgment was given against them, *Quod capiantur*. And in Error assigned for that Cause it was reversed, tho' the Trespass is *Vi & armis*; and Judgment. Capiatur.

so *Son tort demesne*, *Cro. Jac.* 274. *Holbrook* and *Doyly*.

Assault and Battery against Three: Error was brought, That all the Three appeared by Attorney, and pleaded, whereas one was within Age, and ought to have pleaded by his Guardian, and Judgment entirely was given against them all, and it being void as to the Infant, must be void against all. So Judgment was reversed for the whole, *Stiles* 121, 125. *Aylet* and *Oats*.

By Default.

If Judgment be given against an Infant by Default, after the Default he shall have a Writ of *Error*, and reverse the Judgment for his Nonage; but if he make Default after Appearance, Judgment shall be given against him. *Vide supra.*

No Execution against an Infant Heir on Recognizance, Stat. Merch. or Staple.

No Execution shall be sued against the Heir within Age.

If a Man hath a Judgment given against him for Debt or Damages, or be bound in a Recognizance, his Heir within Age; or having two Daughters, the one within Age; no Execution shall be sued of the Lands by *Elegit*, during the Minority, albeit the Heir is not specially bound, but charged as Tertenant.

So against an Heir within Age, no Execution shall be sued upon a Statute Merchant, or Staple, or Recognizance, upon the Statute of 23 *H.* 8. for it is excepted in the Process against the Heir.

Neither if the Heir within Age endow his Mother, shall Execution be sued against her during

during his Minority, 1 *Inst.* 290. *a.* 3 *Rep.* 13. Sir *William Herbert*'s Case.

Note, By the Statute of 27 *Ed.* 3. the Execution of Lands upon a Statute-Staple, is referred to the Statute-Merchant; and by the Statute *De Mercatoribus*, no Execution shall be had against the Heir, so long as he is within Age.

The Trial of full Age in *Ætate probanda*, must be by Jurors of Forty two Years old, or upwards, *Hob.* 325. 1 *Brownl.* 45. Trial in *Ætate probanda.*

CHAP. XIX.

Remedies for Tortious Acts done to Infants.

Action in the nature of a Ravishment of Ward. A famous Case of a clandestine Marriage. Marriage to Infant Maiden by force, against the Custom of London, *Stat.* 24 Car. 2. *If the Father shall have an Action for the Loss of his Sons Marriage. Of a Boy being Spirited, Stat.* 4 & 5 Ph. & Mary. *Of marrying without the Parents Consent, and what shall be a sufficient Refusal. Of* Homine replegiando. *Rape, what. Of Maintenance of poor Children.*

IF a Ward be taken out of the Possession of the Guardian, an Action in the nature of a *Ravishment of Ward* lies.

By the Statute of 4 & 5 *Ph. & M. cap.* 8. It shall not be lawful to take away any Maid or Woman-Child unmarried, being within the Age of sixteen Years, out of the Custody and Governance, and against the Will of the Father, or of such Persons to whom the Father by his last Will and Testament, or other Act executed in his Life-time, shall appoint, under pain of Imprisonment for two Years; and the Penalty for taking away and marrying such Woman-Child, is Imprisonment for five Years, or Fine.

In

In the Case of the King against *Moor*, 2 *Mod.* 128. Information; It was objected that *B. R.* could not fine the Offender upon this Statute, because when Informer entitles himself by a Statute, he may take the Remedy therein prescribed, and here it's limited to the *Star-Chamber*. But *per Cur.* tho' the *Star-Chamber* is taken away, yet those Offences which were punished there, are punishable here in *B. R.* because there are no Negative Words in the Statute to abridge the Authority of this Court.

B. T. seised in Fee of 700 *l. per Annum*, had Issue a Son and four Daughters, the Son had Issue *Ruth*, his only Daughter, who was married to the Defendant *Gore*. Her Father died in the time of her Grandfather, and her Mother fearing that this Daughter might be stolen from her, applies to my Lady *Gore*, and intreats her to take this Daughter into her House, which she did. My Lady had then a Son in *France*, she sent for him, and married him to this *Ruth*, she being then under the Age of 16, without the Consent of her Mother, who was then her Guardian. The Question was, if this be a Forfeiture of her Estate? *Per* Ch. Justice, The Statute was made to prevent Children from being seduc'd from their Parents or Guardians, by Flattering or Enticing Words, Promises or Gifts, and married in a secret Way to their Disparagement; and no such Thing appeared in this Case, for Dr. *Hascard* proved the Marriage to be at St. *Clement*'s Church in a Canonical Hour, and that ma-

ny

ny People were preſent there, and the Church Doors were open when he married them, 3 *Mod.* 84. *Hicks* verſus *Gore.*

If any Woman-Child above the Age of Twelve, and under the Age of Sixteen Years, conſent to ſuch Marriage, then the next of Kin, to whom the Inheritance of ſuch Maiden ſhould deſcend, ſhall enjoy the ſame during her Life.

This is meant of Heireſſes, or other conſiderable Fortunes: But the Cuſtoms of *London*, as to Orphanage, are ſaved.

And in *Paſch.* 20 *Car.* 2. the Caſe was:

Father and Son were indicted for taking with force *M. T.* out of the Poſſeſſion of *Corriter* a Brewer in *London*, and marrying her to *B.* the Son within the Age of ſixteen Years, again the Will of *C.* the Guardian, contrary to the Statute.

And upon the Trial, the Caſe appeared to be:

That *T.* the Father of the Infant, a Freeman, an Alehouſe-keeper of *London*, by his Will deviſed the Cuſtody of this Infant to *C.*

C. obtains a Warrant from the Mayor of *London*, for taking the Infant; and he was taken, but reſcued: And after he had a Warrant from the Lord Chief Juſtice.

Upon

Upon this Evidence they were acquitted of this Indictment:

Becauſe the Deviſe was void; and the Indictment ought to have been, for taking her out of the Poſſeſſion of the Lord Mayor, &c. And,

2. There ought to be a Taking out of the actual Cuſtody of the Guardian; and he ought to be the right Guardian, *Sid.* 362. *The King* againſt *Baſtian.*

And in 24 *Car.* 2. the Court fined *Story* 100 *l.* and bound him to his good Behaviour for five Years, on Information for deceitful taking away out of her Mothers Cuſtody Miſtreſs *Gibbon*, under ſixteen Years of Age, with intent to marry her, and Riot, &c.

G. was fined 50 *l.* and good Behaviour for a Year, who was a Woman aſſiſtant in the Exploit, and found only guilty of Deceit, 3 *Keb.* 101.

This is puniſhable, as a Riot too, at Common Law.

Whether the Woman be Widow, or not, ſhe is under the Protection of this Law.

And though this Statute ſhould be repealed as to the Fine, yet an Information lies for the Contempt againſt the Prohibitory Part. Averment.

It

It was said, *Existens* of fourteen Years of Age, and under Sixteen, it's a sufficient Averment.

As on Custom of *London*, to devise in Mortmain *existens* a Freeman is sufficient, referring only to the Quality of the Person, 3 *Keb.* 708, 715. *Rex* verſ. *Moor.*

Treſpaſs vi & armis. Plaintiff covenants, that the Defendant, *Tiel jour & ayn*, did thrust a Woman named *M. H.* upon his Son named *M. H.* being Infant under the Age of Discretion, by which his Thigh-Bone was broke, and the Plaintiff was enforced to expend great Labour and divers Sums of Money to cure him *ad Damnum.* And *per Raymond*, the Father cannot have this Action, it not being laid *Per quod ſervitium amiſit*, but the Child ought to have the Action as in *Gray* and *Jeoffreys* Case, 3 *Crok.* 55. for Beating and Battering of the Son, whereby he became Lame and Decrepit, and so lost his Marriage. Treſpaſs doth not lie for the Father, and the Father shall not have an Action for the Loss of the Marriage of his Son and Heir, except when a Stranger takes him by force and marries him; but if the Son marries himself, or a Stranger procures him to marry one, the Father has no Remedy, *Stiles* 398. but *Mountague* and Chief Justice *Atkins contra totis veribus.* And Judgment was given for the Plaintiff, *Raym.* 259. *Hunt* and *Wootton.*

Deſigny,

Designy, a *Jamaica* Merchant, spirited a Boy from *Merchant-Taylors* School, and upon Information was found Guilty at *Guild-Hall* before the Lord Chief Justice *Pemberton*, and appeared next Term in the *King*'s-*Bench*, and was fined 500 *l.*;

And because he was likely to procure a Pardon, the Court ordered the Father to bring an *Homine replegiando*; and he did so.

And an *Elongatus* was retorned by the Sheriff, and he was charged with it in Prison.

But they would not bail the Prisoner upon the *Withernam*; but upon his bringing a Thousand Pounds in to be forfeited, if he produced not the Child within six Months, *Raym.* 474. *Designy*'s Case.

The Husband seised in Fee, had Issue two Daughters, and died, and his Wife survived, who was the Guardian in Socage to her Children; one of which under the Age of sixteen Years married Mr. *B.* without her Parents Consent, by reason whereof, her Estate became forfeited during Life to her Sister, by the Statute 4 & 5 *Ph.* & *M.*

Per Cur. There must be a continued Refusal of the Mother; for if she once agree, though afterwards she dissents, yet it is an Assent

Assent within the Statute. There must likewise be Proof of the stealing away, 3 *Mod.* 168. *Calthrop* and *Axtell.* *Vid. supra Hicks* and *Gore.*

Homine replegiando was brought for a young Woman taken out of the Parents Custody, and married against her Consent, cited in *Calthrop* and *Axtell*'s Case.

Rape. Rape, is an unlawful and carnal Knowledge of any Woman above the Age of ten Years, against her Will; or a Woman-Child under the Age of ten Years, with her Will, or against her Will, it is Felony without Clergy, 18 *Eliz.* *c.* 6. 3 *Inst.* 60.

Cornwall and his Wife were indicted for seducing an Apprentice to an House of Debauchery, and causing him to consume great Sums of Money of his Masters.

And after the Defendants were found guilty by Verdict, and put a Demurrer into Court, and shew for Cause, That this is not indictable.

But *per Cur.* Demurrer shall not be upon Indictment after Verdict; notwithstanding *Co. Ent. p.* 363. *a. b.* which Precedent is not Law, *Sid.* 208. *Le Roy* versus *Cornwall and his Wife.*

Of

Of Maintenance of Poor Children.

A Widow having ſeveral Children by a former Husband, who lived in the Pariſh of St. *Buttolph* without *Aldgate*, which Pariſh lies in two Counties, *viz. London* and *Middleſex*, marries a ſecond Husband, and they put out the Children to Nurſe at *Enfield* in *Middleſex*; the Mother dies, and then the Father in Law; the Nurſe applies her ſelf to the Pariſh of St. *Buttolph*, the Woman died in that Part which lies in *Middleſex*, who contended with the other Part of the Pariſh that lies in *London*. The Juſtices at the *Old-Baily* Reſolved, That without particular Uſage to the contrary, the Pariſh in both Counties ought to contribute their Shares towards the Relief of the Children, becauſe the Statute of 43 *Eliz. c.* 2. names only Pariſhes. But in regard it was made appear, That each Part of that Pariſh had diſtinct Officers, and made diſtinct Rates, and had uſed Time out of Mind to make diſtinct Accounts to the Juſtices of each County; the Court did look upon each Diviſion as a ſeveral Pariſh, and thereupon ordered, That that Part of the ſaid Pariſh which lies in *Middleſex* ſhall pay the Nurſe, and provide for the future for the Children. And no Notice can be here taken of the Birth of the Children, but of their laſt Settlement, by 43 *Eliz. c.* 2. becauſe they are only poor Children, and not Vagabonds: But they which are Rogues and Vagabonds within

39 *Eliz.*

39 *Eliz. c.* 4. ſhall be provided for by the Place where they were born, *Raym.* 476, 477.

Indictment for taking a *Feme* Infant out of the Poſſeſſion of the Guardian, and marrying her *contra Stat.* The Father made a Will, and deviſeth the Cuſtody of his Daughter to C. the Indictment was void, for it was, That he took her out of the Cuſtody of *C.* whereas it ſhould have been, out of the Cuſtody of the Mayor and Aldermen of *London*, for her Father was a Freeman, and his Deviſe of the Cuſtody of her was void, and there are *Proviſo's* in the Statute to ſave the Cuſtom of *London* concerning Orphans, *Vide pluis*, 1 *Sid.* 363. *Le Roy* verſus *Baſtian*.

CHAP.

CHAP. XX.

Of Childrens Portions, either by Wills or Settlements; and Resolutions at Common Law or Equity concerning the same.

AS to the Constructions of Last Wills and Settlements, concerning Portions and Legacies left and given to Children, our Law is full of Reason, Justice and Equity: And I durst challenge the profoundest Doctors of the Civil Laws to shew more firm and solid Resolutions in all their Codes, Pandects and Volumes, upon those Points. I shall produce some, which are and may be of daily Use, and therefore ought not in a Treatise of this Nature to be totally omitted.

Vide supra, Tit. Devises.

Lord *Pawlet* had made a Settlement of his Estate, and had charged by Deed his Land for Payment of 4000 *l.* to two Daughters at their respective Ages of One and twenty Years, or Day of Marriage, and left himself a Power of otherwise ordering it by his Will: And he, by his Will in Writing, made some short Time after, devised thus:

Portion in Money devised according to a Settlement, and Legatee dies before the Time limited for Payment, who shall have it.

I bequeath to my two Daughters A. *and* B. 4000 l. *apiece, to be respectively paid to them for their Portions in such Manner as I have provided by the said Settlement.*

One of the Daughters died before Marriage, or the Age of One and twenty Years.

The Lady *Pawlet*, Mother of the said Daughters, took out Letters of Administration to the Daughter that died, and preferred a Bill in *Chancery* against the Trustees for the 4000 *l.* and against the Heir to whom the Benefit of the Land (after the Money raised) was appointed.

The Question was, If this Money raised should go to the Administratrix, or the Lands be discharged thereof, and accrue to the Benefit of the Heir?

It was agreed, That if this had been a Legacy, or Sum of Money bequeathed by the Will, although the Party had died before the Age of One and twenty, or Marriage, the Administratrix should have had it; for the Legatee in such Case is to have it as a present Interest, though the Time of Payment be future, because it chargeth the personal Estate which is in being at the Time of the Testator's Death; and if the Legacies by such an Accident should be discharged, it would turn to the Benefit of the Executors, whereas the Testator did never intend it.

But

But here this Sum of Money is appointed to be paid by a Deed, and is a Trust charg'd upon the Land; and Trusts are guided and governed by the Intention of the Parties, and the personal Estate is not charg'd: And this Sum of Money doth not lie in Demand by a Suit, as where a Legacy is devised, only a Bill may be preferred to have the Trusts performed. Trusts.

And tho' it was much insisted on for the Plaintiff, that here the Will bequeaths the Money, yet that refers to the Deed, and orders it to be paid in such Manner as was thereby appointed.

And the Court decreed it for the Heir at Law, 2 *Ventr.* 366.

So was *Wood* and *Caley*'s Case, 13 *Car.* 2.

The Will was,

That the Executor should sell the personal Estate of the Testator, and by the Money raised thereout, to purchase Lands for the Use of *A.* and her Heirs.

A. dies without Issue before any Purchase made.

It was decreed, That the Administrator of *A.* should have the Moneys out of the Hands of the Executors.

Who shall be said younger Children to take Benefit of a Devise.

C. P. by his Will devised Lands to his Trustees, that they should, out of the Profits thereof, pay unto the younger Children of his Daughter *M.* Four hundred Pounds, equally to be divided; and she had six Children, so that five of them are within the Intent of the Will, to have 80 *l.* apiece.

And so it was decreed by the Court, tho' the Heir at Law insisted, That they are elder in Seniority of Years than he himself, being a younger Child than any of them, and that younger Children in this Case is to be taken as distinguish'd from the Heir at Law, 14 *Car.* 2. *Mead* and *Cave.*

The Question was, upon this Clause in a Will, [Item, *All the rest of my Lands, Goods,*
Disposition on Trust to Children. *and personal Estate, I give to* A. B. *on Trust, to give it to my Children and Grandchildren according to their Demerits.*] The Devisee, who was Heir and Executor, gives the Lands to one, omitting the rest; If this were a Disposition according to the Trust?

Lord Chancellor. I sit not here to make Men's Wills, nor to interpret them farther than the Wills go; and therefore, as to the Settlement of the Lands on one, and not on all, I cannot alter. It is clear, the Children are not to come in by the Will immediately, but by the Act of the Devisee; and he is to give or distribute according to their Demerits, therefore he is a Judge: And though the Words of the Will amounted not to give the Plaintiff the Lands, yet the Words were not idle, but put a Restraint on the Devisee; for tho' he might give the Lands as he did, yet he could not give them in Possession or Remainder to any Stranger, but only to the Family. He remembred, and cited a Case in the Lord *Egerton*'s Time, where one possessed of Leases for Years, devised them to

his

his Wife, and hoped ſhe would leave them his Son, and died. Her ſecond Husband granted the Leaſes away; the Son ſued to be reliev'd, but was diſmiſs'd, for it was no Truſt for the Son, 1 *Caſes in Chancery* 309. *Civil* verſus *Rich*.

Corbet and *Morris*, 17 *Car.* 2.

The Plaintiff, as Executrix to her Huſband, ſets forth,

That Sir *J. Corbet*, Father of *Vincent Corbet*, the Plaintiff's late Husband, by Settlement made 1652. appoints 1000 *l.* apiece to every one of his Children named (of which *Vincent* was the eldeſt) as ſhould be then unmarried, or not provided for at the Time of the Deceaſe of Sir *John Corbet*, at their reſpective Ages of One and twenty Years ſucceſſively, according to the Seniority of Age.

Vincent was married to the Plaintiff in 1642 privately. He had Three hundred and fifty Pounds with his Wife, and had no Proviſion made for him, but Thirty Pounds *per Annum* for Seven Years, if the Father lived ſo long.

Vincent makes his Will, and deviſeth, That if Sir *J. Corbet*, his Father, die, and leave him any real or perſonal Eſtate, that the Rents and Profits thereof ſhall be to his Wife for her Life; and all the reſt of the Eſtate he gave to his Wife, and made her ſole Executrix, and dies.

Devisee and Executrix to have the Benefit of a Portion limited to her Husband.

Sir *John* dies without altering the Settlement, and there is received out of the Profits of the Lands One thousand Pounds over the Debts of Sir *John*, but not enough to pay the other Children.

The Question is, Whether the Plaintiff, Devisee and Executrix of *Vincent*, who was married, and died without Issue in his Father's Life-time, shall have the Thousand Pounds limited to her Husband?

The Court decreed, She being Relict, Devisee and Executrix of *Vincent*, ought to have the Benefit of the said Portion and Interest limited to her Husband.

In *Hartwell* and *Ford*'s Case, the Words of the Will upon which the Question arose, were these:

If it happen my Daughter Charity *to die before she shall have accomplished the Years of a Lawful Age, then the whole Profits of the Premisses (being a Lease) to remain and be to* William *my Son; and if* William *die before the like Lawful Age,* Charity *and* William *having no Issue of their Bodies, then all the whole Term and Profits I give and devise to all my Sisters Children, to be equally divided amongst them.*

Charity made a Will at Eighteen, and died.

The Question was, Whether the Plaintiff, as Executor to *Charity*, had Right to the Premisses, or the Heir of *William* the elder, who administred to *William Ford* the younger, Brother to *Charity*; or whether the same belonged to the Sisters Children of *Lionel Ford*?

And the Chancellor and Judges decreed, That a Lawful Age, in general Words (unless it be in a particular Case) must be construed and taken to be One and twenty Years; and that the said remaining Term, according to the Construction of the Will, belongs to the Sisters Children of the said *Lionel Ford* only.

The Construction of the Word (*Lawful Age*) in a Will.

J. M. by his Will devised the Rents, Issues and Profits of all his Messuages, during his Interest therein, to his Wife for Life; and if she died before the Expiration of his said Interest, then the same to come amongst all his Children equally.

And the Testator conceiving his Wife to be with Child, devised to the Child she then went with, a Lease of two Houses, and ordered a Moiety of the Profits thereof to be put out by the Overseers of his Will, as a Stock for the Benefit of such Child, and the other Moiety for its Maintenance till Age, or Marriage.

Devise to an Infant in *Ventre sa Mere*.

And by his Will further declared, That if all his Children should die before Marriage, or Age of One and twenty Years, then the Premisses devised to his Children should remain to Brothers and Sisters Children; and that Four of the Testator's Children died before One and twenty, or Marriage, and *Alice*, who was not born at the Time of the Testator's Death, is only living.

The Court conceived, That the collateral Line have nothing to do with the Estate of the Teſtator during the Life of *Alice* the Daughter, *Marſh* and *Kirby*, 10 *Car.* 1. *in Canc.*

A Woman, who was poſſeſs'd of a Term for divers Years, had Iſſue two Daughters, the one married to *A.* the other to *B.* *A.* had Iſſue four Daughters, and *B.* had Iſſue alſo.

Legacies deviſed to Children, the Money decreed to the Parent, the Executor refuſing to give Security.

She deviſed Legacies to the Children of *A.* out of the Rent of the Leaſe, and made *B.* Executor, and died.

A. required *B.* (in Behalf of his Children) to pay the Money to him, that he might employ the ſame for the Benefit of the Children, which he refuſed.

Whereupon he ſued him in the Spiritual Court, and there Sentence was given for the Plaintiff.

B. the Executor, moved for a Prohibition, and alledged for the Ground of it, That he was Executor, and chargeable for the Money in Account; but it was denied, becauſe he came after Sentence, and becauſe he refuſed to give Security for the Payment of the Legacies to the Children, *Godb. p.* 243. *Pl.* 337. *Ayliff* and *Browne.*

A. M. makes his Will in Writing, *An.* 1649, and gives a Legacy to his Neece, in theſe Words:

I do give to my Neece H. L. *the Sum of Five hundred Pounds, which my Siſter the Lady* Cholmley *hath now in her Hands of mine, and by her Bond made to me appears.*

And

And makes no Executor, and dies in *Octob. Anno* 1669. About ten Years before his Death, the Lady pays him in the Five hundred Pounds.

The Question is, Whether this Legacy was due?

And *per Cur.* It is due, tho' the Security was altered.

So was *Hill.* 1671. *Skib* and *Chichley*'s Case, where the Lady *Verney* gave Legacies out of Moneys then at Interest, and called in before the Testator's Death, *Raymond* 335. *Pawlet*'s Case.

If the Father devise Lands to his youngest Son by Will in Writing, and the eldest Son knowing this, enters into the Land, and disseiseth the Father, and so continues till the Death of the Father, by which the Will is void; yet for that this is made void by Deceit and Covin, it shall be made good in *Chancery*, *Roswell*'s Case *in Cancellar. Mich.* 16 *Jac.* 1. Will void at Common Law, made good in Equity.

If an Infant sell Lands for Money, and purchase other Lands with the Moneys, yet this Sale made by the Infant shall not be avoided by the *Chancery*, because the Person of the Infant is disabled by a Maxim in Law, *Roswell*'s Case in *Chancery*. Sale by Infant not aided in *Equity*.

A Copyhold was surrendred to the Use of an Infant, to the Intent he should pay an Annuity to another at full Age, which he refused to do; and it was declared he should pay it and the Arrears, *Sawyer*'s Case. Infant decreed to pay an Annuity.

In

Infant of 12 Years old bound by a Decree.

In the Case of *Wadham* and *Moore*, an Infant was bound by Decree, albeit he was but 12 Years of Age.

Infants foreclosed.

The Court of *Chancery* will sometimes decree Infants to be foreclosed before they come of Age, and yet but rarely, 2 *Ventr.* 351.

The *Ecclesiastical Court* may hold Plea of a Child's Portion, but not of the Custody of the Body, 3 *Keb.* 834.

When Lands to be charged or not with Portions upon the Word of a Will.

The Lands were devised by Will to Trustees for 99 Years on Trust, if he left no Son, or such as should die before 21 Years without Heirs Males, and should leave one or more Daughters, 12000 *l.* if but one Daughter, or if two or more Daughters, then 20000 *l.* to be raised for their Portion, payable at 21 Years, or Day of Marriage, 29 *Car.* 2. *Staweb* and *Austin* in *Chancery*.

The Testator dies, having only three Daughters, *Ursula*, *Elizabeth* and *Anne*. *Anne* died since her Father. The Testator's Relict married *S.* she on *Anne*'s Death administred to her, and died, leaving *Anne*'s Portion in the said 20000 *l.* unadministred. The Administration of *Anne*'s Estate was granted to *Ursula* and *Elizabeth*: And the *Quære* was, If the whole 20000 *l.* were to be raised, or any more than 12000 *l.* *Anne* being dead before 21 Years, and unmarried.

Per Cur. The whole 20000 *l.* shall be raised, for the Words of the Will are, If he had two Daughters or more.

A per-

A perſonal Eſtate is deviſed amongſt four Children by Name, and as to the real Eſtate, it was to be added to his perſonal Eſtate for all his Children's Portions; and a fifth Child is born, the Land is to be ſold, and ſhe ſhall have a Share, 32 *Car.* 2. *Cole* and *Hancock*'s Caſe.

Children born, to have a Share when born.

The Commons prayed, That an Infant within Age levying a Fine, may have a Reſpite two or three Years after his full Age to reverſe the ſame.

The King anſwered, *He would be adviſed thereof.*

If an Infant of the Age of 20 Years, and hath Reaſon and Wiſdom to govern himſelf, ſells his Land, and with the Money thereof buyeth other Lands of greater Value than the firſt was, and taketh the Profits thereof, he may have his firſt Lands again in Equity, as he may at Law; for the Vendition made by the Infant ought not to be ſupported or aided by a Court of *Equity*, becauſe that the Infant is diſabled by a Maxim in the Law; and the Court of *Equity* will not give Relief againſt a Maxim, and a Maxim of the Law ought to be obſerved to be of as great Strength as any Statute, which is framed by a triple Aſſent. But in *Equity*, the Infant ought to be bound to repay the Money by him received, with reaſonable Coſts.

An

An Infant may have a Writ out of *Chancery*, to recover his Guardian, directed to the Justices, and to recover another, *&c.*

The King by his Letters Patents, may make a General Guardian for an Infant to answer for him in all Actions, or Suits brought, or to be brought in all manner of Courts, or may make two or three Guardians jointly to answer for him, or to bring any Action for him; and that the said Guardian may make another Guardian.

Inspectio corporis person' infra ætatem.

MArtis 22 die Junii Anno Regni Regis Jac' Angl' &c. Habita isto die per Cur' hic inspectiõe corporis p'd querentis videtur dicte curie hic eundem querent' infra etatem viginti & unius Annorum modo existere sed quia dicta Cur' hic se advisare vult priusquam ad judiciũ in hac pte reddend' pcedatur ordinat' est per eandem Cur' hic q'd p'd Quer' possit pducer' ad dictam Cur' hic testes quoscunq; & alias pbationes ad veritatem in premissis proband'.

Legatees to have Maintenance.

The Plaintiffs were Legatees, their Legacies to be paid at 21 Years of Age; they suggest they had no Maintenance, and pray by Guardian, That the Defendant who is Executor of the Will may allow them Maintenance. The Defendant demurred, because the Plaintiffs are under Age, and their Legacies were not to be paid till they were 21 Years

Years of Age, and ſo had no Cauſe of Sail. The Demurrer was over-ruled, *Ter. Mich.* 16 *Car.* 2. in *Cancellar. Renneſ.* & *Parot.*

Ter. Hill. 17 & 18 *Car.* 2. in *Canc. Osburn, Baker* againſt *Shelbury*; The Bill was to be relieved againſt an Apprentice's Bond and Articles, and to have them up. Upon Hearing, Ordered, That the Defendant do within a certain Time, (*viz.* one Year) bring his Action, and go to Trial thereupon for his Damages, or in Default thereof, the Bond and Articles to be delivered up. And the Reaſon that was given was, That if it were at the Defendants Choice to ſtay his Action as long as he pleaſed, he would ſtay till the Plaintiffs Witneſſes were dead. And it was ſaid, it was uſual in the Caſe after Apprentices were out of their Time, to exhibit a Bill to put their Maſter to ſue their Covenants within a certain Time, or elſe to deliver up their Indentures.

A Bill to force the Maſter to ſue his Covenants on Indentures of Apprentiſhip.

Paſch. 23 *Car.* 2. 15*th* of *May*, *Patt and Hatton.* A Citizen and Freeman of *London*, deviſeth to his Son a groſs Sum, which did exceed the cuſtomary Part, and deviſeth, That if his Son die before 21 Years of Age, that Sum over to another, the Queſtion was, If the Deviſe over was good?

A Citizen of *London* cannot deviſe his Child's Part over to another, in caſe the Child die in Minority.

It was adjudged, and ſo decreed by the Lord Keeper, That the Deviſe over for ſuch as was the cuſtomary Part, was void; and that the Orphan dying within Age, his Adminiſtrator was intitled to ſo much as was the cuſtomary Part, and the Surplus of that

that groſs Sum to go to thoſe to whom it was deviſed over.

A Child's Legacy paid to the Father, who failed the Payment decreed.

A Legacy of 125 *l.* was given to the Plaintiff, being but 10 Years old, and at that Age was paid to the Plaintiff's Father, who after died *Inſolvent*. The Infant at full Age ſued the Executor of the Deviſor for the 125 *l.*

The *Lord Keeper* held it good Payment.

But was preſs'd very much by the *Attorney General* of the ill Conſequence; for the Law muſt be the ſame if it were 1000*l.* and extends to other Caſes of the like Nature, and not to Legacies only.

Lord Keeper. What ſhould the Executor do?

Attorney General. He may take Security to repay it to the Infant, and ſue to have it paid.

Lord Keeper. It may be ſo, where a Legacy will bear the Charge of a Suit, but not elſe. And he delivered his Opinion accordingly.

But the Defendant being put to prove the Payment, did prove likewiſe, That the Executor took a Bond; which the Court preſs'd the Defendant to ſhew: Whereupon the Sollicitor in the Cauſe ſaid, He had it not, but would produce it by the next Day, but ſaid it was a Bond to the Executor to ſave him harmleſs.

Lord Keeper. Then he paid the Security at his own Peril.

Churchil. It may be, it is to pay the Infant at his Age.

Lord Keeper. I ſhall believe the Worſt, unleſs you ſhew the Bond; and therefore decreed

creed the Executor to pay it, *Hill.* 26 & 27 *Car.* 2. *Holloway* and *Collings.*

Leech and *Leech*, *Hill.* 26 & 27 *Car.* 2.

The Bill was, by Trustees to guide and direct them in divers Trusts, and to protect them executing the same, which the Court did, (*viz.*) The Father made a Lease in Trust with Reference to his Will, and thereby devised to several of his Daughters 500 *l.* to each, to be paid at 21 Years, or Marriage; and if any or all die before, then to others. The Daughters had no other Portion, nor no Maintenance, and Direction was prayed by the Trustees, whether they might allow the Daughters Maintenance.

Where Maintenance shall be allowed to Legatees or not.

Lord Keeper. No, because of the Devise over, or else it might have been done.

William Lord Gray had Issue, *Thomas* his eldest Son, and *Ralph* his second Son; *William* their Father, for 13000 *l.* purchased the Manor of *Gosfield*, in the Name of *Thomas* and his Heirs, and he enjoyed it, and took the Rents: And *Thomas* declared several times, That the Land was his Fathers, and not his. But on the other Side, divers Speeches of the Father were proved, that it was his Sons, and the Son by his Will gave the Manor to his Father. And it was decreed, That this Purchase was not a Trust in *Thomas* for the Father, but an Advancement by the Father to the Son. And whereas the Father, after the Death of *Thomas*, did convey *Gosfield*, and three other Manors in Trust, to raise 2000 *l.* for two other of his Grand-chil-

Not a Trust, but an Advancement to the Son.

children, *Ralph* and *Charles Gosfield*, he was not liable thereunto.

Another Queſtion in the Caſe was, *Ralph* Father of *Ralph* and *Charles*, and of *Ford*, did make a Conveyance of *Gosfield* to Truſtees and their Heirs, to pay his Debts and Legacies; and after, for Performance of his Will, and at the ſame time made his Will, and thereby did deviſe the Truſtees to pay 2000 *l.* apiece to *Ralph* and *Charles*, and ſo 6000 *l.* to *Catherine* his Daughter, the Surplus after to his Heir *Ford*, and made his Wife Executrix, but gave not thereby in Terms the perſonal Eſtate, but only made her Executrix, and deviſed, that his ſaid three Children ſhould releaſe to his Executrix all ſuch Actions and Demands of his perſonal Eſtate to his Executrix. Now, whether the Executrix ſhould be liable to the Legacies of the Children in Aid of the Heir, who had the Surplus of *Gosfield* that was to be ſold. As to the Creditors, it was agreed, ſhe muſt be liable; but as to the Children Legatees, there ought to be no Aid for the Heir, for when the Legatees by the Will were to releaſe all Demands out of, or to the perſonal Eſtate, they could make no Demand out of it; which ſhews his Intent, that therefore, as to the Intereſt and Legacies, the perſonal Eſtate was to be diſcharged, and the Executrix to enjoy the Eſtate free againſt them; and therefore, the Heir not to charge the Executrix as for thoſe Legacies of which he diſcharged his Executrix, eſpecially having

4 other-

otherwise provided for their Satisfaction, and the Surplus to the Heir is expresly after Debts and Legacies paid, therefore not before.

Against which it was said, that regularly the personal Estate must Aid the Heir, and an implied Intent must not without clear Expression alter the equitable general Law.

And there was other Reasons for the Release to be given (*viz.*) The Estate which was in the Province of *York*, was liable to the Children for Portions.

The Lord Chancellor decreed the personal Estate to be accounted for in Aid of the Heir, in order to Aid him for what he should be charged withal, not only as to the Creditors, but as to the Legacies charged on *Gosfield*, (*viz.*) the 6000 *l.* to the younger Children, *Hill.* 28, 29 *Car.* 2. Lands devised for Payment of Debts and Legacies, the personal Estate shall be first applied.

Ford Lord *Gray*, *contra Dominam Gray & al.*

A. deviseth, That 300 *l.* shall be paid to the Child which he shall have at the Time of his Death, and if he have none, then to his Sister. Afterwards three Children are born to him; Then by a Codicil he deviseth 200 *l.* to each of the said Children, to be paid at their respective Ages of 21 Years.

The Lord Chancellor decreed the 300 *l.* to be devised to the Child, *&c.* and though there be Three, the Devise is not void for Uncertainty, but all three Children shall have Share in it; and that the Devise of 200 *l.* being without Words signifying the same to be of their Portions, nor any thing one way or another, to revoke or affirm the former Gift of 300 *l.* it shall be taken by way of Accumulation, and the Children shall have both Legacies, *Mich.* 29 *Car.* 2. *Pit versus Pidgeon.*

Legacy and Accumulation.

The Father deviseth to his Wife, Mother-in-Law to his Son, the Custody or Tuition of his Son an Infant of seven Years old, and died. The Wife marries meanly, (*viz.*) her own Servant; *Forster*, the Uncle of the Boy, gets Possession of him, and sends him into *France*, where he placed him in a Protestant College for his Education.

The Court, on Information that the Child was eloined by the Uncle, sued out a Writ *de homine Replegiando*, and it was argued why the Writ should not be discharged.

Writ *de homine replegiando.*

Guardian is named by Will, the Court will not remove him.

Lord Chancellor. Where there is a Guardian by the Common Law, this Court will intermeddle and order it. But being here Guardian by act of the Party, I cannot remove him from her. But in this Case, and all other the like Cases, they shall give Security not to marry the Child *infra Annos nubiles*, or consent to be aiding to the Marriage *post Annos nubiles*, during Minority, without acquainting this Court therewith. But I cannot restrain the Infant to marry *ad Annos nubiles*; and the Uncle was ordered in this Case to send for the Boy home, *Mich.* 29 *Car.* 2. *Duke and Foster.*

By Statute 1 *Anne*, *Seſſ.* 1. *c.* 30. Act was made to oblige the *Jews* to provide for, and maintain their Proteſtant Children. It was Enacted, ‘ That if any Jewiſh ‘ Parents, in order to the compelling his or ‘ her Proteſtant Child to change his or her ‘ Religion, ſhall refuſe to allow ſuch Child ‘ a ſufficient Maintenance ſuitable to the ‘ Degree and Ability of ſuch Parent, and ‘ to the Age and Education of ſuch Child. ‘ That then, upon Complaint made thereof ‘ to the Lord Chancellor, Lord Keeper, or ‘ Commiſſioners of the great Seal, for the ‘ Time being, it ſhall and may be law- ‘ ful for the ſaid Lord Chancellor, Lord ‘ Keeper, or Commiſſioners, to make ſuch ‘ Order therein, for the Maintenance of ‘ ſuch Proteſtant Child, as he or they ſhall ‘ think fit.

CHAP. XXI.

Where Payment or Tender of Money for an Infant is good, and at what Age.

A Man makes a Feoffment, on Condition that if he, his Heirs or Executors, do pay the Rent of 100 *l.* before such a Day, that he may re-enter. The Feoffor dies, his Heir within Age; the Mother (without any Notice of the Son) requests *J. S.* that he would pay the Money for her Son. All this was found by special Verdict; but it was not found of what Age the Son was. *Per Cur.* If the Infant were within the Age of 14 Years, the Tender of the Money by the Mother had been good: But *contra*, if he had been more than 14 Years; and therefore they advised the Party to begin *de Novo*, and that it may be found that the Infant was within the Age of 14 Years. *Per Wray*, If a Bond be upon Condition that the Obligor, or his Heirs, should pay 100 *l.* and the Obligor dies, his Heir within Age, I conceive, Payment by the Guardian, or some other Friend, is good, *Owen* 197. *Watkins*'s Case; *Moor* 22. 1 *Leon.* 34. 3 *Cr.* 132.

Who shall have Benefit of the Nonage of another, or not, *Vide supra.*

Privies in Blood shall have Benefit of the Nonage of another, 8 *Rep.* 42. *b.* 44.

Justice

Justice *Dodderidge*, in his Arguments in *Darcy* and *Jackson's* Case, *Trin.* 20 *Jac.* *B. R.* said, If Infant Donee in Tail make a Feoffment, and die without Issue, that the Donor shall enter; for the Donor may not have a *Formedon*, because it is not a Discontinuance; and then if he should not enter, he shall be prejudiced without any Default in him, and for this he cited 6 *H.* 4. 3. *b.* *per* two Judges, and denied the Opinion in 8 *Rep.* 43. *a.* But it seems to me he may have a *Formedon*, although it is not a Discontinuance, and by this admitted to be a Discontinuance, as in 3 *Rep.* 85. *a.*

Donor in Tail.

It was held by *Dodderidge* in the same Argument, That if Infant Donee in Tail make a Feoffment, and is attainted of Felony, and dies, his Issue shall enter, and avoid the Feoffment. The Issue is as a meer Stranger, for his Blood is corrupt, 8 *Rep.* 43. *a.*

Issue in Tail by the Attainder of the Father.

He also then agreed, *Anderson's* Case in *Dyer*, 1 & 2 *P.* & *M.* 104. *a.* to be good Law. In a *Præcipe* against three Jointenants, they lose by Default, and brought a Writ of Error for the Nonage of two of them, and upon this the Judgment was reversed for all three, and so one takes the Advantage of the Infancy of another.

Jointenants.

If Baron and Feme are Jointenants, and the Husband, being an Infant, makes a Feoffment, and dies, the Wife shall have Benefit of his Nonage, and shall enter into the whole; and yet she is not of his Blood, because *alias* there being a Wrong done, one shall sustain Prejudice without Default in him.

Baron and Feme.

him. Baron shall have Benefit of the Nonage of the Wife.

Debt against Baron and Feme, the Parole shall demur for the Nonage of the Wife.

Where Age shall be granted, and Suit stay for the Nonage of the Plaintiff or Demandant. Vide supra.

In all Cases where it may be presumed to be for the Benefit of the Infant, though but a bare Right discend; as in all real Actions Ancestrel of the Possession of his Ancestor, (and in all Cases where a bare Right in Fee-Simple discend from any Ancestor to an Infant) there in any Action Ancestrel brought by Infant, the Tenant, without pleading any Plea, may pray that the Suit may stay. As in a Writ of Right as Heir, so in a *Formedon* in Reverter as Heir to the Donor. So if an Infant alien within Age, and his Heir, being an Infant, sues a *Dum fuit infra Ætatem.* In Wast, or *Quid Juris clamat,* by Infant, the Tenant pleads a Lease without Impeachment of Wast, and offers to attorn, saving his Priviledge, and prays the Suit may stay, it shall stay, *Cok. sup. Litt.* 64.

But in all Cases where it cannot be presumed to be for the Benefit of the Heir within Age to have the Suit to stay, there Age shall not be granted for the Nonage of the Plaintiff or Demandant; as in all real Actions Possessory, as where the Ancestor died seised, and the Land discended to the Infant,

Infant, and he hath entred and took the Profits, here the Suit shall not stay. In a Writ of Entry *sur Disseisin*, of a Disseisin made to the Infant himself in *Cessavit*, *Droit sur Disclaimer* in a *Formedon in Discender*, it shall not demur, unless something be pleaded against him to which he cannot be Party to try it within Age; as in a Writ of Entry *sur Disseisin* to the Ancestor, if fresh Suit be made to the Ancestor, and after the Writ brought, the Ancestor died before Trial could be had, 6 *Rep.* 39. 85.

Where Age shall be granted to him who prays for the Nonage of the Defendant or Tenant.

In most Cases where the Heir is sued for the Land he hath by Discent, or for something out of, or concerning it, and he be an Infant, there (upon Prayer made) his Age shall be allow'd him; as in a *Cui in Vita*, Writ of Debt brought upon an Especialty; as for an Obligation, a Statute, or for a *Nomine Pœnæ*, a Writ of Error if he be Tenant, a Writ of Formedon in Discender, 6 *Rep.* 85. 1 *Inst.* 290.

But in such Actions where the Infant is supposed to come to the Land by his own Wrong, as if he be a Disseisor. In a *Per quæ Servitia* against Infant that hath Tenancy by Discent, and in a *Patronæ facienda* where they are both in Possession, and in a Writ of Dower, or of an Appeal, and in a Writ of Execution sued against his Lands upon a Judgment had against his Father; in all these Cases, he shall not have his Age allowed him, neither shall the Suit stay for that Cause. So it is for personal Actions: An Infant may be sued for a Trespass, and for divers other Cases. *Vide supra*, 9 *Rep.* 85. 1 *Inst.* 239.

Where an Heir born after, shall put out another Heir born before, or not.

The Difference lies between Discent and Purchase.

In all Cases where a Daughter, or other Person Heir, cometh to Land by Discent, there the Son, or more immediate Heir, that shall be born after, shall out her, and have the Land; as if one seised of Land in Fee, and have but one Daughter, but his Wife is with Child of a Son, and dies, and the Daughter enters, and after the Son is born, in this Case he may out the Daughter, and have the Land. So where the Wife doth discontinue the Land of the Land she hath by her Husband, and so make a Forfeiture of it within the *Stat.* 11 *H.* 7. *c.* 20. and she hath at that Time a Daughter, and is with Child of a Son by her deceased Husband, and the Daughter enters, the Son shall after out her. So if a Gift be in Tail to a Man, and the Heirs Males of his Body, and the Donee die without Issue, having a Brother that is next Heir *per Formam Dom.* but the Wife of the Donee is privily with Child of a Son, and the Brother enter, in this Case the Issue, when he is born, shall have the Land,

Land, and put out his Uncle. So if Tenant in Tail having Issue two Sons, and the elder die in the Life-time of the Father, leaving his Wife with Child of a Son, and then the Tenant in Tail suffer a Recovery to the Use of himself for Life, and after his Death to a Stranger for 20 Years, and after of the Heirs Males of the Body of the Tenant in Tail, and after the Tenant in Tail die, and then the youngest Son enters, and after the Son of the eldest Brother is born, in this Case he shall have the Land, and out his Uncle. So if there be Son and Daughter, and the Son purchase Land, and die without Issue, it shall go to the Daughter; but if there be a Son born after, he shall have the Land; and if he have another Daughter, she shall be Copartner with her Sister, 3 *Rep.* 61. 1 *Rep. Shelley*'s Case; *Plo.* 375. 1 *Inst.* 11.

But in all Cases where the Daughter and Female Heir, or other Heir, cometh into the Land by Purchase, or in the Nature of a Purchaser, there the Son, or other more immediate or next Heir, that shall be born after him, shall not oust him: As if Land be given to one for Life, the Remainder to the right Heirs of *J. S.* and *J. S.* hath a Daughter, his Wife with Child of a Son, and the Remainder fall before the Son is born, in this Case the Daughter shall have the Land for ever, and never be put out by the Son. So if an Estate be made, on Condition that if the Feoffor, or his Heirs, pay 20 *l.* that they shall have the Land again, and

and the Daughter pay the Money, and after a Son is born, he ſhall never have the Land. *Qui ſentit Onus, ſentire debet & Commodum.* But if the Condition were to be performed on the Part of the Feoffee, or it were broken in the Life-time of the Anceſtor, in ſuch Caſes it ſeems the Son may enter afterwards, and put out the Daughter.

If one by his Will deviſe to *J. S.* and his Heirs, and the Deviſee had then a Daughter when the Deviſor died, his Wife being privily with Child of a Son, and the Deviſee dieth, and the Heir doth enter, in this Caſe the Son that is after born ſhall not out her, but the Daughter ſhall have the Land, 3 *Rep.* 61, 95, 99.

Forecloſing Equity of Redemption.

In the Caſe of *Sayle* and *Freeland*, the Court would not decree Infants to be foreclosed of Redemption till they came of Age, though ſometimes 'tis ſo done, and the rather in this Caſe, becauſe the Mortgage depended on a diſputable Title, and ſo no Money could be expected on Aſſignment of it over, 2 *Vent.* 351.

Of Puniſhment of Infants for Criminal Matters.

If Infant be indicted of Felony, and arraigned, and pleads Not guilty, and found Not guilty, yet the Juſtices may diſmiſs him by by their Discretion, if it appear to them to be of such an Age that he had not Discretion, 35 *H.* 6. 11. *b.* And the Reason is, that in Felony he had no other Remedy but to plead Not guilty, for Felony may not be justified.

Per Doctor and *Student* 149. *a.* If Infant commit Felony at such an Age that he had Discretion to know the Law, he shall have Punishment of the Law. One of 12 Years or over kills another, this is Felony; if he were but of 9 Years, if by any Signs it may be intended that he had Conisance of Good and Evil; as by his Excuses, or any other Act that he did after the killing, to wit, in hiding the Dead in any secret Place; for in such a Case *Malitia supplebit Ætatem, ut patet,* 3 *H.* 7. 12. *b.*

Per Doctor and *Student* 149. *a.* If Infant does a Trespass at such an Age that he had Discretion to know the Law, he shall have Punishment of the Law.

Com. 19. *a.* Infant of tender Years kills one, it is not Felony, because he had not Discretion to understand.

Cok. 3 *Inst.* 47. Murder is when one of Age of Discretion kills one: So of Homicide.

Abstracts

Abstracts of Acts of Parliament in this Treatise not in the former Edition.

21 *H.* 8. *c.* 7. Servants imbezelling their Masters Goods of 40 *s.* or above, Felony; not so in Apprentices.

39 *El.* *c.* 4. Infant under Seven, no Vagrant.

12 *Car.* 2. *c.* 24. Of the Disposition of Infants by their Fathers Wills.

Stat. 4 & 5 *Phil.* & *Mar.* Of conveying Maids under Age, or marrying them.

Stat. 6 & 7 *W.* 3. Rates on Burials, chargeable upon Infants, by whom to be paid.

Stat. 10 & 11 *W.* 3. Enables Posthumous Children to take Estates as if they were born in their Fathers Life-time.

Stat. 7 *Annæ*, Enables Infants who are seised, or possess'd of Estates in Trust, or by way of Mortgage, to make Conveyances of such Estates.

Stat. 2 *Annæ*, *c.* 6. Of Infants Apprentices bound to Sea-Service.

1 *An-*

1 *Annæ, c.* 2. An Act made to oblige the *Jews* to provide for and maintain their Children that turn Protestants.

8 *Annæ*, The Rates and Duties upon the Money given or contracted for, with Clerks, Apprentices or Servants.

P R E-

PRECEDENTS

AND

PLEADINGS

CONCERNING

INFANTS.

AN APPENDIX.

Of Precedents and Pleadings concerning Infants.

Bar per deins Age, al Det sur Bond.

ET predict' J. per R. B. Attornat' suum venit & defendit vim & injuriam, Quando, &c. Et dicit quod predicti N. & E. actionem suam predict' versus eum habere non debeant, quia dicit quod ipse tempore confectionis Bille predicte fuit infra etatem viginti & unius Annorum. Et hoc parat est verificare, Unde petit judicium si predicti N. & E. actionem suam predictam versus eum habere debeant, &c.

Replicat' & Issue, que Def. est de plein Age.

ET pdict' N. & E. dicunt, Qd ipsi per aliqua pallegata ab accone sua pdicta inde versus pdictum J. hend' pcludi non debent quia dicunt qd J. tempore confect Bille pdicte fuit plene etatis viginti & unius annorum, & non infra etatem prout pd J. superius allegavit, Et hoc petunt quod Inquiratur p priam, Et p d' J. silit, Ideo Preceypt est Vic, &c.

Bar al Trespass per deins Age, & qd' non Narravit versus Def. per Gardianum.

PEtrus C. nuper de C. in Com, &c. Attachiatus fuit ad respondend' J. R. jun de plito quare Vi & armis claus ipsius J. fregit & herbam suam ibid crescen' ad valentiam centum solidorum pedibus suis ambulando conculcavit & consumpsit, & alia enormia, &c. ad damnum, &c.

ET pdict' P. per J. A. Attornat suum venit & Def. vim & injuriam, Quando, &c. Et dicit quod pd' J. R. (tali die & anno) in Nart pdict' superius specificat (scil) 20 die Octob. Anno Regni Dom Regis nunc quinto & die impetrationis brevis Originalis ipsius R. (scilt) die [illegible] Anno septimo dicti Dom

Dom̄ Regis nunc fuit infra etatem viginti & unius annorum; Et qd̄ pd' J. K. narravit versus pd' P. C. in pl'ito pd'ico per Attornat' situm ubi per debitam legis formam p Gardianum suū narrasse debuit. Et hoc parat' est verificare. Unde petit Judicium.

Replicat' al deins Age, quod Mercimonia fuer' propter necessarium apparatum, & Rejoinder.

PRecludi non debet, quia dicit qd̄ pd'icta Mercimonia per p'fat' D. de eodem Querente ad requisic̄on̄ p'dic' Def. in forma p'dict empt' fuer' empt' p necessario apparatu & vestitu corporum p'dict' D. ac cujusdam F. adtunc uxor' ejusdem D. gradibus eorum ea requirenᵭ, Et hoc, &c.

ss. ET p'dict' D. dicit, quod p'd'ca Mercimonia p ipsum in forma p'dict' empt' non empt' fuer' p necessar' apparatu & vestitu corporum ipsius D. & p'dic' F. uxoris put, &c.

Vel sic:

——K. B. Vid' Executrix, &c. J. B. port Action sur Case sur several Assumpsits versus O. L. Armig', for Taylors Work, and Necessaries provided.

Def. plede Nonage.

ACtio non, quia dicit qd pdictis seperalibus temporibus quibus seperales promissiones & assumpcon pdicte facte fuer' ipse idem Def. fuit infra etatem 21 annorum. Et hoc, &c. Unde, &c.

Repl. Quod vestimenta fuer' necessarium pro Def.

PRecludi non, quia dicit Qd predicta seperalia vestimenta in Narracone pd superius specificat' fuer' necessar' & convenien' apparat' & vestit' p corpore ipsius Def. videlt apud London in paroch & warda predict', Et hoc, &c. Unde, &c.

Rejoinder & Issue.

ET pdict' Def. dicit', Qd pdicta sepalia vestimenta in Narracone pdict' superius specificat' non fuer' necessar' & convenien apparat' & vestit' p corpore ipsius Def. modo & forma prout pdict' Querens superius replicando allegavit. Et de hoc ponit se super patriam, &c.

Lond

Lond ss. Count in Debt by Administrator upon a Bond against the Heirs in Gavelkind, T. W. J. W. & W. W.

The Defendants pray, That the Parol may Demur for the Infancy of one, in this Form :

ET pdict' T. & W. per J. P. Attornat suum & pd J. W. per pdict' J. P. qui admissus est per Curiam dict' Dom Regis hic ad Defend p eod J. W. infra etatem existen ut Gardianus ipsius W. ven & def. vim & injur quando, &c. Et idem J. dicit qd ipse est infra etatem 21 annorum (videlt) etatis undecim annor & octo mensium & non amplius; Et hoc paratus est verificare; Unde non intendit quod ipse durant minoritate sua pfat' T. E. (Quer) in plito pdicto respondere debeat, &c. Et petit quod loquela pdicta inde remaneat usq; plenam etatem pdict' J. W. &c. Et quia pdict' T. E. (Quer) non dedicit quin pdict' J. infra etatem est, ideo loquela pdict' remanen usq; ad plenam etatem ipsius J. &c. Postea scilicet 4 die Junii Anno, &c. venit hic in Cur pdict' T. E. p Attornat suum pdict' & dic qd pdict' J. W. modo plene etatis existit & per bre dom Regis Vic Lond dirigend ad resum tam pdict' J. W. quam pdict' T. W. & W. W. filios es- Resummons.

sendi hic auditur judic' suum de loquela pdict'; & ei conceditur retornab hic tres Trin, &c. ad quem diem hic ven pdict T. C. per Attornat suum pdict'. Et Vic videlt A. B. modo mand qd pred' T. W. & J. nihil habent in balliva sua p quod resum possint. Et super hoc Testatum est in eadem Curia hic qd pred T. W. W. & J. satis hent in predict' Com Kanc unde sum possnt. Ideo Precept est Vic K. qd resum p bonos sum pred T. W. & J. essendi hic in Octab S. Michaelis auditur judic suum de loquela pdict'. Idem dies dat est pfat T. C. &c. Ad quem diem hic ven pdict' T. C. per Attornat suum pdict', & obtulit se quarto die post versus pfat T. W. & J. de plito pdict' & ipsi non vener'. Et Vic Kanc videlt T. S. modo mand qd sum fecit pred' Def. essend hic ad hunc diem per J. S. & J. N. &c. Super quo Precept est prefato Vic K. qd distring pfatos Def. p omnes terras, &c. & qd de exit, &c. ita quod heret corpora cor hic in Octab Hill ad respond prefat T. C. de plito pred; Et aud' judic suum de plur. defalt', &c. idem dies dat est prefat T. C. hic, &c. Et modo hic ad hunc diem scilt ad pdict' Octab S. Hill ven tam pred T. C. per Attorn suum pred quam predict' Def. p T. S. Attornat suum. Et super hoc pd T. C. per qd pred Def. ad Parr suam pred respondeat, &c. Et pred Def. ut prius Def. vim & injur' quando,

Nihil Retorn.

Testatum.

Resummons.

Vic' retorn' Summon'.

Def. appere.

quando, &c. & pred' Def. plitant riens p discent generalit. Placit. riens per discent.

Cornub ss. J. M. versus J. W. & S. Ux' ejus, & J. C. Et Eliz. Ux' ejus filias & heredes T. J. gen de debo sup Obligat.

Parol demur prie pur deux Infants pur Infancy del un.

ET pdict' J. Wl. & S. ux' ejus, Et J. C. per E. S. Attornat suum, Et pdict' Eliz' p A. & B. qui admissi sunt per Cur dicti Dom Regis hic ad defend p ead Eliz' infra etatem existen ut Gardiani ipsius E. ven & def. vim & injur quando, &c. Et dicunt qd pdict' J. M. accoem suam inde versus eos here non debant quia protestando qd ipsi non heant aliqua terras seu tenementa p discensum hereditarium de prefat J. C. patre ipsar S. Et E. in feodo simplici nec huer die impetracon bris Original ipsius quer nec unquam postea; p plito tamen iidem def. dicunt qd pdict' Eliz' est infra etatem 21 annorum (videlt) viginti annorum & non amplius. Et hoc parat sunt verificare. Unde non intendunt qd durante minori etate pdict' Eliz' iidem def. in plito pdict respondere debeant; Et petunt qd loquela pdict' remaneat usq; plenam etatem pdict' Eliz'; Et quia pdict' quer non dedicit quia pdict' Eliz' infra etatem existit.

Ideo loquela p̄dicta remaḋ usq; ad plenam etatem ipsius Eliz', &c. Resummons p̄rie, &c.

Count d'avoyder Recognizance pur Nonage del Conisor. B. C.

DOm̄ Rex mandat Justiciar' suis de Banco bre suum clausum in hec verba:

Carolus, &c. Justiciariis nostris de Banco salutem. Ex gravi Querela, &c. Et modo hic ad hunc diem scilt 25 diem Januarii Anno, &c. veṅ hic in Curia p̄dict' quer' in propria persona sua, & dicit qd ipse p̄dict' primo die Martii Anno 36. supradict' apud Lond' in paroch, &c. coram p̄fat' P. P. Mil Cap' Justic' dict' dom̄ Regis ad plita coram ipso Rege tenend' assignat' & ad capiend' recognitiones debitor̄ deputato, per procurationem persuasionem & instigationem dicti def. ductus fuit; & idem quer' coram prefat' P. P. Mil' cognovit seipsum debere prefat' def. 400 l. quas ei solvisse debuit ad certum tempus in ead' Recogn̄ content' secund' formam Statuti apud Westm̄ p recuperacone debitor̄ edit & pvis', prout in eadem Recupac' plenius continetur. Et idem quer' ulterius dicit, qd ipse tempore recognitionis p̄dict' cogn̄ fuit, & adhuc est infra etatem viginti & unius annorum; Et hoc paratus est verificare; Unde pet' judici-

judicium, & qd ipse per Curiam hic esse infra etatem 21 annoꝝ adjudicari possit, & qd recognitio pdicta esset vacua & nullius vigoris, & qd ipse idem quer' de recogn pdict' p Curiam hic exoneretur: Et sciend est qd 9 die Febr' Anno 36 supradict' ad pband allegaconem & querelam pdict' fore veram ptulit hic in Curia testes sequentes (videlt) E. Y. N. O. & F. B.

Qui quidem E. Y. N. O. & F. B. dicto 9 die Febr' Anno 36 supradicto in eodem Termino coram E. N. Mil & Sociis suis Justic dicti dom Regis de Communi Banco hic super Sacram suum separatim p seips. onerat' jurat' & examin ad veritatem de & super pmissis dicend deposuerunt modo & forma sequen. Quarum quidem Depositionum tenor sequitur in hec verba: Testimoinage produce.

ff. Depositiones capt' coram, &c. Et quia Justic hic se advisare volunt de & super pbationes pdict' & quia expediens est & necesse qd pdict' def. p interesse suo in hac parte pmunic foret priusquam Curia hic ulterius pcedat ad recognicon pdict' adnulland & evacuand Precept' est Vic, qd Venire fac hic pfat' def. ad ostend quare recogn pdict' (in forma pdict' capt' & recogn) rone per ipsum quer' pallegat adnullari & evacuari. Et idem quer' eadem rone exonerari non debeat & ulterius ad faciend & recipiend Ven' fac. Def.

eius qd dicta Curia in ea parte consid, Idem dies dat est eis quer hic &c. Et super hoc ulterius dictum est pfato quer qd tunc sit hic & secum afferat alias pbationes dictarum allegaconis & querelesuis, &c. Et modo hic ad hunc diem scilt, &c. (tali retorno) venit pdict' quer in ppria persona sua, ducens secum Librum Parochial. (Anglicè the Church-Book) paroch de B. in Com S. per quem plenius liquet Curie hic qd ipse idem quer baptizatus fuit apud B. pdict' 27 die Octob 1696. Et idem Vic modo mand' qd pdict' def. nil het, &c. Et super hoc idem quer ut prius dicit, qd ipe tempore recogn pdict' fuit & adhuc est infra etatem 21 annorum. Et hoc paratus est verificare. Unde ut prius pet judic & qd ipse per Cur hic esse infra etatem 21 annorum adjudicari possit, & qd recognitio pdict' evacuetur & penitus pro nullo heatur. Super quo quia Justiciar hic tam per inspection dicti quer quam examinacon testium & pbationum pdictarum satis liquet & apparet ipsum quer tempore recognitionis pdict' fuisse & adhuc esse infra etatem 21 annorum. Ideo consideratum est, qd recognit pdict' p pdict' quer pfac def. in forma pdict' recognit vacua & penitus p nullo heatur. In B. C.

Judgment que Recognizance serra void.

Count

Count sur Bill Obligatory per Administratorem durante minori Ætate Executoris.

J. C. nuper de, &c. att' dict', &c. ad respondend' T. H. gen' Administratori omnium bonorum & catallorum que fuer' W. G. durante minoritate W. C. Executoris Testamenti pdict' W. de plito qd reddat ei 12 l. quas, &c. Et unde, &c. per quandam billam, &c. cognovisset se debere pfato W. in vita sua 6 l. solvend' eidem W. Executoribus, &c. (tali die) tunc px' sequen' dat' Bille pdict' & p vera soluc̃one bene & fideliter faciend' pdict' J. C. obligasset se, &c. in pdict' 12 l. per eandem Billam. Et pdict' J. H. in facto dicit qd pdictus J. C. non solvit pfat' W. in vita sua (tali die) in Billa pd superius specificat' pdict' 6 l. quas idem W. Executoribus, &c. ad & super pdictum diem solvisse debuit secundum formam & effectum Bille pd p quod actio accrevit pfato W. in vita sua ad exigend' & hend' de pdict' J. C. pd 12 l. pd tamen J. C. licet sepius requisitus pd 12 l. pfato W. in vita sua seu eid' J. H. post pd W. mortem (cui Administratio omnium bonorum & catallorum que fuer' pd W. tempore mortis sue p Ricum Providentia divina, &c. apud London in parochia Beate Marie de Arcub' in ward' de Cheap durante minoritate pdicti Walteri

teri qui adhuc superstes (videlt) apud D. predict' & infra etatem existit post mortem pred W. commissa fuit) non reddidit sed ill ei reddere omnino contradixit & ill eidem J. H. adhuc reddere contradicit ac injuste detinet, Unde, &c. Et pfert. &c.

Al Count sur Obligation ove Condition pur performance des Covenants in Indenture de Apprentiship.

Bar.

Per Stat. 5 Eliz. que nul Merchant prendra ascun Apprentice nisi son pere ad terres al value de 40 s. per Annum destre certifie south les Maines & Seals de 3 Justices.

ss. Et pd Robertus per R. A. Attornat' suum ven & Def. vim & injuriam quando, &c. & petit auditum Scripti pred & ei Legitur, &c. petit etiam auditum Conditionis ejusdem Scripti Obligatorii & ei Legitur in hec verba.

ss. The Condition of this Obligation is such, That if the above-bounden *Robert Leigh* pay, and keep all and singular the Covenants, Grants, Articles, Clauses, Provisoes, Payments, Conditions and Agreements whatsoever, which on the part and behalf of the said *James Leigh* are, and ought to be observed, performed, fulfilled, accomplished, paid

paid and kept, compriſed and mentioned in one Pair of Indentures, bearing even Date with theſe Preſents made, or expreſſed to be made, between the ſaid *Robert Leigh*, and *James Leigh* of the one part, and the above named *Anne Wade* and *Samuel Wade* of the other part, in all Things according to the true Intent and Meaning of the ſaid Indentures; Then this preſent Obligation to be void and of none Effect, or elſe to be and remain in full Power and Vertue.

Quibus Lectis & auditis idem Robert dicit qd ipſe de debo pred pretextu Scripti Obligatorii pred onerari non debet quia dicit qd Indentur pred in Condition pred ſuperius ſpecificat fact' fuit apud Civitat Exon pred in comit ejuſdem Civitatis pred viceſimo tertio die Julii Anno Regni dict' Dom Regis nunc primo ſupradicto inter ipſum Robertum Leigh & pd Jacobum Leigh in Conditione predicta ſuperius nominat per nomina R. L. &c. & J. L. filii ſui ex una parte & prefat Annam & Samuel per nomina A. W. de civitat Exon vid & Samuel W. de civitat Exon pred mercatoris ex altera parte cujus quidem Indenture alteram partem ſigillis ipſor' Ann & Samuelis ſigillat geren dat iiſdem die & Anno idem R. hic in Curia profert per quam quidem Indentur Teſtat exiſtit qd predict' Jacobus Leigh tam de electione ſua propria quam per & cum conſenſu patris ſui per Indentur

dentur pred posuisset & obligasset seipsum Apprenticium ad & cum predict' Ann & Samuel habitare remanere & servire a dat Indentur predict' pro & durante Termino Septem Annorum plenarie complend' & finiend' durante omni quo tempore ipse pdict' Jacobus Leigh per Indentur predict' convenit & promisit ad & cum pdict' Anna & Samuel secreta sua concelare mandat suis legitimis & honestis in promptu obedire & performare Bona ejusdem Magistri & Magistre suorum non accomodare devastare fucare imbezillare seu consumere sed in omnibus ut vero & fideli Apprentic doceret seipsum erga ipsos gerere & pdict' Anna W. & Samuel per Indentur predict' pro Bonis causis ipsos moven convener & promiter ad cum Apprenticio predict' ipsum docere & instruere vel ipsum doceri seu instrui causare Secundum optimum modum quo potuere in arte Merchandizandi durante Termino predict' Et causarent & procurarent qd predict' Jacobus L. resideret in Bilboa in Regno Hispanie & ibidem foret educat in negotiis mercatorum sub aliquo experto mercatore duran tribus ultimis Annis Termini predict' Et invenirent & providerent pro dicto Apprent suo sufficien apparat & victum & omnia al' res apt & necessar tam in egritudine quam in valetudine duran Termino pdict' & in fine ejusdem relinquerent ipsum apparat

rat' in decent' modo Et ipsum liberum facerent de societate mercatorum (Comuniter vocat' Gallica Societas) prout per Indent' pdict' plenius liquet & apparet Que sunt omnia & singula Conventiones Concessiones Articuli & Agreament' in Indentur' pdict' content' Et idem Robertus ulterius dicit qd ipse die & Anno supradictis in narratione pdict' spec' apud Civitat' Exon' pdict' in Comitat' ejusdem Civitatis fecit & deliberavit eisdem Ann' & Samuel' pdict' Scriptum Obligatorium p performacone conventionis barganie & agreament' in Indentur' pdict' spec' ex parte pdict' Jacobi Leigh performand' Quique diu ante Confectionem Scripti Obligatorii pdict' & Indentur' pdict' per quendam actum in Parliamento apud Westm' in Comit' Middx duodecimo die Januarii Anno Regni Dom' Elizabethe nuper Regine Anglie Quinto tent' edit' (int' alia) provisum & inactitatum fuit Authoritate ejusdem Parliamenti qd non Liceat alicui persone inhabitan' in aliqua Civitat' sive Villa Corporat' utenti sive exercenti aliquod mysteriorum sive Artium (Anglice Crafts) mercatoris negotian' (Anglice Trafficking) per commercium (Anglice Traffick) in aliquas partes transmarinas merceri pannarii aurifabri ferrarii (Anglice Ironmonger) Segmentarii (Anglice Embroiderer) sive pannularii (Anglice Clothier) qui ponit aut poneret pannum ad confection' & vendition' caper' aliquem

aliquem Apprenticium aut servien̄ fore instruct' sive doct' in aliquibus occupationum artium (Anglice Crafts) sive mysteriorum nisi talis serviens aut Apprenticius sit filius suus aut aliter quod pater & mater talis Apprenticii sive servien̄ haberent ad tempus capc̄onis talis Apprenticii vel servien̄ terras Tenem̄ta seu alia hereditamenta clari annui valoris quadragint' solidorum de statu hereditario sive libero Tenement' ad minus fore certificat' sub manibus & sigillis trium justiciarior̄ ad pacem Com̄ vel Civitat' ubi hujusmodi terre Tenementa seu hereditatum jacent seu jacerent Majori Ballivis aut aliis Capital Officiar' talis Civitat' sive Ville Corporat' Et fore irrotular' inter recorda ibidem Et ulterius per eundem actum inactitat' fuit per authoritatem ejusdem Parliament' Quod omnes Indentur' convention̄ promission̄ & barganie de aut pro retentione capc̄one sive custod̄ alicujus Apprent' aliter tu̅ imposteru̅ fiend̄ aut capiend̄ quam per Stat' p̄d Limitatur ordinatur Et appunctuatur penitus vacue forent in Lege ad omnes intenc̄ones & proposit' put per eundem actum (inter alia) plenius liquet & apparet. Et idem Robertus in facto dicit q̄d p̄dict' Civitas Exon̄ in Indent' p̄dict' superius spec' est & tempore confection̄ Indent' p̄dict' nec non a tempore cujus contrar' memoria hominum non existit fuit antiqua civitas Incorporat' Et q̄d quidam Jacobus

 Walker

Walker Arm̄ tempore confectionis Indentur' p̄dict' & capcionis Apprent' p̄dict' fuit major p̄dict Civitat' Exon̄ scilicet apud Civit' Exon̄ p̄dict' in comit' ejusdem Civitatis ac quidam Michael Pyne Benjaminus Ivey Rogerus Mallock & Thomas Boyland adtunc & ibidem fuer' Ballivi ejusdem Civitatis Qd̄que p̄dict' Anna Ward & Samuel p̄dict' tempore confectionis Indenture p̄dict' ac retencon & capcon̄ Apprenticii p̄d Inhitabant & adhuc inhabitant infra Civitat' Exon̄ p̄dict' & adtunc & ibid̄ utebantur & exercebant & adhuc utuntur & exercent mysterium & artem mercatoris negotian̄ per commercium & negociation̄ apud Bilboa in partibus transmarin̄, &c. scilicet apud Civit' Exon̄ in comit' ejusdem Civitat' Qd̄que p̄dict' Jacobus L. Apprenticius adtunc & ibidem fuit filius p̄dict' Roberti Leigh & Marie uxor ejus patris & matris ipsius Jacobi Leigh & non filius Anne W. & Samuelis vel eorum alicujus Qd̄que nunquam certificat' fuit sub manibus & sigillis aliquorum Justic' ad pacem Dom̄ Regis conservand̄ assign̄ Majori Balliis sive al' Capital' Officiariis p̄dict' seu eorum alicui qd̄ pater & mater p̄dict' Jacobi huer' Terras Tenementa seu al' Hereditament' clari annui valoris quadragint' solidorum de Stat' Hereditario sive libero Tenement' Qd̄que aliqua talis certificat' nunquam irrotulat' fuit inter record̄

Civitat' pdict' ibidem Secundum formam in Statut' in hujusmodi casu edit' & provis. Et sic idem Johes dicit qd Indentur' pdicta ac clausule & convencon' pdict in eadem content' & spec' fuer' & sunt per retencon' capcon & custod' Apprenticii aliter & alio modo quam per Stat' pdict limitatur ordinatur & appunctuatur per quod Indentur' pdict' hic in Curia prolat' ac in Narracone pdict' superius spec' ac omnes & singule conventiones clausule concessiones articuli & agreement' in eadem content' mencionat' specificat' & comprizat' nec non pdict' Scriptum Obligatorium in forma pdict' occacone pdict' deliberat' pro performatione conventionis pdict' vigore Statuti pdict' in hujusmodi casu edit' & provis. penitus vacue & nullius vigoris sive validitatis in Lege devener' & existunt. Et hoc idem R. paratus est verificare. Unde petit judicium si ipse de debito pdict' virtute Scripti Obligatorii pdict' onerari debeat,

Narr' versus Apprenticium qui decessit è Servitio Magistri sui illicite sine Licentia sua & seipsum abstinuit à Servitio suo per 3 annos & recusavit servire quer' pro residuo Termini.

Lond' ss. Memorand' qd alias scilicet Termino Sci Michaelis ult' pdict' coram Dom Rege apud Westm venit W. A. per R. J. Attorn' suum Et protulit hic in curia dicti Dom Regis tunc

tunc ibidem quandam Billam suam versus C. T. in custod Marr', &c. de placito convencon fract' Et sunt plegii de prosequend scilt Johes Doe & Ricus Roe Que quidem billa sequitur in hec verba.

Lond ss. B. A. queritur de C. T. in custod mar' marcesch Dom Regis coram ipso rege existen de placito convencon fract' pro eo videlicet qd cum Civitas Lond est Antiqua Civit in qua quidem Civitate hetur & a tempore cujus contrar' memoria hominum non existit habebatur quedam consuetudo usitat & approbat' in eadem videlicet qd si aliqua psona existen Libere conditionis & etatis quatuordecim Annorum & ultra & infra etatem viginti & unius Annorum & non maritat' seipsum posuerit Apprenticium alicui civi & libero homini Civitat' pdict' aliqua arte mysterio sive manuali occupatione ibidem uten per Indentur' inter hujusmodi Apprentic' & hujusmodi civem & liberum hominem confect' pro Termino septem Annorum incipiend a die dat' Indenture pdict' ad artem hujusmodi civis & Liberi hominis erudiend & secum more Apprenticii commorand pro pdict' Termino septem Annorum ac per J. hujusmodi Indentur convenirect cum magistro suo ad deserviend eidem magistro suo more Apprenticii durante hujusmodi Termino in hujusmodi Indentur specificat' Ac si talis Apprenticius per Indentur suam pdict' Custom de *London*. con-

conveniret cum pdict' magro suo qd ipse fideliter deserviret dicto magro suo secreta sua celaret precepta sua ubiq; faceret Dampn dicto Magistro suo non faceret nec ab aliis fieri viderit quin illud pro posse suo impediret vel statim dicto magro suo premonition daret bona magri sui non devastaret nec ea alicui illicite accomodaret fornicationem non committeret nec matrimonium contraheret infra terminum pdict' ad Chartas Pictas Aleas (Anglice Dice,) Tabulas Lusorias, (Anglice Tables,) vel aliqua alia joca illicita non Luderet per quod magister suus pdict' aliquod Dampn haberet cum bonis suis propriis vel alienis durante Termino pdict' sine Licentia magistri sui pdict' nec emeret nec venderet Tabernas vel Dom Lusorias (Anglice Playhouses) non frequentaret nec se a dicti sui magri servitio die sive nocte illicite abstineret sed in omnibus tanquam fidelis Apprenticius se gereret erga magrm suum & omnes suos durante Termino pdict' in hujusmodi Indentur specificat' Ac si talis magister per hujusmodi Indentur conveniret cum tali Apprenticio suo ad docend & instruend eundem Apprenticium in eadem arte qua tunc utebatur optimo modo quo posset doceret & instrueret invenien dicto Apprenticio cibum potum apparat' lectum & omnia alia necessar' Secundum consuetudinem Civit' pdict' per totum pdict' Terminum in hujusmodi In-

Indentur' menconat' quod tunc talis Apprenticius pro consider' pdict' teneretur & obligaretur & a toto tempore supradict' cujus contrar' memoria hominum non existit teneri & obligari usus fuit & consuevit ad hujusmodi magrm̄ suum more Apprenticii sui deserviend' p Termino in Indentura illa menconat' & ad performand' alias Convencones pdict' in Indentur' pdict' menconat' ex parte sua performand' Et si talis Apprenticius in contrarium faceret & durante dicto Termino Annorum in Indent' pdict' specificat' infringeret aliquas Convencones in hujusmodi Indentur' specificat' qd tunc magister talis haberet & habere consuevit & debuit tale remedium versus hujusmodi Apprenticium suum per accõnem de Convencone fract' pro fraccione seu non performacone hujusmodi Convenconis qualis haberet seu habere potuisset versus eundem Apprenticium si talis Apprenticius tempore confeccionis Indentur' pd' foret plene etatis viginti & unius Annorum & amplius. Et idem B. ulterius dicit qd pdict' consuetudo & omnes alie consuetudines Civitat' London pdict' in eadem Civitat' diu usitat' Authoritate Parliamenti Domini Rich nuper Regis Anglie post conquestum secundi apud Westm̄ in Com̄ Middx Anno Regni sui Septimo Majori & Civitat' & Communibus dict' Civitat' & successoribus suis ratificat' & confirmat' fuere Et idem B. ulterius dicit qd pdict' C. C. modo Def. existen etatis quatuordecim Annorum & amplius & Libere Conditionis ac existen infra etatem viginti & unius Annorum ac non maritat' nono die Februarii Anno Dom Millimo sexentesimo quinquagesimo octavo quod Lond pdict' videlicet in Paroch beate Marie de Arcubus in Warda de Cheap Secund' consuetud Civitat pdict' per quandam Indentur adtunc & ibidem fact' inter pdict' B. per nomen B. A. civis & mercatoris scissor Lond ex una parte & pdict' C. per nomen C. C. filii R. C. de Dowpton in Comit' Wiltes clerici ex altera parte cujus quidem Indentur' alteram partem sigillo ipsius C. sigillat' idem B. hic in curia profert cujus dat' est iisdem die & anno posuit seipsum Apprenticium pfat' B. ad artem ejus erudiend & secum more Apprenticii a die dat' Indentur' pdict' usque plenum finem & Terminum septem Annorum extunc prox' sequend plenarie complend & finiend deserviend durante quo Termino pdict' Apprenticius per Indentur' pdict' convenit cum pfat' magro suo qd ipse pfat' magrum suum fideliter serviret secreta sua celaret precepta sua Legitima ubique faceret damnum prefat' magro suo non facere nec ab aliis fieri videret quin ille pro posse suo impediret & statim magro suo pdict' premoneret bona magri sui non devastaret nec ea illicite alicui accomodaret Fornicationem non committeret nec Matrimonium

nium contraheret infra Termin̄ p̄dict' ad Pictas Chartas Aleas (Anglice voc' Dice) Tabulas Lusorias (Anglice Tables) vel aliqua alia joca illicita non Luderet per quod dictus magister suus aliquod Damnum haberet cum bonis suis propriis vel alienis durant̄ Termino p̄dict' Sine Licentia p̄dict' magri sui non emeret nec venderet Tabernas vel Lusorias Domos non frequentaret nec seipsum a servitio dicti magri sui die seu nocte illicite abstineret sed in omnibus tanquam fidelis Apprenticius seipsum gereret erga dictū magrum suum & omnes suos durante p̄dict' Termino Et p̄dict' magister convenit per Indentur p̄dict' cum p̄fat' Apprenticio suo qđ ipse dict' Apprenticium suum in eadem arte qua tunc utebatur optimo modo quo possit doceret & instrueret inveniend̄ dicto Apprenticio suo cibum potum apparatum lectum & omnia alia necessar' secundum consuetud̄ Civitat' London durante Termino p̄dict' & p vera performacone omniū & singulorum convencon & agreament p̄d alteruter partium p̄dict' obligabat se alteriorum per Indentur p̄dict' put per eand plenius liquet & apparet. Et p̄dict' B. ulterius dicit qđ ipse tempore confeccionis Indentur p̄dict' & continue postea hucusque fuit & adhuc existit liber homo Civitat' p̄dict' ac Inhabitans infra libtatem ejusdem Civitat' a tempore confeccionis Indentur p̄dict' hucusque videlicet in Parochia Warda p̄dict' ac

per totum tempus p̄dict' artem scissoris
(Anglice Taylor) ibidem usus fuit Ac
idem B. ulterius dicit qđ licet ipse be=
ne & fideliter servavit performavit per=
implevit & custodivit omnes & singulas
conventiones Et agreeamenta in Inden=
tur p̄dict' superius specificat' ex parte
ipsius B. performand perimplend & cu=
stodiend secund forma & effectum Inden=
tur p̄dict' predictus tamen C. post con=
fection Indentur p̄dict' & ante finem
Termini 7 Annorum scilicet sexto die
Septembris Anno Regni Dom Caroli
Secundi nunc Regis (Anglie, &c) Deci=
mo quinto, apud Lond p̄dict' in Paroch
& Warda p̄dict' decessit (Anglice did de-
part) a servitio ipsius B. illicite & sine
Licentia & contra voluntate p̄dict' B.
& ab eod sexto die Decembris Anno su=
pradict' usque finem p̄d Termini 7 An=
norum in Indentur p̄dict' superius
mencionat' p̄d C. seipsum abstinuit a ser=
vitio p̄d B. Et recusavit servire p̄dict'
B. magro suo p residuo Termini 7 An=
norum secund tenorem & effectum In=
dentur p̄dict' neque p̄dict' B. dicit qđ
Licet sepius requisit', &c. conventionem
suam p̄dict' de eo qđ ipse idem C. Se=
cundum morem Apprenticii prefat' B.
serviret a die dat' Indentur p̄dict' ad
plenum finem & terminum 7 Annorum
nec seipsum a dicti magri sui servitio
die seu nocte illicite abstinere non tenuit
sed infregit & illi ei tenere omnino con=
tradixit & adhuc contradicit Ad dampnum
ipsius

ipsius. B. ducentar librarum Et inde produc sectam, &c.

Barr.

Protestando qd' non est talis Consuetudo prout, &c. nec qd' ipse decessit a quer' prout, &c. pro placito qd' Def. obtulit servire Quer' durante Termino & quer' recusavit ipsum recipere absque hoc qd' ipse recusavit servire quer' prout, &c.

ET idem C. dic qd pdict' B. actio non quia protestando qd in Civitate Lond pdict' non hetur nec a tempore cujus contrar memoria hominum non existit hebatur talis consuetudo usitat & approbat in eadem quas pdict' B. per Narrationem suam pdict' superius suppon protestando etiam qd idem C. non decessit a servitio dic B. prout idem B. superius allegavit pro placito idem C. dicit qd ipse obtulit seipsum servire dicto B. magro suo durante Termino Annorum in Indentur pdict' superius specificat Secund formam & effectum Indenture illius Quodq; pdict' B. eundem C. in servitio suo recipere penitus recusavit absque hoc qd idem C. recusavit servire pdict' B. magro suo pro Resid Termini Septem Annorum Secund tenorem & effectum Indenture pdi put pdict B. superius inde narrando allegavit Et hoc paratus

tus est verificare. unde petit judicium, &c.

Demurrer general ad hoc plitum, Trin. 22 Car. 2. Rot. 1559.

Narr' in Appel' Murdri per Infant versus un' Accessary.

R. B. nuper de, &c. alias dic', &c. Attach' fuit p Corpus suum ad respond' D. S. filio & hered' T. S. simul cum R. D. nuper, &c. & R. B. de, &c. de morte pd T. S. quondam patris sui unde eos appellat. Et sunt pleg' de pros. E. W. de, &c. N. F. & E. W. de, &c. & unde idem D. per J. R. custod suum hic in Curia admiss' instant appellat pdic' R. B. qui modo compet de eo qd pdict' T. S. fuit in pace Dei & Dom. Regis nunc apud N. &c. Secundo die, &c. Anno Regni, &c. ad horam undecimam ante meridiem ejusdem diei ubi venit tam pdic' R. B. quem quidem R. B. pd D. S. alias scilt termino, &c. cor eod dom Rege apud West' de felon' & murd pdic' aliter appellavit ac pdic' R. D. qui modo non compet quem quidem R. D. pd D. de morte pdic' aliter appellaret si presens esset quam pdic' Rog. B. qui modo compet felonice ut felo dic' dom Regis nunc insidiando ex eorum malitia precogitat contra pacem ejusdem dom Regis coron' & dignitates suas Die Anno Hora Loco &

Com

Com̄ Mid. Vi & Armis videlt Gladiis, Baculis & Sceptis, & aliis armis defensoriis, Et in p̄dict' T. S. apud N. p̄dict' in p̄dict' Com̄ Mid. insultum fecer' & p̄dict' R. D. cum quodam Gladio vocat' a Two-handed Sword, pretii duorum solidorum quem ipse tunc & ibid in manu sua dextra tenuit felonice percussit & dedit ei adtunc & ibid unam plagam mortalem de qua quidem plaga mortali idem T. S. apud N. p̄dict' in p̄dict' loco in Com̄ Mid. instant' obiit Et sic p̄dict' R. D. p̄d T. S. iisdem Die Anno Hora Loco & Com̄ Mid. p̄d in forma p̄dict' felonice interfecit & murdravit contra pacem dict' dom' Regis coron' & dignitates suas, & q̄d p̄dict' Ro: D. apud N. p̄dict' in Com̄ Mid. p̄dict' secund' die Decembris Anno 29. supradict' & ad horam supradict' fuer' felonice presentes abettantes confortant' & auxiliantes p̄fat' D. ad feloniam & murdrum p̄dict' in forma p̄dict' faciend' & perpetrand' Et sic p̄dict' Roulandus Rogerus & Robertus p̄fat' T. S. iisdem Die Anno Hora Loco & Com̄ Mid. p̄dict' modo & forma p̄dict' felonice interfecere & murdraver' contra pacem dict' dom̄ Regis coron' & dignitates suas. Et quam cito idem felo qui modo comparet feloniam & murdrum p̄dict' sic in forma p̄dict' fecisset fugiit dictusq; D. ipsum recenter insecutus fuit de Villa in Villam usq; Quatuor Villas propinquiores & ulterius quo-

quousq;, &c. Et si idem felo qui modo compet feloniam & murdrum p̃dict' ei in forma p̃dict' imposit' velit dedicere pro D. hoc paratus est versus ipsum probare prout Curia, &c.

THE

THE

TABLE.

A.

Ability.

Account.

Actions.

Administrator dur' Minoritate.

Acti-

Age.

Apprentice.

Where

Of the Infant's Agreement to a Devise.

B.

C.

Conditions.

Copyhold Estates.

May

Covenants.

D.

E.

F.

Fines.

G.

 Guar-

Guar-

I.

Of

Inſpection.

Judg-

Judgment.

L.

Of

M.

N.

N.

O.

Orphans.

P.

Pleading.

R.

Of

S.

Statutes.

T.

Nonage.

U.

W.

Wills.

Devise

A

TABLE

OF THE

APPENDIX.

Barr.

A Table of the APPENDIX.

FINIS.

---

www.ingramcontent.com/pod-product-compliance
Lightning Source LLC
LaVergne TN
LVHW091523200926
848483LV00002B/284
* 9 7 8 1 5 8 4 7 7 8 3 3 2 *